KW-553-020

READING BOROUGH LIBRARIES

Askews

£19.99

THE LAW

OF

RTY WALLS

AND

FENCES,

INCLUDING

The New Metropolitan Buildings Act,

WITH NOTES.

BY

HUMPHRY W. WOOLRYCH,

OF THE INNER TEMPLE, ESQ., BARRISTER-AT-LAW.

LONDON:
WILLIAM BENNING & CO., LAW BOOKSELLERS,
(LATE SAUNDERS AND BENNING,)
43, FLEET STREET.

1845.

LONDON:
PRINTED BY RAYNER AND HODGES,
109, Fetter Lane, Fleet Street.

PREFACE.

This Work contains the Law of Party and other Walls under the new Act of Parliament for regulating Metropolitan Buildings.

It likewise, in a separate portion, treats of the Law of Fences generally, in which Term Party and other Walls are included.

It has been thought right to give a general outline of the new Statute, and then to proceed with a more particular description of the Walls, which are a principal feature in it.

There is also an Appendix, containing the Act above referred to, with Notes illustrating and explaining its provisions where it has appeared necessary.

Amongst other tables and indexes, a table mentioning the duties and liabilities of persons under the Act will be found, and a table of time is also added.

H. W. W.

Hare Court, Temple,
December, 1844.

CONTENTS.

THE LAW OF PARTY WALLS.

CHAPTER I.

Of the Ownership of Party Walls, and other Incidents.

CHAPTER II.

Of Party and other Walls under the Buildings Act, 7 & 8 Vict. c. 84.

CHAPTER III.

CHAPTER IV.

APPENDIX.

Metropolitan Buildings Act.

THE LAW OF FENCES.

CHAPTER I.

CHAPTER II.

CHAPTER III.

CHAPTER IV.

TABLE

OF THE

CASES CITED.

A

TABLE OF STATUTES

REFERRED TO IN THIS TREATISE,

MORE ESPECIALLY OF THE VARIOUS SECTIONS OF THE NEW BUILDINGS ACT, 7 & 8 VICT. Cap. 84.

SCHEDULES.

A TABLE

OF THE

NAMES, DUTIES, AND LIABILITIES, &c., OF PERSONS,

UNDER THE METROPOLITAN BUILDINGS ACT,

7 & 8 Vict. c. 84.

Adjoining Owner, who uses a raised wall, to pay his proportion of costs, s. 31.
the like as to a *fence wall*, s. 32.
liable to reimburse building owner, s. 46.

Appellant, in cases of appeal concerning offensive trades, see sects. 57, 58, 59.
how to conduct his appeal, s. 105.

Architect, see Builder.

Assistant Surveyor, under what circumstances appointed, s. 75.

Builder, to execute his contracts, subject to modification, s. 10.
to give two days' notice to surveyor of works to be performed, under a penalty, s. 13.
so if the work be stopped and recommenced, or the builder be changed, *ib.*
to give notice to official referees when certain buildings of the higher classes are in a forward state, s. 15.
to amend insufficient parts of the same upon notice from the official referees, *ib.*
upon the completion of the building, to give fresh notice to the referees, *ib.*, see also s. 16.
to enter into recognizance to abate nuisance, and pay costs, s. 18.
to deliver an account of work done, to the adjoining owner, s. 47.
payment of surveyor's fees, s. 77, see s. 110.

Building Owner, sect. 20.
- to give notice to adjoining owner before work done, s. 21.
- to signify his assent to, or dissent from, modification, s. 22.
- may not commence work till the decision of official referees, in cases of non-consent, as to modification, has been given, *ib.*
- to signify his assent to, or dissent from, delay, s. 23.
- may not commence work till the opinion of referees, in case of non-consent, has been had in cases of delay, *ib.*, see s. 25.
- may rebuild a *sound* party wall, but he must make all good, and pay all costs and fees, s. 26.
- when to build up an external wall against a party wall, s. 27.
- and in such case he must make good damage, s. 28.
- and also rebuild the party wall if damage arise through his own carelesness, s. 29.
- when to build up party wall in the event of *raising* a building, s. 31.
- to pay costs of raising a *fence* wall, s. 32.
- or of pulling it down, *ib.*
- when he may pull down timber partitions, s. 33.
- power of entry to execute works, s. 36.
- his duty when he builds on *vacant ground*, s. 38.
- as to chimney breasts, &c., when adjoining owner consents, s. 39.

Commissioners of Works and Buildings, sect. 2.
- appeal to regarding special suspension, s. 6.
- their approval required to the modification of building leases, s. 10.
- may make general orders respecting modification, s. 11.
- may order modification in the case of existing buildings to be rebuilt, s. 12.
- to appoint examiners of surveyors, s. 66.
- to appoint the registrar of Metropolitan Buildings, s. 89.
- and make rules for his guidance, *ib.*
- and appoint a temporary registrar in case of illness, *ib.*
- to appoint a place of office for such registrar, s. 92.

Copyholder, may recover contribution for costs of works, s. 50.

Defendant, sued for matters done in pursuance of the act, how he is to proceed, s. 108.
- when he may apply to compel plaintiff to give security for costs, s. 109.

Deputy Surveyor, his appointment and duties, s. 73.

Examiner of surveyors, see sect. 66.

Excise, see sect. 63.

Freeholder, may recover contribution for costs of works, s. 50.

Gas Companies, see sect. 63.

Judge, to give effect to the awards of official referees, s. 86.
- to require, in certain cases, security for costs, s. 109.
- to take notice of act as a public act, s. 119.

Official Referees—continued.
to assist in examining surveyors, s. 66.
to approve of deputy surveyor, s. 73.
in cases of vacancy to make an appointment *ad interim*, s. 74.
when necessary, to appoint an assistant surveyor, s. 75.
their appointment, s. 80.
may not act as arbitrators and referees in the same case, nor as surveyors, *ib.*
their functions, s. 81.
to settle disputes with the registrar, s. 82.
power of their awards, s. 83.
may proceed in the absence of parties to reference, s. 84.
to take evidence and summon witnesses, s. 85.
to make declaration of official fidelity, s. 87.
where one may act without the other, s. 88.
their remuneration, s. 94.
see sect. 89.
how disqualified, s. 95.
notices, service of upon referees, s. 116.
to give certain consents where owner, occupier, &c., cannot be found, s. 117.
certificate and award of, free from stamp duty, s. 118.

OVERSEERS,
to give notice of extending the act, s. 4.
in cases of ruinous buildings to apply to referees for a survey, s. 40.
and upon receipt of surveyor's certificate from referees to cause the building to be shored, and a hoard to be put up, *ib.*
and, after notice to owner, to cause, upon his neglect, the destruction of the ruinous building, *ib.*
and the like, upon appeal and award to that effect by referees, *ib.*
to sell materials of such buildings, &c., s. 41.
and pay surplus to owner, *ib.*
in cases of dispute to refer to referees, *ib.*
if no demand made, to add the amount to the poors' rate, *ib.*
but at any time within six years, to pay it out of the rate if duly demanded, *ib.*
to place deficiency of monies received, after a sale of materials, to the poors' rate account, s. 42.
to pay for ruinous chimneys when there is no known owner or occupier, s. 43.
and recover the amount when an owner or occupier can be found, *ib.*
to report to referees concerning underground rooms or cellars, s. 53.
when to raise a sum, by way of rate or otherwise, for the purchase of an offensive trade, s. 62.
see sect. 72.

Owner, of ruinous buildings, to pay any deficiency after sale of materials, s. 42.
of building, liable for damage done by the falling down of chimney pots, &c., s. 44.
when liable to costs of works, s. 49.
liable to contribution, s. 50.

A

TABLE OF TIME

UNDER 7 & 8 VICT. CAP. LXXXIV.

	Months.	*Weeks.*	*Days.*	*Hours.*
Sect. 1. As to districts and officers, to come into operation, ...	.. *September* 1, 1844.			
Id. As to buildings, streets, and other matters,	.. *January* 31, 1845.			
Id. Acts in schedule A. repealed, ..	.. *January* 1, 1845.			
Sect. 2. Term "already built," used in reference to buildings by interpretation clause, to mean buildings built before, ...	.. *January* 1, 1845.			
Or commenced before that day, and covered in and rendered fit for use thereafter, within	12			
Id. Used in reference to streets and alleys, to apply to all streets and alleys made or laid out before, ...	.. *January* 1, 1845.			
And which shall be formed and rendered fit for use thereafter within	12			
Id. Term "hereafter to be built," used in reference to buildings to apply to all buildings built after	.. *January* 1, 1845.			
Or not covered in afterwards within ..	12			
With reference to streets and alleys, to apply to streets or alleys not laid out before ..	.. *January* 1, 1845.			
Or not rendered fit for use afterwards within	12			
Sect. 4. Notice of extending limits of act, before the said extension shall be taken into consideration, to be published previously by royal proclamation	1	..	..	..
Id. Copies of proclamation to be fixed on church doors, &c. before the same is considered	..	3	..	..
Sect. 13. Notice to surveyors of works under the act before they are commenced ..	..	..	2	..
Id. If builder suspend progress for any time exceeding	3	..	..	..
And then go on with the work, there must be a notice to the surveyor of	..	..	2	..
Id. But upon an emergency, work may be done if notice be given afterwards within	..	..	..	48

	Months.	Weeks.	Days.	Hours.
Sect. 14. Notice to amend irregularities in building to be given by surveyor to builder within	..	..	..	48
Id. Surveyor to advertise official referees if builder do not amend within such ..	..	..	..	48
Sect. 15. Official referees to survey buildings subject to special supervision, after notice from builder that the walls are built up; within	..	..	7	..
Id. And if they approve, to certify within ..	..	..	7	..
Or otherwise, after their survey, to give notice to builder to amend within	..	.	7	..
Id. Then after such amendment, upon a fresh notice by builder, to inspect the same within	..	..	7	..
Id. Next, upon completion and fresh notice, the referees to survey within	..	..	7	..
And, after such survey, if they approve, to certify within	..	..	14	..
And the building must not be used till the lapse, after such survey, of	..	..	14	..
Sect. 16. Certain works mentioned therein being amended, official referees are to inspect them within	..	..	7	..
Id. Official referees, upon completion of the said buildings, are to survey within ..	..	..	7	..
After survey, and no notice that official referees are not satisfied, still building may not be used without express authority from them, till the lapse from such survey of		..	14	..
Sect. 20. Workmen offending against the provisions of the act may be committed in default of payment of penalty for	1	..	..	.
Sect. 21. Notice of pulling down, repairing, &c., of party walls and party fence walls to be given by building owner at the least ..	3	..	..	..
Id. So with respect to intermixed walls and timber partitions a notice of	3	..	..	..
Sect. 22. If adjoining owner express a wish for modification within	2	.	..	..
Id. Then building owner must assent or dissent after such notice within	..	..	7	..
Id. If he do not assent or dissent, application is to be made to the official referees within ..	..	..	7	..
Id. And they must give their decision thereupon within	..	..	10	..
Id. However, the building owner may proceed with the work if no objection or requisition of any kind be made by the adjoining owner within ..	3	..	..	..
Sect. 23. If, after notice from building owner, adjoining owner express a desire that the work should be delayed, within	3	..	..	..
Then building owner must express his assent or dissent after such notice within	..	..	7	..
If he do not assent or dissent, application is to be made to the official referees within ..	..	..	7	

	Months.	*Weeks.*	*Days.*	*Hours.*
And they must decide within	..	..	10	..
However, building owner may proceed with work, if no objection or requisition be made by adjoining owner within	3			
Sect. 24. Notice of survey by surveyor for the purpose of certifying concerning works ..	..	[*Forthwith.*]		
Certificate of surveyor as to works, to be confirmed by official referees, if not appealed from within	..	..	7	..
Sect. 25. [Repair of walls at joint expense.] *See* Schedule M., No. 8, notice of . ..	3	..	..	..
Sect. 26. [Rebuilding of party walls by building owner.] Schedule M., No. 14, notice of ..	3	..	..	..
Sect. 28. [Cutting into footings and chimneys.] Before building owner does this, he must give to adjoining owner a notice of	1	..	..	..
Sect. 29. Building owner to make good, damage	..	[*All due dispatch.*]		
Sect. 32. [Repair or rebuilding of party fence walls.] Notice must be given to adjoining owner of	1	..	..	..
Sect. 33. [Pulling down timber partitions.] Building owner to give to adjoining owner a notice of	3	..	..	..
Schedule M., No. 11.	..	..	..	..
Sect. 36. Power for building owner, &c. to enter upon premises to effect works, and abide during the usual times of working ..	[*Between* 6 *a.m. and* 7 *p.m., Sunday excepted.*]			
Sect. 37. [Stopping up openings in external walls.] Adjoining owner may require such stopping upon giving a notice of . ..	1	..	..	..
Schedule M., No. 3.	..	..	..	..
Sect. 38. [Building upon vacant ground.] Notice by building owner to adjoining owner or occupier of vacant ground, of ..	1	..	..	..
Id. Building owner may build on the line of junction, if assent be given by adjoining owner within	1	..	..	..
Sect. 39. Then, consent being given, a notice of the beginning to build party wall must still be given of	..	..	10	..
Sect. 40. Upon receiving information of ruinous buildings, surveyor and overseers to apply to official referees for a survey. *See* s. 13.	..	[*Forthwith.*]		
Id. Upon receiving certificate of surveyor, Lord Mayor, &c. and overseers to cause ruinous building to be shored, &c.	[*With all convenient speed.*]			
Id. And to give notice to owner to repair or pull it down within	..	..	14	..
Id. And Lord Mayor, &c. and overseers may themselves pull down or repair if the owner neglect to begin the work within ..	..	..	14	..
Sect. 41. Materials to be sold, and surplus to be accounted for	..	[*Upon demand.*]		

	Months.	Weeks.	Days.	Hours.
Sect. 41. If owner claim such surplus at any time from the deposit of such surplus within ..	..	6 *Years.*		
Sect. 42. On the contrary, if there be a deficiency, owner to pay it	..	[*On demand.*]		
Sect. 43. Ruinous chimney pots must be repaired by occupier, &c. after a notice by surveyor of	..	..	..	36
Sect. 47. After completion of works, an account in writing of the expenses of such works to be delivered to adjoining owner within ..	.	..	21	..
Id. But he may appeal against the account to the official referees, after such delivery within ..	..	..	10	..
Id. If no appeal, the money must be paid within	..	..	10	..
Id. So, after certificate of approval by official referees, the money, being first demanded, must be paid within	..	..	10	..
Sect. 53. No underground rooms or cellars to be occupied as dwellings after . ..	..	[*July* 1, 1845.]		
Id. Report to be made to official referees by overseers as to the number and situation of such dwellings	[*On or before Jan.* 1, 1845.]			
Sect. 54. Buildings dangerous with respect to fire prohibited within certain distances, but a period allowed to discontinue them of ..	..	[20 *Years.*]		
Id. Penalty for disobedience to this order. Upon failure of payment, offender may be imprisoned for a term not exceeding ..	6	..	..	..
Sect. 55. Businesses noxious or offensive. Period of discontinuance for . ..	..	[30 *Years.*]		
Id. Penalty, &c. as above, and imprisonment, &c., *see* s. 56	6	..	..	..
Sect. 57. But the party may appeal to the general Quarter Sessions within	..	..	4	..
Id. Such Quarter Sessions to be holden within	4	..	..	..
Id. But he must give notice of the grounds of appeal after entering into the recognizance within	1	..	..	..
See s. 58.	..	..	..	..
Sect. 59. Adjournments of sessions for trying appeals within	..	6	..	..
And further adjournments within ..	..	3	..	.
Sect. 61. Obnoxious trades may be purchased by means of a memorial to the Queen in Council	..	..	..	..
Compensation to be settled by jury. Then, after verdict, if the inhabitants of the parish or neighbourhood pay or tender the compensation assessed, within	3	..	..	..
Id. It shall not be lawful for the owner or occupier to continue the aforesaid business for a longer time afterwards than within ..	3	..	..	..
Must be abated after verdict, within ..	6	..	..	..
Sect. 66. A certificate must be produced by candidate for the office of surveyor, before the election	..	..	..	..

	Months.	Weeks.	Days.	Hours.
Sect. 72. Surveyor to attend at his office from	[10 *a. m. till* 4 *p. m. Sundays, Christmas Day, and Good Friday excepted.*]			
Sect. 74. Upon the death or removal of surveyor, his successor to be appointed by Lord Mayor and Justices, within	1	..	..	..
Sect. 77. After roof of building has been covered in and walls built up to their full height, &c.	1	..	..	..
Surveyor may deliver his account of fees at the expiration of	1	.	..	.
Id. So after the completion of any addition, alteration, or repair the like, at the expiration of	..	..	14	..
Id. So after each special service performed, the like, at the expiration of	..	..	14	..
Sect. 78. Surveyor to make a return of works &c. to the registrar of Metropolitan buildings, within	[7 *days after the first of any month.*]			
Sect. 79. Notice of complaints against surveyor to be served upon him by complainant before the hearing, at the least	..	..	10	..
Sect. 85. No person need attend official referees as a witness under a summons for more days consecutively than	..	..	2	..
Sect. 96. Official referees to be paid their salaries each year in	[*June and December.*]			
Sect. 103. [Proceedings for penalties,] Offenders may be committed upon failure of payment, for any period not exceeding	3	..	..	..
Sect. 105. Party convicted may appeal to the General Quarter Sessions, within	..	..	4	..
Such Quarter Sessions to be holden within	4	..	..	..
Sect. 106. Prosecutions for penalties must be instituted within	6	..	..	..
Sect. 108. No action to be brought against any person for any thing done in pursuance of the act, after	6	..	..	..
Id. And notice in writing of the intention to bring such action must be given before the commencement thereof, at the least . ..	..	..	21	..
Id. There must be a verdict for the defendant, if such notice be not given of	..	.	21	..
Sect. 110. Penalty for *default* in complying with the provisions of the act, to be sued for within	3	..	..	..
Id. However, if any other than the surveyor or official referees take such proceedings, there must be left previously at the office of the surveyor and of the registrar, a notice of ..	..	..	7	..

ERRATUM.

Page 2, (*note*), omit "See likewise Schedule D., Part VI."

ADDENDA.

Page 112, note (*z*), and see likewise, Peake, Add. Ca. 15, *Lukin and another* v. *Godsall.*

Page 303.—Under 5 & 6 Wm. 4, c. 50, s. 53, a certain notice is to be given before the surveyor can take materials from any "*inclosed land or ground.*" A similar provision appears in the Turnpike Act, 3 Geo. 4, c. 126, ss. 97 and 98. These words "inclosed land or ground," gave rise to a decision of the Court of Exchequer, by which a plaintiff, whose sheep down, although it was private property, was not fenced off on all sides, was deemed not to have an inclosure within the Act, 3 Geo. 4, c. 126. The surveyor, therefore, who was the defendant in an action for taking materials from inclosed lands, succeeded in obtaining a rule to enter a nonsuit. (*a*) But now, by 4 & 5 Vict. c. 51, all lands and grounds which shall be in the exclusive occupation of one or more persons for agricultural purposes, shall be deemed and taken to be inclosed lands or grounds within the meaning of the recited Acts (3 Geo. 4, c. 126, and 5 & 6 Wm. 4, c. 50), although the same may not be separated from any adjoining lands or grounds of other persons, or from the highway, by any fence or inclosure. And note, that where the surveyor makes any pits or holes in getting materials, he must cause such pits or holes to be fenced off, and must support and repair such fence whilst the pit or hole continues open. If no materials are found, he must cause such pits or holes to be filled up within three days after the opening thereof. If found then, within fourteen days after having dug up sufficient materials, he must cause such pits or holes to be filled up, or sloped down, and fenced off, if required by the owner of the land, and so continued. Every surveyor, likewise, upon coming into office, shall cause all unnecessary pits and holes to be filled up, and sloped down, and, if further useful, to be secured by posts and rails or other fences to prevent accidents to persons or cattle. For every default he may be fined 10*s*. And if he neglects to do these acts after notice from a justice, or from the owner or occupier of any ground, &c., or from any person having a right

(*a*) 7 Mees. & Wels. 441, *Tapsell* v. *Crosskey.*

of common, he may be fined 10*l.* at a special sessions, to be laid out in fencing, sloping down, &c. and towards the repair of the road. 5 & 6 Wm. 4, c. 50, s. 55. And see sects. 101, 102, 103. Similar provisions will be found in the Turnpike Act, 3 Geo. 4, c. 126, s. 99, the forfeiture being not less than 40*s.* and not exceeding 10*l.*

Page 304, note.—As to making new ditches and fences where narrow ways are widened, see 5 & 6 Wm. 4, c. 50, s. 82.

Page 313, [*Return to Mandamus.*]—Turnpike trustees had carried a road over certain private grounds, but had not fenced them according to the statute. Upon a writ of mandamus being issued, a return was made, 1. Denying the ownership of the land; upon which issue was joined, and a verdict found for the crown; 2. Alleging that satisfaction had been made by the trustees to the owner of the land under 3 Geo. 4, c. 126, s. 83, which satisfaction had been accepted; and further, that the owner had taken security for the amount, and had proceeded to enforce the security. 3. Alleging want of funds on the part of the trustees. These latter allegations were not answered, but, notwithstanding, a peremptory mandamus was ordered to issue. The trustees, having made the road, could not excuse themselves from the duty; if they had not adequate funds, they ought not to have made the road, and the acquiescence of the prosecutor for a long time was held to make no difference (*a*).

(*a*) 1 Q. B. Rep. 860, *R.* v. *Luton Road Trustees.*

THE

LAW OF PARTY WALLS,

&c.

CHAPTER I.

Of the Ownership of Party Walls, and other Incidents.

Ownership of party walls, and of the land whereon they stand.

We must consider the question of the Ownership of Party Walls with the aid of the Building Act (*a*). This act is limited within certain boundaries (*b*), so that buildings and walls situate without those boundaries, must be referred to the common law. Now it is a good doctrine that the building ensues the nature of the tenure of the land on which walls are built (*c*). So that a joint tenancy, for instance, or a tenancy in common of the land would govern the house and walls. "There must be a conveyance to pass the property of the soil, it will not pass by parol agreement." (*d*) Therefore, as a

(*a*) 7 & 8 Vict. c. 84. (*b*) Sect. 3.

(*c*) 5 Taunt. 23, by Heath, J. "And an award, directing that a wall shall be built at the joint expense of adjoining owners, will not alter the right of soil. So that the direction of a Judge was held right, who told the jury, notwithstanding the award, that if they believed the ground upon which the wall had been built, to be the exclusive property of the defendant, it should find for the defendant." 1 Alc. & Napier, 155, Hutchinson *v.* Mains.

(*d*) 5 Taunt. 23.

Ownership of party walls, and of the land whereon they stand.

general principle, whether the Building Act be called into the question or not, a party cannot meddle with the wall of his neighbour under the pretence of his being equally interested in every portion of the erection, in that, for example, which stands upon the land of his neighbour. This point came under discussion some years since, when every argument was resorted to in order to make out a case in favour of a defendant who had pulled down part of a fence wall which displeased him. Nevertheless, in reading this case, we must bear in mind the 32nd section of the new act (*e*), which makes it lawful for the owner of any of the premises parted by a fence wall to repair, pull down, and rebuild the same; and if the wall be below the height of nine feet above the ground on either side, he may either raise it to that height, or pull it down and rebuild it to that height; upon condition, nevertheless, that he pay all the expenses thereof. And further, if a building be to be erected against such party fence wall, and such wall be not conformable to the requisites prescribed for a proper party wall for a building of that class and rate, the building owner may pull down such party fence wall, upon condition of his paying all the expenses of the same. The plaintiff and defendant owned adjoining premises on which there was a party [fence] wall. The plaintiff, without any communication with the defendant, began to raise this wall higher than it had formerly been, in order to add to certain buildings on *his* side of the wall, when the defendant thought proper to pull down the wall to its former height. Upon this, trespass was brought, and it was proved for the plaintiff that this was a party fence wall, built above twenty-five years before, at

(*e*) See the section, *post*, in the Appendix. ~~See likewise Schedule D., Part VI.~~

Ownership of party walls, and of the land whereon they stand.

the joint expense of both proprietors, and that it stood on the boundary line, so that half of the wall was on the ground of each proprietor. The defendant contended at the trial,—1st. That the plaintiff had no right to add to the wall, as he had done, without giving notice (*f*) to the defendant under section 38 of the Building Act (*g*); and 2ndly, that the defendant was tenant in common with the plaintiff of this wall, so that no action could be supported by the plaintiff against his companion for pulling down the common property. The jury found for the plaintiff, damages 40*s*. and *Mansfield*, C.J., reserved the points. It was urged for the defendant, that much inconvenience would ensue if it were competent for one man to make a severance by splitting his neighbour's wall, for the necessary consequence would be, that the other proprietor's half of the wall would fall down. To be sure, a Court of Equity might interfere to prevent this destruction; but it would be upon the principle that the parties are tenants in common, and that being so, an action of trespass cannot be maintained. The Court, however, decided for the plaintiff, and discharged the rule to enter a nonsuit. Mr. Justice *Chambre* said, "that the statute which gave each party certain rights in a wall built in this way, did not make it a common property; it only conferred on each a right to use it for certain purposes. There had been here no transfer of property, and the parties were severally owners of their respective land as before." The Court said, that these parties had no tenancy in common of this wall, that the joint expenditure in building the wall originally was no evidence of such a tenancy, that the Building Act did

(*f*) Three months' notice in writing of the plaintiff's intention to repair or build the party wall.

(*g*) 14 Geo. 3, c. 78.

Ownership of party walls, and of the land whereon they stand.

not alter the relation of the plaintiff and defendant in this respect, and that, for any injury done to the wall which stands upon the land of either party, there must be the ordinary remedy (*h*). Nevertheless, there may be, and there often is, a tenancy in common of party walls, and in such a case, one tenant, who sustains an injury by interference, cannot succeed in an action of trespass as in *Matts* v. *Hawkins*(*i*). The ownership in the event of a tenancy in common consists of an undivided property in both walls, and this is a matter of evidence, for in order to make out the point, a joint use of the wall by both proprietors must be shewn. Then the presumption arising from acts of enjoyment is, that the wall is the property of the two owners as tenants in common, and here again the property in the wall clearly ensues the nature of the tenure of the land where it is erected. If the evidence shows a separate interest, and a distinct user, the ownership is several, but if a joint interference comes out in proof, a tenancy in common is the ownership, with all the incidents attached to that tenure (*k*). A covenant with a party that he shall build a wall of such a height, as seven feet, for instance, shews that the possession of the land on which the wall is to be built is in that party, unless there be something to rebut the presumption (*l*).

These authorities will be cited in all cases to which they may apply beyond the limits of the new act. And

(*h*) 5 Taunt. 20, Matts *v.* Hawkins.

(*i*) See *post*, Chap. III.

(*k*) See 8 B. & C. 259, Wiltshire *v.* Sidford; S. C. 1 Man. & Ry. 403, cited there. 8 B. & C. 257, Cubitt *v.* Porter; S. C. 2 Man. & Ry. 267. 8 Adol. & El. 138, Murly *v.* McDermott; S. C. 3 Nev. & P. 356. See also 1 Man. & Ry. 63, Noye *v.* Reed; and *post*, Chap. III., where these points are fully discussed.

(*l*) 1 Arnold, 341, in Alexander *v.* Bonnin.

Ownership of party walls, and of the land whereon they stand.

they will probably hold as governing decisions within the scope of that act, where there is an old sound fence wall. For the original common law right of property in respect of walls of this nature, although modified by the permission to rebuild, is not taken away, and it may be added, that if the owner, desirous of making an alteration, does not abide by the various provisions of the statute, he will be liable to an action of trespass, independently of any penalties which the act itself may have pronounced against him. When we come to speak more particularly of party fence walls under the act, we shall have occasion to enter at large into the mode of building them, and it may, therefore, be sufficient for the present to observe, that a partial alteration of the fence wall may take place under the statute, if the owner chooses to rebuild or repair, and that a total destruction of the wall may be effected if it be not conformable to the act, when such owner is desirous of raising a structure against it. Perhaps, as it is not expressly declared that a party fence wall shall not exceed nine feet, it may be made a question, whether a wall above that height is a nuisance, or whether a building owner may not go higher than nine feet. Now if a wall of this kind may exceed nine feet, the original rights of ownership seem to remain unimpaired, at all events in respect of old walls above nine feet, as long as the wall requires neither repair nor rebuilding, and trespass will lie for an invasion of such a wall. And if an old wall above nine feet be repaired or rebuilt, there seem to be no words in the statute to forbid its being rebuilt to its former level. And, moreover, if any damage be done unnecessarily, or if there be an illegal interference with a wall, whether it be of the height of nine feet, or more or less than nine feet, so as to produce a consequential injury, an action on the case may probably be maintained.

Ownership of party walls, and of the land whereon they stand.

Whereas, on the other hand, supposing that the new statute will bear the interpretation that a fence wall may be more than nine feet in height, a party who raises his wall above that measurement *to the detriment of his neighbour*, may be liable to an action upon the case, or of trespass, if he meddle with that portion of the wall which belongs to the tenant in common with himself, although the statute may not disallow the elevation. The ownership seems to be broken in upon by the statute only when a fence wall is out of repair, of whatever height it may be, or when it is not nine feet high; in these cases any owner may repair it on the one hand, or raise it on the other, subject to the notices and provisions ordained by the respective clauses.

But as the maxim, *expressio unius est exclusio alterius*, is one which the law recognises and approves, it may be considered very unsafe to raise a wall above nine feet which has been always below that level, however reasonable it may be to assume, on the other hand, that an ancient wall above nine feet is not affected by the statute.

It might be conceived that the property of a party wall would be exactly divisible into two equal parts, where there are only two owners. That which we have already said upon the subject would seem to favour this view. The common custom is very much to the same end. And the statutes which so frequently speak of a moiety evidently recognise this joint right of equality. But this division into half is not to be trusted as a principle, neither where the statute rules, nor without the limits of its range. The principle most worthy of acceptation both at common law and by statute concerning this matter, seems to be that existing rights of ownership shall, if possible, be deemed inviolate. If, therefore, there be a just ground for admitting a proportion, more

Ownership of party walls, and of the land whereon they stand.

or less, than half of the property of a wall, the Legislature has sanctioned rather than invaded the unequal claim. Now as the act declares that a party wall shall be built half upon the ground of one owner, and half upon that of the other (*m*), it might possibly result, that the owner of the ground adjoining the new wall might claim a moiety of the soil, and so encroach upon the property of his neighbour. Wherefore, by Sect. 30 (*n*), with regard to any sound party wall against which an external wall shall have been built, and which shall have been suffered to remain, so far as relates to the rebuilding thereof, it is enacted, that if while such party wall continues sound, the adjoining buildings be pulled down or rebuilt, and such party wall be pulled down, then the owner of such adjoining building shall not be entitled to more than his just proportion of the materials thereof, nor to more than his just proportion of the ground on which such party wall was built, nor shall he build on more than his just proportion of the said ground, unless he shall have agreed with and satisfied the owner of the building so previously rebuilt for his half thereof (*o*). The external wall, therefore, shall not count so as to enable the adjoining owner to reckon from the middle of the original sound party wall to the exterior of the external wall, unless he make compensation; for otherwise he would encroach upon the land of his neighbour. The only instance in the act of an exception

(*m*) Schedule D., Part III., "Site of Walls."

(*n*) See the section, *post*, Append.

(*o*) Disputes are referred to the official referees; for if the said owners cannot agree concerning the division of the said materials, or of such ground, or of the building thereon, or concerning the reimbursement of the party first rebuilding as aforesaid, then the price, and all matters in difference, including the sale and purchase of the ground in question, shall be settled by a reference to the official referees, whose award shall be final.

Ownership of party walls, and of the land whereon they stand.

to this rule, (and even then it is more like a suspension of right than an extinguishment of it) is where a party wall has been legally built by an individual owner, and the adjoining owner, being liable, has not paid his contribution. Here, until the expenses are duly paid, the right of soil and the sole property of the wall are declared to be vested entirely in the person at whose expense such party structure shall have been built. And the Legislature thus divests the original right till the money is reimbursed (*p*). The same principle obtains with respect to contribution: for by the 46th section, the person building a party wall is to recover a sum of money proportionate to the value of so much of the party structure made use of, whether it be a new wall, or an unsound wall rebuilt, or a wall built in lieu of a timber partition, or a wall used by an adjoining owner after having been built or rebuilt. So again, the same principle is carried on in respect of houses of different rates which adjoin to each other. For, if a building of a lower rate be enlarged or altered so as to become one of a higher rate, the owner of the same must make a proportionate compensation to the building owner according to the increased rate of his structure. This modification was admitted in disputes concerning contribution under the 14 Geo. 3, c. 78, where the evidence made it clear that the rates of adjoining buildings were unequal (*q*). But beyond the boundaries of the statute, no such arrangement can of course be insisted on.

Ownership of party walls.

Ownership of Party Walls.]—Then it may be added, that in the country, or beyond the reach of

(*p*) Sect. 46, at the end. See likewise sect. 38, where there is a similar provision concerning party walls raised next to vacant ground.

(*q*) 2 Taunt. 66, Philp *v.* Donati.

Ownership of party walls.

the statute 7 & 8 Vict. c. 84, the wall will usually be found to belong in equal moieties to both owners, and the cases in London and its neighbourhood—which may happen to deviate from this rule, will probably at no distant period be rare exceptions. The common law leans strongly towards the equal division—in the one case, and the Schedule of the new Act above referred to expresses the same arrangement particularly in the other. The 38th section also follows the same rule where an owner proposes to build upon vacant ground, and seeks the consent of the neighbouring owner to build the party wall at their joint cost (*r*). Whereas the 30th section, and the reimbursing clause, maintain the exception above adverted to in cases where it is clear that there cannot be an equal right to each portion of the party wall. And, of course, an external wall, being built wholly upon the ground of a single owner cannot be the subject of joint property. However, as we shall see by and by, this ownership of the external wall will not allow of opening windows or other apertures without the consent of the adjoining owner (*s*). It should not escape remark that the word, "owner," means "every person in possession or receipt either of the whole or any part of the rents or profits of any ground or tenement, or in the occupation of such ground or tenement, other than a tenant from year to year, or a tenant at will" (*t*).

A wall is not the less an external wall because another house adjoins to it. There was a dispute between a lessor and lessee as to the repairs of a house

(*r*) See 2 Sir Wm. Bl. 959, Barlow *v.* Norman, where the same law obtained under the old acts, 12 Geo. 3, and 14 Geo. 3.

(*s*) Sect. 37.

(*t*) Sect 2, "Interpretation Clause."

Ownership of party walls.

which had been damaged by the act of a corporation. The lessor had covenanted with his tenant to keep in repair all the external parts of the demised premises except the glass and lead of the windows. The premises were in the High-street, Exeter, and they adjoined the Swan Inn there. The Corporation of Exeter pulled down the Swan Inn, and, in so doing, exposed the wall which had divided the Swan Inn from the house in question. It was said likewise, that the injudicious manner of removing the beams belonging to the Swan was the cause of the wall of the house being unsafe. Upon that the lessee removed, and upon his landlord's refusal to repair or rebuild, he did the necessary repairs himself, and brought his action upon the covenant. The jury found for the plaintiff. But it was contended, upon a rule to enter a verdict for the defendant, amongst other points, that the wall pulled down was not an external wall within the meaning of the covenant; for that the external parts were those which were exposed to the air and to the view of the landlord. But the Court gave judgment against the objection. "We think," said Lord Denman, "that it (the wall) was an external part of the premises before the Swan was pulled down, but certainly afterwards. The external parts of premises are those which form the inclosure of them, and beyond which no part of them extends: and it is immaterial whether those parts are exposed to the atmosphere, or rest upon and adjoin some other building which forms no part of the premises let" (*u*).

(*u*) 2 Ad. & El. N. S. 225, Green *v.* Eales.

CHAPTER II.

Of Party and other Walls under the Building Act, 7 & 8 Vict. c. 84.

Building Acts.

THE chief principle of the Building Acts seems to have been the preservation of dwellings from fire, and the main cause of them arose, most probably, from the great Fire of London, in 1666. For, in 1667, 19 Car. 2, we find an act for rebuilding the city of London (*a*); and again, in 1670, 22 Car. 2, another act, entitled, "An additional Act for the Rebuilding of the City of London, uniting of Parishes, and Rebuilding of the Cathedral and Parochial Churches within the said City" (*b*). Again, in 1707, 6 Anne, we have an act to prevent mischiefs that may happen by fire (*c*). In 1724, party walls in particular had given rise to so much inquiry and to such litigation, that the mode of reimbursement came to be a matter of more accurate legislation (*d*). In 1759, the widening of streets attracted attention, and an act was passed which made regulations for this purpose (*e*). In this statute also party walls, the ruinous condition of buildings, and the state of pavements were subjects of attention (*f*). Another act, giving still more extensive powers, passed in 1763 (*g*); and one other to amend and make more effectual the 33 Geo. 2, c. 30, succeeded

(*a*) 19 Car. 2, c. 3.
(*b*) 22 Car. 2, c. 11.
(*c*) 6 Ann. c. 31. See likewise 7 Ann. c. 17.
(*d*) 11 Geo. 1, c. 28.
(*e*) 33 Geo. 2, c. 30.
(*f*) See Sect. 24, *et seq.*
(*g*) 4 Geo. 3, c. 14.

Building Acts.

three years afterwards (*h*). A more general act now engrossed the attention of the Legislature, repealing some of the earlier statutes upon the subject (*i*), till at length the whole ripened into the 14 Geo. 3, c. 78, the late Building Act: "An Act for the further and better Regulation of Buildings, and Party Walls; and for the more effectually preventing Mischiefs by Fire, and for the Indemnity of Builders under certain circumstances." This act, which was not very intelligible to the learned Judges who did not hesitate to express their disapprobation of its obscurities (*k*), incorporated the leading principles of the law concerning these matters, and embraced all the material provisions of the former statutes. The safety of premises against fire, the architectural disposition of the party walls, the compulsory process to make parties assent to such erections, the duties of surveyors, the mode of apportioning expenses, the rewards given for activity in bringing up engines to a fire, and the general forms of procedure necessary towards the carrying out of the act—all these were prominent features in this statute. But notwithstanding the care bestowed upon it, this consolidation of the building law was not a work of skill. The Judges seem never to have missed an opportunity of censuring its provisions, they even advised parties to avoid so intricate an act; and had parties rightly understood their own interests, it is probable that many harassing lawsuits would have been saved. There was, in particular, one clause which abounded in litigation—it was the 41st section, and it related to the important question of reimbursing individuals who should build party walls at their own cost. The compensation was to

(*h*) 6 Geo. 3, c. 27. (*i*) 12 Geo. 3, c. 73.

(*k*) 1 Bos. & Pul. 305, Eyre, C. J. 5 Taunt. 99, Mansfield, C. J. 2 Marsh, 436, Gibbs, C. J. 4 Bingh. 554, Best, C. J.

Building Acts.

be made by the owner or owners who should be entitled to the *improved* rent of the adjoining building or ground, and who should at any time make use of such party wall (*l*). These words, "Owner or owners of the improved Rent," occasioned a very considerable amount of discussion in the Courts. Sometimes the term, "improved rent," was confounded with "improved value" (*m*); very frequently a landlord sought to load his tenant with the burden, upon the ground of improvements made by the tenant, sometimes, amidst a multiplicity of interests, it became difficult to discover the proprietor of this improved rent, and, indeed, no subterfuge was left untried on the part of the person charged with the claim of reimbursement to cast the obligation from his own shoulders and repose it upon those of another as the legal owner of the improved rent. Taking, therefore, this constant theme of dispute into our consideration, together with other difficulties of a less important nature, it is not surprising that the Legislature should have resolved upon introducing an entirely new act for the regulation of buildings in or near the Metropolis, and the only matter for wonder is, that such a step should have been so long delayed. We must, consequently, take leave of this statute, 14 Geo. 3, c. 78, with its intricacies and embarrassments, and apply ourselves to the provisions of an act which professes to have avoided the blunders of the old one, and to have introduced, moreover, considerable improvements in the clauses more particularly devoted to the science of build-

(*l*) See 5 T. R. 130, Peck *v.* Wood. 1 Bos. & P. 303, Sangster *v.* Birkhead. 4 Bingh. 551, Collins *v.* Wilson. 2 B. & Adol. 878, Williams *v.* Pocklington; and 3 T. R. 461.

(*m*) See 3 T. R. 458, Southall *v.* Leadbetter. 8 T. R. 214, Beardmore *v.* Fox. 2 B. & Ald. 467, Lambe *v.* Hemans. 6 Taunt. 139, Taylor *v.* Reed. See 7 Taunt. 159.

Building Act. 7 & 8 Vict. c. 84.

ing. This new act repeals the existing laws upon the subject (n). Its preamble expresses the propriety—1. Of extending the limits within which building regulations may be enforced; 2. Of improving the drainage of the metropolis and its neighbourhood; 3. Of securing a sufficient width of streets and ways; 4. Of discouraging and prohibiting the use of dwellings unfit for habitation, and whereby disease is fostered and propagated; 5. Of controlling explosive or inflammable works; 6. Nöisome or deleterious works; and 7. Of regulating the office of surveyor, and of modifying the rules laid down for building where the strict execution would be impracticable or inconvenient (o). The act then goes on to define certain terms and expressions used in it, an alphabet of which, with the respective constructions directed by the statute, as far as walls are concerned, is appended in the note (p).

(n) That is to say, 14 Geo. 3, c. 78, except as to bygone penalties incurred, and fees due, and matters relating to fires; 50 Geo. 3, c. 75, 3 & 4 Vict. c. 85, as far as relates to the construction and regulation of chimneys within the limits of the act: all which are repealed by the 1st section of the new statute, referring to schedule A.

(o) Sect. 1. The act, with regard to districts and officers, was fixed to come into operation on the 1st of September, 1844; and as to buildings, streets, and other matters, on the 1st of January, 1845.

(p) "Interpretation Clause," sect. 2:—

Alley.]—See the act, *post*, Append.

Already built.]—Used, in reference to buildings, to apply to buildings built before 1st January, 1845, or commenced before that day, and covered in and rendered fit for use within twelve months thereafter.

Commissioners of Works and Buildings.]—The Commissioners of her Majesty's Woods, Forests, Land Revenues, Works, and Buildings.

External Wall.]—To comprise all outer walls of buildings now or hereafter to be built, which shall stand wholly upon ground of the owner of such buildings, and shall not be used or intended to be used as party walls, under the definition hereinafter contained,

For it is desirable to confine the matters of this chapter as strictly as possible to the consideration of walls, and if, for the sake of understanding the subject better, we

Building Act.

whether the same shall adjoin or not to other outer, or to party walls.

Floor.]—To mean the horizontal platform forming the base of any story, and to include the timber or boarding, or any other substance which constitutes such platform.

Hereafter to be built.]—Used in reference to buildings, to apply to all buildings to be built or commenced after 1st January, 1845, or which, being commenced, shall not be covered in within twelve months thereafter.

Justice of the Peace.]—To mean a justice of the peace for the county, division, or liberty within which the building or other subject-matter, or any part thereof, is situate; unless it be situate within the city of London, or the liberties thereof, in reference to which any matter or thing elsewhere required or authorized to be done, either by one, or by two or more justices of the peace, may be done either by the Lord Mayor of the city of London, or by any one, two, or more justices of the peace for the said city; or unless the subject-matter be situate in the district of any Police Court of the metropolis, in reference to which any matter or thing elsewhere required or authorized to be done by two or more justices, may be done by one magistrate.

Month.]—A calendar month.

Official Referees.]—To mean the persons appointed in pursuance of this act to be official referees of metropolitan buildings.

Owner.]—To apply to every person in possession or receipt, whether of the whole or of any part of the rents or profits of any ground or tenement, or in the occupation of such ground or tenement, other than a tenant from year to year, or a tenant at will.

Party wall.]—To comprise all walls which shall be used or built in order to be used as a separation of two or more buildings for the occupation of different families, or actually occupied by different families, and also all walls which shall stand upon ground not wholly belonging to the same ownership or occupation.

Square.]—One hundred superficial feet. See the act, *post*, Append.

Story.]—See the act, *post*, Append.

Street.]—See the act, *post*, Append.

Surveyor.]—To apply to all surveyors to be appointed in pursuance of this act, or whose appointment is confirmed by this act;

Building Act.

step, for a moment out of the way to mention the provisions of the various sections, there will be but a brief notice of them, and we shall proceed, afterwards, to enter fully into the examination of those clauses which bear upon the law of party and other walls.

Limits.

Limits.]—By section 3, the limits of the act are defined to be all such places lying on the north side or left bank of the Thames, as are within the exterior boundaries of Fulham, Hammersmith, Kensington, Paddington, Hampstead, Hornsey, Tottenham, St. Pancras, Islington, Stoke Newington, Hackney, Stratford-le-Bow, Bromley, Poplar, and Shadwell: and to such part of Chelsea as lies north of Kensington: and to all such parts and places lying on the south side or right bank of the Thames as are within the exterior boundaries of Woolwich, Charlton, Greenwich, Deptford, Lee, Lewisham, Camberwell, Lambeth, Streatham, Tooting, and Wandsworth: and to all places lying within two hundred yards from the exterior boundary of the district hereby defined (*q*). However, by the next section, the act may be extended, by an order

and also to all deputies or assistant surveyors to be appointed under this act.

The Surveyor.]—Used without any addition, to mean the surveyor in whose district the buildings, street, or alley, or other subject-matter shall be, or any deputy or assistant surveyor duly acting in his behalf.

And, generally, the name of "officer," having local jurisdiction, shall mean the officer having jurisdiction in the place where the building or other subject-matter is situate. See the act, *post*, Append.

Lastly, the singular number shall include the plural, the masculine gender the feminine, and words importing an individual, shall apply to a corporation or company, or other body of persons, subject to the context, and to the nature of the subject-matter. See the act, *post*, Append.

(*q*) See the section, *post*, Append.

Limits.

in council, to any place within twelve miles of Charing-cross, and the provisions of the act shall extend thereto, so far as they shall be capable of application to such places (*r*); and notice of the time of considering such extension shall be given by proclamation in the *London Gazette* one month at least before such consideration, and three weeks before such consideration the official referees and overseers of parishes shall cause notice of such proclamation to be fixed on the doors of the churches and chapels, and every order in council made in pursuance of the enactment shall be published in the *London Gazette*.

The 5th section refers all buildings within the limits above prescribed (except certain buildings comprised in Schedule B. (*s*) and except sewers) to certain schedules annexed to the act (*t*). Every such building is to be built, rebuilt, enlarged, or altered in reference to the walls, whether external or party walls, and to the fences, and the party fence walls, &c. in conformity with the particulars set forth in these schedules. Subject, nevertheless, to any other rules and directions of the act, and subject also, in cases of dispute, to the determination of the official referees (*u*), upon a reference made to them in that behalf (*x*). Section 6, notwithstanding, retains a certain list of important buildings, and places them under what is called a special supervision. The official referees, as well as the surveyor, are to control the building of this class of structures, and they are to decide whether any particular structure shall be such as to come under their supervision, subject nevertheless to an appeal to the

(*r*) See the section, *post*, Append.

(*s*) See Schedule B., *post*, Append.

(*t*) See Schedules, C. D. E. F. G. H. I. K., *post*, Append.

(*u*) These official referees, two in number, are introduced to us in the 80th section.

(*x*) See the section, *i. e.* sect. 5, *post*, Append.

Building Act. commissioners of works (*y*). Section 7 places the excepted buildings mentioned in schedule B., Part I., under the special supervision of the official referees, and exempts every building mentioned in schedule B., Part II., from supervision (*z*). Then, if there be a building desired by any person which will not fall under any class or rate, it may be built (by section 8) under the direction of the surveyor, subject to an appeal to the official referees (*a*). The next clause modifies contracts which may happen to clash with the provisions of the act, permitting a reference to the surveyor and official referees (*b*). So, again, there is a modification with respect to building leases which must be executed in conformity with the act (*c*). There is, next, a general power of modification, which is committed to the commissioners of works, in order to secure the adoption of improvements (*d*). And, as to existing buildings proposed to be rebuilt, if a compliance with the act, would produce "extreme loss and inconvenience;" there is again a power to modify, subject to the report of the official referees, and the consent of the commissioners of works, *provided that the party walls and the external wall be of the required height and thickness* (*e*). The 13th is an important section with regard to notice: a heavy penalty is awarded against builders and others who shall build, or alter, or pull down, without giving two days' notice (*f*), and the 14th provides for irregu-

(*y*) See the section, *post*, Append.
(*z*) See the section, *post*, Append.
(*a*) See the section, *post*, Append.
(*b*) See section 9, *post*, Append.
(*c*) See section 10, *post*, Append.
(*d*) See section 11, *post*, Append.
(*e*) See section 12, *post*, Append.
(*f*) See *post*, in this Chapter, "Party Walls;" and see the section, *post*, Append., and Schedule M., "Summary of Proceedings respecting Notices."

Building Act.

larities in building, due notice being first given by the surveyor (*g*). Next comes the 15th section, watching over the highest rate buildings, except the buildings exempted in schedule B. First, notice is to be given to the official referees that the structure is ready to be covered in (*h*). They are then to survey it, and should they approve, to give a certificate of approval within seven days after survey, or, on the other hand, to give within such seven days a notice in writing to the builder of their disapproval. The amendment must then be made, and notice given to the official referees of such amendment. The official referees must then inspect the same within seven days, and in default thereof all such amended parts of the building may be covered up at the end of such seven days. Secondly, when the building is finished a fresh notice must be sent to the official referees, upon which, within seven days, there shall be a new survey, and certificate (*i*), if the structure be approved of. Moreover, such building may not be used till the certificate last mentioned has been obtained, or until fourteen days after such survey shall have elapsed, without the official referees having given notice in writing that they are not satisfied, without the express authority of the referees under their hand, and the seal of office of the registrar. Then follows the penalty for using the building without such certificate or authority, or for

(*g*) See *post*, in this Chapter, "Party Walls;" and see the section, *post*, Append.

(*h*) See Lofft, Rep. 330, Payne *v*. Hill. The offence, under the old acts, was completed as soon as the wall was finished, at least, as soon as the shell was finished, after which, nothing done to the inside could make any alteration, especially as the action, under the old law, must have been brought within three months.

(*i*) Under their hand, and under the seal of office of the registrar of metropolitan buildings.

Building Act.

using the same without giving notice to the official referees within fourteen days after the completion of the building. Upon conviction before two justices, the owner or occupier shall forfeit a sum not exceeding 500*l.* for every day during which such building shall be so used. In determining the amount of the penalty, the justices shall have regard to the size and character of the building, and to the nature and extent of danger involved in the use of such building, and to the amount of profit which might be derived from such use thereof (*k*). Now, having excepted certain buildings in schedule B., the statute, nevertheless, by section 7, has subjected them to special supervision, and section 16 carries out the plan of this supervision which is not very dissimilar to the provision of the last section (*l*). A power of entry is ordained for the surveyor and referees in all these cases (*m*).

To proceed: all buildings, walls, projections, drains, and other works which are not constructed in accordance with the act are declared to be nuisances, and shall be prosecuted as such (*n*). The 19th section punishes offending workmen (*o*).

We now come to several clauses concerning party walls, including party fence walls, and walls where there are intermixed properties, and likewise external walls, which, upon many occasions have a near relation to party walls. These respective walls, form, of course, a very principal part of this chapter; so that the reader

(*k*) See the section, *post*, Append.

(*l*) See the section, *post*, Append. The penalty, however, for disobedience, may not exceed 100*l.*

(*m*) See *post*, "Party Walls;" and see section 17, *post*, Append.

(*n*) See *post*, "Party Walls;" and see section 18, *post*, Append.

(*o*) See the section, *post*, Append.

will be satisfied here with a mere reference to the clauses belonging to those walls (*p*) and will look forward to the full setting out of those sections presently. Building Act.

The three sections ensuing relate to ruinous buildings, (which may be said to include walls,) to the disposal of the materials of such buildings when pulled down, and the indemnity to the public for the expense of condemning them (*q*). Then comes the repair of ruinous chimnies, roofs, and projections (*r*), and the mode of compensating persons upon whose property anything may happen to fall and do damage, as chimney shafts, pots, parapets, &c. (*s*). Here, it is the duty of the owner of the building from which such chimney shaft, &c. shall fall, to reimburse the owner or occupier of the injured building for the damage done, in like manner as is directed concerning the reimbursement of the expenses of ruinous party walls (*t*), and such costs shall be recoverable in the manner directed for the recovery of the costs and expenses of executing works in pursuance of the act (*u*).

Having expressed the nature of the works to be done, the statute proceeds to shew how the money expended upon certain of them, as party walls, for instance, is to be recovered from the adjoining owners. And first, we have the Court of Mayor and Aldermen holden in the outer chamber of the Guildhall mentioned as a sufficient tribunal to exercise all powers vested by the act in the *Mayor and Aldermen* of London (*x*). Then follow the

(*p*) Sections 20 to 38, inclusive. See *post*, "Party Walls," &c.; and see the sections, *post*, Append.

(*q*) Sections 40, 41, 42. See *post*, in this chapter, "Party Walls." And see the sections, *post*, Append.

(*r*) Section 43, *post*, Append.

(*s*) Section 44, *post*, Append.

(*t*) That is, under section 46, as to the amount of reimbursement.

(*u*) See sections, 46, 47, 48, 49, 102.

(*x*) Section 45, *post*, Append.

Building Act. reimbursement clauses, which most especially regard party and other walls, and will, therefore, appear at length by-and-by (*y*). The 51st section directs the making of drains in conformity with the schedule (H) (*z*). The 52nd section prescribes the width of streets and alleys (*a*). The act then proceeds to forbid the letting of places unfit for habitation, as cellarages, &c., upon pain of forfeiting 20*s*. a-day upon conviction before two justices (*b*). Then ensues a prohibition under penalties for disobedience, (with certain modifications) of dangerous employments, such as the making of gunpowder, or ignitable matches, &c., unless they shall be carried on at a sufficient distance from public ways or human habitations (*c*). Then as there are certain businesses which are deemed injurious to health, no building is to be erected within a certain distance of them, nor may they be newly set up within certain distances of other buildings (*d*). Appeals are, however, given, with reference to trades which are not particularly specified by the statutes as obnoxious, or which have not been adjudged to be nuisances by her Majesty's Courts at Westminster (*e*). Those which the 55th section enumerates cannot be the subjects of appeal, nor can adjudged nuisances be so. The 58th section gives the privilege

(*y*) See *post*, "Party Walls." Sections 45 to 50, inclusive.

(*z*) See the section, *post*, Append., and Schedule H., *post*, Append.

(*a*) See the section, *post*, Append., and Schedule I.

(*b*) Section 53. See the section, *post*, Append. It comes into operation on the 1st of July, 1846. And see also Schedule K.

(*c*) Section 54. See the section, *post*, Append.

(*d*) Section 55. See the section, *post*, Append., and likewise section 56, *post*, Append., modifying in some measure the above, directing the course of proceedure, and preserving the jurisdiction of the superior Courts.

(*e*) Sections 57, 59, *post*, Append.

Building Act.

of a trial by jury, if the party complained against desire it before conviction. He must enter into a recognizance to try the matter without delay, and pay all the costs of the trial, in case a verdict should be found against him. The trial must be at the next practicable Quarter Sessions, and power is given to such sessions to summon witnesses. There may likewise be a view if the Court think fit. The jury shall then determine whether the business be offensive or noxious, and whether the party in question has done any act whereby the penalty has been incurred: upon which, subject to the power hereinbefore conferred of mitigating the penalty, suspending their judgment, order, or determination thereon, or making such order touching the carrying on of the business aforesaid, the Court shall give judgment according to the verdict, and shall award the penalty, (if any) and likewise costs to either of the parties. Such verdict, judgment, and award, order, or determination, shall be thereupon binding and conclusive. The next clause is a proviso, saving the powers of any public, local, or private act of Parliament, with regard to offensive trades, and the rights, likewise, of all persons to prosecute either civilly or criminally for nuisances of this nature (*f*). These unpleasant trades may, moreover, be bought up by the public, and the owners of them may thus be compelled to accept a compensation, and to remove (*g*). However, as far as relates to the operation of the act with respect to businesses dangerous in respect of fire or explosion, or which are offensive or noxious, public gas works are excepted by sect. 63 (*h*), and also the extension of such works, and any additional works, as far as their

(*f*) Section 60, *post*, Append.

(*g*) Sections 61, 62, *post*, Append.

(*h*) See the section, *post*, Append.

Building Act.

present limits are concerned. Premises entered or used for the distillation or rectification of spirits under the survey of commissioners of excise or their officers are also excepted by the same section.

The attention of the Legislature is now turned to the public officers appointed to carry out the provisions of the act, and to their respective duties and emoluments. First, there are the districts (*i*), and next the nomination and appointment of surveyors (*k*), their practical qualifications, together with the examination of candidates for the office as to their fitness (*l*), and their tenure of office, which is to be at will (*m*). Their functions are specially set forth in the 68th section (*n*). There are certain disqualifications connected with these officers (*o*), but the present surveyors are not disqualified by the new act, although they may be removed (*p*). The surveyors hereafter appointed must make the declaration prescribed by the act (*q*), and regulate their attendance according to the provisions laid down in that behalf (*r*). There may be a deputy surveyor in cases of illness, or other unavoidable circumstances (*s*), and likewise assistant surveyors, if the district be too large (*t*), and the 74th section provides for the filling up of vacancies (*u*). No surveyor is to survey buildings built,

(*i*) Section 64, *post*, Append.
(*k*) Section 65, *post*, Append.
(*l*) Section 66, *post*, Append.
(*m*) Section 67, *post*, Append.
(*n*) See the section, *post*, Append.
(*o*) Section 69, *post*, Append.
(*p*) Section 70, *post*, Append.
(*q*) Section 71, *post*, Append.
(*r*) Section 72, *post*, Append.
(*s*) Section 73, *post*, Append.
(*t*) Section 75, *post*, Append.
(*u*) See the section, *post*, Append.

Building Act.

rebuilt, enlarged or altered under his professional superintendence, as far as relates to the supervision of buildings, but such survey must be done by another district surveyor, or by another surveyor appointed by the official referees for that purpose (*x*). The next sections relate to the fees of surveyors (*y*), to returns of the business done by them (*z*), and to penalties which they are to incur for extortion or other misconduct (*a*).

Official referees are now the subjects of enactment. Two of these are to be appointed by the Secretary of State for the Home Department, for the purposes of superintending the execution of the act, of determining sundry matters incident thereto, and of exercising, in certain cases, a discretion in the relaxation of the fixed rules and directions of the act, where the strict observance of it may be impracticable, or would defeat its object, or would needlessly affect with injury, the course and operation of any branch of business. These referees may be removed by such Secretary of State, and others appointed. The referee, moreover, is not to act as surveyor either alone, or with any partner, or by an agent; nor is he to act as referee in any case where he shall act as architect. If he be the architect upon such an occasion, he must report the fact to the commissioners of works and buildings, upon which some other person shall be by them appointed to act in conjunction with the other referee in the particular matter (*b*). Their functions and the matters to be referred to them follow next in order (*c*). The principal of these matters of reference are disputes

(*x*) Section 76, *post*, Append.
(*y*) Section 77, *post*, Append., and Schedule L.
(*z*) Section 78, *post*, Append.
(*a*) Section 79, *post*, Append.
(*b*) Section 80, *post*, Append.
(*c*) Sections 81, 82, *post*, Append.

Building Act.

between parties, or between a party and a surveyor, or between two surveyors, as to any act done or to be done in pursuance of the statute; or as to the effect of the provisions thereof in any case; or as to the mode of carrying out the act. And particularly as to whether the requirements implied in terms of qualification applied to sites, to soils, to materials, or to workmanship, or otherwise, and denoting good, sound, fit, proper, or sufficient, are fulfilled in certain cases; or as to the district in which any building, matter, or thing is to be deemed to be situate, especially in case where such building, &c. is partly in one district, and partly in another; or as to the expenses to be borne by the respective owners of premises parted by the same party walls, or the proportions thereof; or as to the proportions of the expense to be borne by the occupier, or by the owners of premises, in respect of any work executed, or any other matter whatever.

The powers of these persons are extensive, their awards, if in writing, being of equal value with orders of reference by the Court of Queen's Bench, and binding and conclusive upon all, not excepting the Queen's Majesty (*d*). The reference to such referees is not to be revocable without the consent of all parties thereto, and although any party may not attend upon such reference, the official referees may, nevertheless, proceed with the reference, and make their award (*e*). The next section enables the referees to compel the attendance of witnesses, whose neglect shall be punished as a contempt of Court. But the parties attending shall be compensated. Moreover, they shall not be compelled to produce any document or writing which they would not be compelled to

(*d*) Section 83, *post*, Append.

(*e*) Section 84, *post*, Append.

Building Act.

produce at a trial, nor shall they be compellable to attend on more than two consecutive days to be named in the summons. The referees may administer oaths or take an affirmation where the law will permit, and persons giving false evidence shall be guilty of perjury (*f*). Copies of these awards, when produced under the seal of the registrar are to be *primâ* evidence before all Judges, justices, and others of the matters therein contained (*g*). The referees are to make a declaration of official fidelity before the Lord Chief Baron, or a Baron of the Exchequer (*h*). The 88th section regulates the business of their office (*i*).

The next clauses respect another officer, who is called the Registrar of Metropolitan Buildings (*k*). He is to make a declaration of official fidelity (*l*), to keep the awards, certificates, and other documents of the referees, to permit inspection of the same and give copies (*m*), to keep likewise a register of all matters referred to the referees, to keep all documents connected with the duties of official referees, and receive, file, and number all notices requiring any act to be done by them (*n*). The remuneration of the referees and of the registrar is provided for by the 94th section (*o*). By section 95, the following disqualifications of an official referee and of the registrar are declared. If he become commissioner, receiver, steward, or agents for any owner of houses within

(*f*) Section 85, *post*, Append.
(*g*) Section 86, *post*, Append.
(*h*) Section 87, *post*, Append.
(*i*) See the section, *post*, Append.
(*k*) Section 89, *post*, Append.
(*l*) Section 90, *post*, Append.
(*m*) Section 91, *post*, Append.
(*n*) Sections 92, 93, *post*, Append.
(*o*) See the section, *post*, Append.

Building Act. the limits of the act. Upon such appointment his qualification shall cease, and the office shall be vacant, without prejudice, nevertheless, to any act done by him in his office, so far as other persons are affected thereby. The money required for these salaries is to be raised out of the city funds, and by a county rate respectively, as far as a stated amount, and the balance is to be made up from the consolidated fund (*p*). However, the expenses of the office of the referees and registrar, and of the remuneration of persons employed under the registrar are to be defrayed by fees (*q*). By section 99, other duties may be assigned to the officers appointed under this act than those which it ordains, and the offices shall be held not only subject to the pleasure of the officers and justices who make the appointment, but likewise subject to the provisions of any future act of Parliament in relation thereto.

We now approach the termination of the statute, which winds up with the usual law clauses: as, that distresses shall not be unlawful for want of form, &c. (*r*), that the plaintiff shall not recover if a tender of sufficient amends be made, and that the defendant may pay money into Court (*s*). Section 102 gives the proceeding by distress, with regard to every sum of money by the act, or by any award or certificate, or other proceeding in pursuance of the act, charged upon any person in respect of any work done in pursuance [of] or in accordance with the act. Any two justices may determine this matter, or any one police magistrate. And in default of a sufficient distress, the party may be committed till the amount of the sum

(*p*) Sections 96, 97, *post*, Append.
(*q*) Section 98, *post*, Append.
(*r*) Section 100, *post*, Append.
(*s*) Section 101, *post*, Append.

Building Act.

due shall have been fully paid, or until the party shall be discharged under an Insolvent Act (*t*). With regard to penalties, one justice may issue the summons, or warrant in default of appearance; but the hearing must take place before two justices, or one police magistrate, and the recovery of such penalties is to be by distress, as under the foregoing section, and in default of sufficient distress, the offender may be committed for a period not exceeding three months, or till the amount of such penalty and costs shall be paid (*u*). Section 104 takes away the writ of *certiorari*, except in cases of conviction for carrying on a trade or business offensive, noxious, or dangerous, and contrary to the act, otherwise than those (*x*) specified (*y*). When the penalty upon a conviction amounts to 50*l.* an appeal to the sessions is allowed from all convictions for penalties. But notice must be given within four days after the decision, and the grounds of the appeal must be stated. There must be a recognizance, with two sureties, conditioned to abide the order of the Court, and to pay costs. The appeal may then go forward at any time within four months from the conviction, and the determination of the Court (who may also award costs) shall be binding and conclusive (*z*). Proceedings for penalties or forfeitures are limited to six calendar months next after such penalty or forfeiture shall have been incurred (*a*). Any person may sue for and obtain a penalty, unless

(*t*) See the section, *post*, Append.

(*u*) Section 103, *post*, Append.

(*x*) This word, "those," of course refers to the previous terms of "trade" and "business," although in the plural number.

(*y*) These trades and businesses are specified in section 55. See the section, *post*, Append.

(*z*) Section 105, *post*, Append.

(*a*) Section 106, *post*, Append. But see section 110, which limits the time to three months, where the default is for not complying with the provisions of the act.

Building Act. there be a specific provision in the particular case to the contrary, one-half of which penalty shall go to him, and the other half to the Crown, and shall be paid over to the sheriff of the county, city, or town where the fine shall be imposed, and all convictions shall be returned to the sessions, under 3 Geo. 4, c. 46 (*b*). Section 108 forbids the bringing of an action against any person for any thing done *in pursuance of the act* until twenty-one days' notice in writing shall have been given, and it limits the bringing of such action to six calendar months next after the fact committed. The trial for the same must be within the city of London, or the liberties thereof, or in the county of Middlesex for causes of action respectively arising within them, and not elsewhere. The defendant may plead the general issue and give the special matter in evidence, and prove that the matter and thing for which the action is brought was done in pursuance of the act. Then, in case any of the above provisions be not complied with, or in case sufficient amends shall have been tendered, a verdict shall be found for the defendant, and if so, or if judgment, under any circumstances shall pass for the defendant, the defendant shall be entitled to full costs of suit (*c*). And it seems that he may have these costs without entering a suggestion on the roll, although it may be the safest course to do so before the roll is carried in (*d*). The fact of a verdict being found for the plaintiff, subject to a reference, will not deprive him of his full costs, the arbitrator having awarded in his favour (*e*).

(*b*) Section 107, *post*, Append.

(*c*) See the section, *post*, Append.

(*d*) See 2 Cr., M. & R. 184, Wells *v* Ody, where judgment was signed, and the Master allowed treble costs, without requiring the entry of a suggestion, and the Court would not disturb the taxation.

(*e*) 6 D. & Ry. 481, Pratt *v*. Hillman.

Building Act.

It is of frequent occurrence to find that the expression, "in pursuance of the act," has been a source of litigation. The old Building Act was not without its difficulties upon this score. The plaintiff had brought trespass against his neighbour for taking down a portion of his party wall between their two houses in London, and building upon it; but the plaintiff was nonsuited, because the defendant had done the thing in question under the provisions of the act. The defendant, having thus succeeded, obtained a rule to shew cause why a suggestion should not be entered on the roll that the action was brought for acts done in pursuance of the statute, and why the Master should not tax treble costs for the defendant. Upon which it was contended for the plaintiff, that these words did not apply to private persons, but to magistrates and surveyors, and other subordinate officers, who were required to do certain acts in the execution of the duties imposed on them. Besides, as double costs only were awarded under the 41st section, for not reimbursing the party who paid the expense of building the wall, it would be unreasonable to place a defendant, who might happen to be sued wrongfully, in a better position than one who brought his action under the statute rightfully (*f*): and *Le Blanc*, J., expressed an opinion that such a case was not within the intention of the Legislature in framing the clause. But a majority of the Court held that the words of the 100th section (*g*) were too general to be got over, especially as the same clause gave the plea of the general issue to any defendant sued for any matter or thing done in pursuance and by the authority of the act, by which alone the defendant

(*f*) That is, to give a plaintiff double costs, and a private person, being defendant, treble costs.

(*g*) "Any person or persons." The same words are in the new clause.

Building Act.

could justify what he had done. And *Le Blanc*, J., admitted that he felt himself hampered by the general words of the statute (*h*). Indeed, as the defendant's counsel insisted *arguendo*, the defendant, but for the act, would have been a trespasser, and if, instead of pleading the general issue, (which was only given by the 100th clause) he had pleaded specially, that what he did was done in pursuance of the act, it must have been found for him, for *if not so done, there must have been a verdict for the plaintiff* (*i*).

Trespass was brought for building a wall on the roof of the plaintiff's house, whereby it was injured. The action was referred, and the arbitrator awarded for the defendants. The ground of his certificate in favour of the defendants was, that it had become necessary to raise the whole party wall between the two houses, that the defendants in so doing intended *bonâ fide* to comply with the provisions of the Building Act, that the wall was examined whilst it was building, and directions as to the mode of building it given by the regular district surveyor: but that the wall was, in fact, not built conformably to the provisions of the Building Act, and that considerable damage had been done to the plaintiff's house by the weight of the new wall; nevertheless, that the plaintiff had failed to give the notice of twenty-one days required by the 100th section of 14 Geo. 3, c. 78 (*j*), before the bringing of an action; and, moreover, that he commenced his action three calendar months after the building of the wall. Upon the propounding of this certificate, the plaintiff moved to set aside the award, and it was contended for him, that as the 42d section

(*h*) 9 East, 322, Collins *v.* Poney.

(*i*) *Ibid.* 323. By Gibbs, Att Gen., Park, and Marryatt.

(*j*) And the same notice of twenty-one days is now required.

of the act provides that no party wall shall be raised unless it can be done with safety to such wall, and to the adjoining buildings, it was a condition precedent to the interposition of the act that this security should have been ascertained. Whereas it did not appear that any inquiry of that nature had been set on foot, and it was stated by the arbitrator that the wall had not been built conformably to the statute. Consequently, the wall was not erected in pursuance of the act. But the counsel for the defendants referred to the certificate of the arbitrator, which shewed that the defendants had intended *bonâ fide* to comply with the act, and of this opinion was *Abbott*, C. J., and he connected the authority under section 42 to raise the party wall, with the 100th section, which demanded the notice, and the rule for setting aside the award was discharged (*k*). Building Act.

With regard to the right of action within six months next after the fact committed, it has been held, that if any part of a trespass happened within the time limited, the action would lie *pro tanto*. Therefore, when a wall had been begun more than *three* months (*l*) before the action, but was not completed till after the three months, the plaintiff was allowed to recover for so much of the latter cause of complaint, and thus became entitled to his costs (*m*).

Section 109 enables the defendant to apply to the

(*k*) 4 B. & C. 269, Pratt *v*. Hillman and others; S. C. 6 D. & Ry. 360. S. P. 7 C. & P. 22, Wells *v*. Ody. S. P. & C. 2 Cr., M. & R. 128. S. P. & C. 1 Gale, 137. See likewise 2 Nev. & M. 340, R. v. Hungerford Market Company, *ex parte* Yeates; S. C. 1 Adol. & El. 668.

(*l*) The time limited by the old Building Act, 14 Geo. 3, c. 78.

(*m*) 5 C. & P. 51, Trotter *v*. Simpson.

Building Act. Schedules.

Schedule H. has the rules of drainage, with regard to buildings hereafter built (*e*); and

Schedule I. the rules concerning streets and alleys hereafter to be formed (*f*).

Schedule K. gives various rules concerning the backs of dwelling-houses, rooms under ground, &c. (*g*)

Schedule L. is the list of fees payable to surveyors (*h*).

Schedule M. is a summary of proceedings to be taken or observed before and after notices in relation to building, and the respective forms applicable to each case are appended (*i*).

Now, although it has been thought best to set forth this statute at some length, giving an outline of the clauses, and referring to those on party and other walls which more nearly concern our subject, it is with these latter clauses alone that we have materially to do upon the present occasion.

Party walls are to a building what hedges and palings may be to a field, so that we shall take care to enter at large into the consideration of all the sections respecting these walls as being closely connected with our main subject of fences; and to enumerate in detail the provisions appropriated to them by the new statute.

The kinds of walls or fences mentioned in the 7 & 8 Vict. c. 84, are,—

I. Party walls, both old and new.

II. External walls.

III. Party fences and fence walls.

IV. Timber partitions.

And these walls and fences will be found to relate, for

(*e*) *Post*, Append., and see section 51, *post*, Append.

(*f*) *Post*, Append. (*g*) *Ibid.* (*h*) *Ibid.* (*i*) *Ibid.*

the most part, to houses already built and divided by a separate entrance; to new dwellings, or buildings having separate owners; to cases of vacant ground, where one party in particular is desirous of commencing a new building; to intermixed properties or places where there are rooms or floors belonging to different owners, without being separated by any party wall, or party arch, or stone floor; and to houses or buildings which project over public ways.

Building Act.

Notices.

It is a very governing principle in the act that sound walls shall support the various structures. It is of the same consequence whether buildings be built, rebuilt, enlarged, or altered. In every case reference must be had to the walls, whether external or party walls, and to the fences and the party fence walls, as well as to other particulars set forth in the schedules(*k*). And in order to ensure obedience to these rules, notice must be given to the surveyor of the commencement of any building, and notice likewise of any irregularity, where it occurs, must be given by the surveyor to the builder. The first notice applies—

Notices.]—Before any building shall be begun to be built.

Before any addition or alteration shall be made.

Before any party wall, external wall, &c., shall be begun to be built, pulled down, rebuilt, cut into, or altered.

Before any opening shall be made in any party wall, or any other matter or thing done which is placed by the act under the supervision of the surveyor.

(*k*) Sect. 5. See the section, *post*, Append., and the schedules, C. D. E., *post*, Append., and *post*, in this chapter.

Building Act. Notices.

The statute declares with regard to this notice, that the builder (by which term the master builder or other person employed to execute the work is to be understood, or if there be no master builder or other such person, then the owner of the building or other person for whom or by whose order such work is to be done,) shall give to the surveyor, at his office, a notice (*l*) of his intention two days before each act or event. The penalty for default is treble the amount of the surveyor's fees for inspection, and also a sum not exceeding 20*l.* (*m*). And further, if the building be suspended beyond three months, or if the builder be changed during the progress of the work, a fresh notice (*n*) must be given to the surveyor, or left at his office two days before the renewal, or proceeding by the new builder, upon pain of forfeiting for every such offence a sum not exceeding 20*l.* (*o*). And, moreover, if the act be disobeyed as aforesaid, or if such surveyor or the official referees be refused admittance to inspect the premises, the building or work may be abated as a nuisance. There is, however, this proviso. If by reason of any emergency any thing placed under the supervision of the surveyor be required to be done immediately, or before notice can be given to the surveyor, then such act may be done, but upon condition that

(*l*) According to the Form, No. 1, schedule M., or, to the like effect, *post*, Append.

(*m*) See Sections 103, 105, 106, 110, *post*, Append. As far as the surveyor is concerned, it seems, that if he should superintend the work, notwithstanding a neglect of notice, he may be said to have waived the notice, (2 Cr., M. & R. 128, Wells *v.* Ody); but this waiver would not apply to the forfeiture.

(*n*) According to the Forms in Nos. 2 and 3, schedule M., *post*, Append.

(*o*) See sections 103, 105, 106, 110, *post*, Append.

Building Act. Notices.

notice be given to the surveyor within forty-eight hours next after the beginning of the work (*p*).

Secondly, the act places as a further guard the notice by the surveyor in cases of irregularity. For, if in building, pulling down, rebuilding, cutting into, or altering any part of any building or party wall, or external wall, &c., the provisions of the act shall not be conformed to, it becomes the duty of the surveyor to give forty-eight hours' notice (*q*) to the builder to amend the irregularity. At the expiration of the notice, the surveyor shall inspect the work, and if he cannot ascertain from the advanced state of the work whether there has been any fault, he may order the work to be cut into, laid open, or pulled down. Moveover, if the builder refuse or fail to amend the work after notice, within the prescribed time of forty-eight hours, or refuse to cut into, lay open, or pull down the work, when ordered, the surveyor shall give information to the official referees. These officers shall then proceed to hear the matter, and if it appear that any breach of the rules of the act has been committed, or if there be good ground for supposing that such breach of rules has been committed, but is concealed, such referees, or one of them, may then make an award, and direct that the building, party wall, external wall, &c., may be amended, removed, cut into, laid open, or pulled down, and that the costs of the same and of the application shall be borne by such party as the official referees shall determine (*r*).

(*p*) Section 13, *post*, Append. The abatement, as a nuisance, is under sect. 18. And see also sect. 68.

(*q*) See the Form, schedule M., No. 4, *post*, Append.

(*r*) Section 14, *post*, Append. And, for the recovery of these costs, see sect. 102. By sect. 19, if any workman, &c., wilfully and without the consent of his employer, shall do anything in or about a building, contrary to the act, he shall forfeit, upon con-

Building Act. — Notices.

We must here also refer to the 15th clause (*s*), which places buildings of the sixth rate of the first or dwelling-house class, and of the sixth rate of the second or warehouse class, and all buildings of the third or public building class (except the buildings before excepted) (*t*), under particular supervision (*u*). All the walls of such buildings are mentioned as subjects of scrutiny amongst other particulars, and a survey of the closest description is ordained by the statute, which forbids the *completion* of any such building, after it shall have had its walls and timbers set up, without a fresh notice from the builder (*x*), and a certificate from the official referees. For disobedience to this clause there is a penalty of not less than 5*l.*, nor more than 500*l.* for every day when such building is used without such certificate, or an express authority in writing, one-half to go to the person giving information, and one-half to the poor of the parish in which the building shall be situate (*y*).

Entry.]—However, notwithstanding these notices, the power of the surveyor would be but imperfect, unless he

viction, a sum not exceeding fifty shillings, and, in default of payment, upon or immediately after conviction, may be imprisoned for any term not exceeding one month. See the section, *post*, Append., and see section 107.

(*s*) *Post*, Append. See also sect. 16.

(*t*) In schedule B. See sections 5, 7, 16, *post*, Append.

(*u*) See the notice by the builder, according to No. 6, schedule M., *post*, Append.

(*x*) According to No. 7, in schedule M., *post*, Append. See the notice, which extends both to amendments required by the referees, as well as to the completion of the building, where no amendments are required. And as to the surveyor's fees demandable when the building attains to this height. See section 77, *post*, Append.

(*y*) See sections 103, 105, 106, 110, *post*, Append.

could resist the consequences of a refusal to allow an inspection of the premises. Therefore, a refusal to permit such inspection by the surveyor or official referees at reasonable hours is made punishable, upon conviction, by a forfeiture not exceeding 20*l.* (*z*), whilst the building in question may be abated as a nuisance (*a*). And, besides, the surveyor and official referees are empowered, with the aid of a peace officer, to enter upon the ground, building, and premises in cases of a refusal to admit them (*b*). Party Walls.

The mode of conducting the supervision of these walls having been noticed, we will proceed to mention the requirements of the act in respect of each kind of fence. And, first,

I. OF PARTY WALLS.

Of Party Walls.

First, with regard to the thickness, foundations, &c. of party walls. The thickness is governed by the class and rate of each house. There are three classes of buildings, and six rates to each of the two first classes. The rates of the third class are regulated accordingly as they correspond most with the first or second class respectively. The first class is called the dwelling-house class; the second is the warehouse class; and the third is the public buildings' class. There are, likewise, insulated buildings, and buildings attached to or detached from others. Now, with regard to the first and second classes, there is assigned to each a table, shewing the requisite

(*z*) Which is recoverable under sect. 103. And see sections 105, 106, 110, *post*, Append.

(*a*) Section 18, *post*, Append.

(*b*) Section 17, *post*, Append.

Party Walls.

thickness of the party wall in each rate (*c*); and the third class being governed, as we have just observed by its agreement, according to circumstances, with the first and second classes, will, of course, have its thicknesses of walls set forth in these two tables, subject only to this addition, namely, that with regard to the walls of public buildings of whatever rate—the width of the footings thereof, and the thicknesses thereof are to be at the least *four inches more* than is hereby required *for party or external walls* of the same rate, unless the official referees, on special supervision thereof, shall otherwise appoint (*d*).

Thickness.]—The thickness of every wall, and of the footing thereof, is to be ascertained by measuring only the thickness of which such walls or footings shall have been originally built (*e*).

The Legislature, as we have seen, has been so careful, to preserve these required thicknesses, as to except them specially from the provisions of the modification clause which relaxes, upon certain conditions, a strict compliance with the act (*f*).

Foundations and Footings.]—The foundations and footings of these walls are provided for. Indeed, there are some general rules concerning the foundations and foot-

(*c*) Schedule C., Part II. and Part III., referring to sect. 5. See the schedule, *post*, Append. And see the measurements of stories, in this schedule.

(*d*) Schedule C., Part V., at the end, *post*, Append.

(*e*) Schedule C., Part I., at the end, *post*, Append. See the rule for ascertaining the areas of buildings, including party walls, schedule C., *ut supra*, tit. "Rule for ascertaining Area," *post*, Append.

(*f*) Section 12, *post*, Append.

Party Walls.

ings of *all* walls which the reader will find in the Schedule referred to. The construction, materials, height, and width of the footings are ordered, together with the depth of such footings below ground and below the lowest floor, and the thicknesses of enclosing walls generally to stories of buildings of whatever rate (*g*).

General Construction of Party Wall.]—The general construction of the party wall is the subject of a separate ordinance (*h*), and the materials of it are pointed out in the same place (*i*).

Height.]—The height of the wall is also regulated, whether it adjoin to a roof, or to a gutter, or if it there be a turret, dormer, &c. within a certain distance of the wall (*k*).

After all this care and detail in raising proper party walls, it will be anticipated that the provisions of the old law requiring such walls to be built or repaired are rather enlarged than narrowed by the present act.

Imperative upon Parties to build or repair Party Walls.]—The 20th section and the schedule D. embrace the subjects of making and repairing party walls. We will take the 20th section in the first instance, which speaks of repair and alterations. With regard, then, to works in relation to adjoining premises, parted by the same party wall or party fence wall, but belonging to different owners, or occupied by different persons, or to

(*g*) Schedule D., Part I., and see the schedule, *post*, Append.

(*h*) Schedule D., Part III., tit. "Construction and Materials," *post*, Append.

(*i*) *Ibid.*

(*k*) Schedule D., *ut supra*, tit. "Height of Party Walls above Roof," *post*, Append.

Party Walls. buildings intermixed, belonging to different owners, or occupied by different persons.

These works, as far as they refer to party walls, are:—

The Reparation of the Party Walls by which such premises shall be parted.

The pulling down and rebuilding of such Party Walls.

The raising of such Party Walls.

Party Walls in lieu of Timber Partitions.

Buildings over Public Ways.

We will, in the first instance, deal more especially with the reparation and rebuilding of the party walls, being the subjects of the two first heads just set out. The section proceeds then to call the owner who desires to execute any of the above works, the "building owner," and the owner of the adjoining premises, the "adjoining owner," and declares the object of the enactment to be the facilitating the execution of such works for the building owner, and the protection of the interests of the adjoining owner. Therefore, *if the adjoining owner shall have consented to the works*, or, if without such consent, the required notice (*l*) of such works shall have been given by or on the part of such building owner to the adjoining owner, then—subject to the modification afterwards mentioned (*m*)—and subject to the provision for supplying the want of the owner's consent (*n*)—and subject to the conditions prescribed by the act, as well as those relating to the payment of the costs of such works, and subject to the sanction or to the award of the surveyors or official referees, it shall be lawful for the building owner to execute such works (*o*).

(*l*) Schedule M., No. 8, *post*, Append.
(*m*) Under section 22, *post*, Append.
(*n*) Under section 24, *post*, Append.
(*o*) Section 20. See the section, *post*, Append.

Party Walls.

An application for consent is indispensable in the first instance. For without such consent, no work can be done till notice shall have been given to the adjoining owner, and every such notice with regard to the pulling down and rebuilding or repairing of party walls, or party fence walls must be given three months at the least, before the work is to be commenced; and every such notice with regard to the pulling down and rebuilding intermixed walls and timber partitions must be given three months at the least before such work is to be commenced; and every such notice must be in the form or to the effect of the notice No. 8, for that purpose contained in the schedule (*p*).

It follows from hence, that if the owners agree, the work may be carried on forthwith, for the sanction or award of the surveyors or official referees seems only to be necessary in cases of difficulty, such as the want of consent, the desire of modification, &c. But the surveyor has a hold over the work, because he is entitled to two days' notice before it is begun (*q*); he is expressly authorized likewise to supervise these works (*r*), and the due watchfulness concerning them is mentioned amongst his functions (*s*).

Want of consent, or modified consent.]—But, perhaps, the adjoining owner may not agree, or may not be found, or he may be willing to agree if the mode of building suggested should be modified or altered. In these cases a fresh expense and more trouble are incurred unless the

(*p*) Section 21, *post*, Append. See the Form of Notice, schedule M., No. 8, *post*, Append.

(*q*) Section 13, *post*, Append.

(*r*) Section 14, *post*, Append.

(*s*) Section 68, *post*, Append.

Party Walls.

building owner should agree to the modification. The fruits of disagreement, or of other difficulties, are a survey, certificate, and award. The words, "subject to such modification," &c. introduce another section which enacts, that in order to render the work suitable to the premises of the adjoining owner and his tenant, if the adjoining owner, at any time within two months after the receipt of the said notice from the building owner, give notice of his desire of such modification, according to the form No. 18 in the schedule, or to the like effect (*t*): then, within seven days after the receipt of such notice, the building owner must signify his consent to, or dissent from, the proposed modification (*u*). If such building owner dissent from, or do not within such seven days signify his consent, the adjoining owner may require the building owner not to commence the work till the official referees shall have determined thereon. If, within seven days thereafter (which would be seven days after the expiration of the first seven days) application in writing be made to the official referees, according to the form No. 19, in the schedule (*x*), or to the like effect, and notice be given to the building owner according to the other form, No. 20 (*y*): then, within ten days after such application it shall be the duty of the referees to signify their decision thereon, and it shall be the duty of the building owner not to commence the work till such decision. But, if the adjoining owner make no objection within three months from the date of the first notice, nor make any requisition in conformity with the act, the building owner may then proceed with

(*t*) Schedule M., *post*, Append.
(*u*) It is not said, "in writing."
(*x*) Schedule M., *post*, Append.
(*y*) *Ibid.*

his work (z), the consent being implied. Then follows a very similar section, only adapting the language to a desired *delay* on the part of the adjoining owner on account of domestic arrangements or otherwise, instead of the modification before spoken of (a). The notice, however, is three months instead of two. Party Walls.

Thus far, if the adjoining owner consent, or the building owner agree to the modification, the ordinary duty of the surveyor seems to be alone necessary. But if the adjoining premises be unoccupied, or if the owner cannot be found, or if, although found, he cannot, by reason of legal disability or otherwise, consent to the work, or if the owner will not consent thereto, or if differences arise between the parties concerned, then, in all these cases, the expense and trouble commence which we have above noticed.

First, in addition to the single notice served on the adjoining owner, or on such other parties entitled to notice under the act upon whom such notice can be served, there must be a notice to the surveyor and official referees (b). On the receipt of this notice, the surveyor must forthwith give notice to the parties by whom the work is to be executed, and to their surveyors or agents as to the day and hour when he will view the premises (c). At the appointed time the surveyor inspects accordingly, and certifies to the official referees:

1st. Whether such work ought to be done, or not.

2ndly. If it ought to be done, whether it should be done in the manner proposed.

3rdly. As to the site of the party wall.

(z) Sect. 22. See the section, *post*, Append.
(a) Sect. 23. See the section, *post*, Append.
(b) See the Form, No. 9, schedule M., *post*, Append.
(c) See the Form, schedule M., No. 10, *post*, Append.

4thly. As to the quantity of ground to be laid to or taken from the respective houses (*d*).

5thly. As to any compensation which the building owner might be liable to pay to the adjoining owner in lieu of the lessening the building in question by the party wall, or as a satisfaction for any injury done.

The surveyor having sent his certificate to the referees, they are to give notice to the parties, or to such as are known. This affords the parties an opportunity of appealing against the certificate, which may be within seven days after such notice. If there be no appeal, and if the referees approve of the works, and of the compensation (*e*), the certificate shall be confirmed by them, and the work may proceed as if there had been a consent of the adjoining owner. But if an appeal be made as to any of the above matters, the official referees shall appoint one of their number to survey the building. This person must give notice to the parties and to their surveyor or agents as to the time of survey, upon which he is to attend, inspect, and give a certificate of his opinion to the referees. The referees shall, thereupon, make their *award*, confirming, reversing, or modifying the *surveyor's* certificate, and appointing by whom and in what proportions the expenses of the surveys and of the reports thereon are to be paid, and such award shall be final and conclusive. And with regard to any works by such award authorized, so far as relates to the proceedings of

(*d*) The words of the act are "laid to or taken from the house of the person desirous to rebuild, to the house of the person permitting him to erect a party wall or party arch."

"Permitting" must be understood only in those cases mentioned by the section where a consent has been virtually given, as where the party may be under disability, where all parties have agreed to build, and yet some unforeseen dispute has arisen.

(*e*) That is to say, if any.

Party Walls.

the building owner, if upon the making of the award the periods of the notices by the act prescribed with regard to works of that nature have elapsed, the building owner, his agents, and workmen, may proceed to execute the works immediately upon the making of the award: but if such period have not elapsed, the building owner must wait till the periods in question shall have elapsed (*f*). The same proceedings are directed where a party wall or party arch is used wholly or in part as a party fence wall. So far as relates to the reparation and rebuilding thereof at the joint expense of the owners of the buildings parted thereby, it is enacted, that if such party structure be so defective or so far out of repair as to render it necessary to pull down and rebuild the same, or any part thereof, then on notice given by the owner of one of the buildings to the adjoining owner, the building owner may require a survey, certificate, and award authorizing the execution of such reparation, or rebuilding, according to the provisions of this act in that behalf (*g*). Thus, if there be a consent, the matter is arranged as we have above shewn in expounding the last sections, but if there arise difficulties, the proceedings by the building owner, in conjunction with the surveyor and official referees, come into play.

Imperative, nevertheless, as is the command to rebuild party walls, an owner may, if he choose, encounter the whole expense, and rebuild the joint wall. He must however, give the required notice of three months (*h*), and he may then pull down and rebuild the party wall, but upon condition that he do reinstate and make good

(*f*) Sect. 24. See the section, *post*, Append.; and see the notices in schedule M., Nos. 8 and 10.

(*g*) Sect. 25. See the section, *post*, Append.

(*h*) See schedule M., No. 14.

Party Walls. all the internal finishings and decorations of the adjoining premises, and pay all the costs and charges thereof, and also the expenses incidental to the execution of the work, including the fees and expenses of the survey, and the fees of surveyors and of official referees, and also such reasonable compensation as the referees may think proper to be given for any loss which the adjoining owner shall have incurred by reason of such works (*i*). Here again, it is presumed, that if the adjoining owner offer no opposition, the ordinary services of the surveyor will alone be necessary. But, in case of opposition (*k*), or of irregularities in the work (*l*), or of subsequent disputes (*m*), the surveyor's extraordinary duties, and the services of the referees may doubtless be called in aid, and it is not quite clear whether a survey, certificate, and award may not in certain cases be demanded under the 24th section, especially where the adjoining owner may desire that the work shall be modified (*n*). However, the 13th section must, under all circumstances, be obeyed (*o*).

Something has been already said concerning the *site* of the party wall in disputed cases (*p*). This leads us to mention for a moment the proceedings where the party wall is new.

New Party Walls.]—We have seen that it is imperative upon parties to have a party wall. The schedule (D)

(*i*) Sect. 26. See the section, *post*, Append.
(*k*) See section 81, "General Functions of Referees."
(*l*) See sections 13, 14, *post*, Append.
(*m*) See section 81.
(*n*) See section 22.
(*o*) See section 27, *post*, "External Walls."
(*p*) *Ante*, p. 47.

which is recognised and referred to by the 5th section, gives a practical statement of this matter. It commences thus: "With regard to walls used to divide single buildings into two or more. If it be intended to divide any building into two or more distinct parts, then every wall for that purpose must be built as a party wall, in the manner and of the materials, and of the several heights and thicknesses for party walls of the highest rate of building to which such party wall shall belong or adjoin, as prescribed in reference to the thicknesses of party walls in schedule (C). And if any building already built or which shall be hereafter built, be converted, used, or occupied as two or more separate buildings, each having a separate entrance and staircase, and each being separately rated to the poor, then every such building shall be deemed to be two or more separate houses, and such separate houses must be divided from each other by a party wall or party arch or arches, built in the manner and of the materials required for party walls or party arches for the class and rate to which the largest of the buildings so divided shall belong (*q*). New Party Walls

The schedule (D) directs the site of walls generally without reference to any difference of opinion. It is as follows:

Site of Walls.]—With regard to party walls, in reference to the site thereof.—

If the buildings be of equal rate, then such party wall must be built on the line of junction of such buildings, one-half on the ground of one owner belonging to one of such buildings, and one-half on the ground

(*q*) Schedule D., Part III., tit. "Division of Buildings."

Site of Walls. of the other owner belonging to the other of such buildings.

If such buildings be of different rates, then such wall must be built on the line of junction thereof as follows; that is to say, one-half of the thickness of the wall required for the building of the lower rate on the ground of each of the adjoining owners; and the whole of the additional thickness of the wall required for the building of the higher rate, on the ground of the owner of such building of the higher rate. And if such building of the lower rate be thereafter enlarged or altered, so as to become a building of a higher rate, then the owner of such first-mentioned building of the higher rate, for the time being, shall be entitled to receive from the owner of such building of the lower rate, such sum of money as shall be a sufficient compensation for the ground occupied by that portion of the party wall, which, according to the rate of the building enlarged, ought to have been built by its owner on his own ground (s), as well as the value of so much of the wall itself as may be more than the owner of such building of the lower rate has already paid for.

Openings in Party Walls.]—The Legislature has not forgotten to anticipate the possibility of a very inconvenient opening in a party wall made to the detriment and annoyance of the adjoining owner. For notice must be given to the surveyor two days before any opening shall be made in any party wall, so that if the adjoining owner should object, or if the work should not be done conformably to the act, an immediate remedy will be

(s) Schedule D., Part III., tit. "Site of Walls." And see chapter I., *ante*, pp. 7, 8.

available. If the first case, the official referees will have the power to stop the work by virtue of their functions (*t*); and, in the second, the building itself may be amended, or even abated, according to circumstances, by the same authority (*u*). And moreover, if the owner who meddles with the party wall should happen to go beyond his proportion, he will be liable to an action of trespass, or upon the case, according to the nature of the injury. However, if dwelling-houses shall happen to be united, the walls may be opened under certain restrictions, that is to say, "with regard to any dwelling-houses which when so united will contain more than twelve squares, and the external and party walls of which are such as are herein prescribed for buildings of the fifth rate of the first class: if such dwelling-houses shall be and continue to be in the same occupation, and if the poor-rates in respect thereof shall be paid by the same person, then upon its being declared by the official referees that in their opinion the stability of any or either of such dwelling-houses will not be endangered by making such openings, they may be made accordingly (*v*). Openings in party walls between one dwelling-house and another, are likewise permitted under restrictions which the reader will find in the schedule referred to beneath (*x*).

Openings in Party Walls.

Party Walls, Warehouses, &c.]—As to buildings of this nature, in reference to the capacity or contents

(*t*) Section 81, *post*, Append.

(*u*) Sections 14 and 18, *post*, Append.

(*v*) Schedule D., Part III., tit. "Openings in Party Walls," *post*, Append. See also *ibid*, tit. "Recesses and Chases."

(*x*) Schedule C., Part IV.

Party Walls.

thereof, within the same inclosing walls: if such building contains more than 200,000 feet, then such building must be divided by party walls, so that there be not in any one part of such building more than 200,000 cubic feet without party walls (y).

Party Walls; Attached Buildings and Offices.]—With regard to buildings or offices now built, or hereafter to be built; (except greenhouses, vineries, aviaries, or such like buildings,—and that, whether the same be attached to or detached from the buildings to which they belong,) every such building is to be deemed, in respect of the external walls thereof, and all other requisites, as a building of the rate to which it would belong if it had been built separately (z).

Insulated Buildings afterwards divided.]—Some mention has been made of insulated buildings (a). If an insulated building of the first or second classes be divided, the Schedule (C) makes a provision for the erection of party walls. Thus, if any such building be hereafter divided into two or more distinct buildings, and the several parts of such buildings so divided be not at the prescribed distance from each other, and from other buildings and ground, then such several parts must be separated by external walls, and be separated from each other by such party walls, as are herein prescribed for the rates to which such several

(y) Schedule C., Part IV., tit. "Warehouses, &c.," *post*, Append. See also *ibid*, tit. "Roofs," and *id.* Part VI., "Rule concerning fire-proof Accesses and Stairs to Buildings of the First and Third Classes."

(z) Schedule C., Part VII., *post*, Append.

(a) *Ante*, p. 41.

Party Walls.

parts, if adjoining, would belong (*b*); and if such requisites be not observed, then such several parts of such buildings in respect of which they are not so observed, shall be deemed a public nuisance, and as such be taken down according to the provisions of this act in that behalf (*c*).

Raising Walls.]—Party walls may be raised under certain conditions. The statute declares, that with regard to every building hereafter built, with regard to the raising thereof, it shall be lawful to raise any building, but so that, nevertheless, the party and external walls and chimnies thereof, when so raised, be of the materials, heights and thicknesses hereinbefore described for such walls and chimnies of the rate such building shall be of when so raised. And as to buildings already built, although the walls be not of the prescribed thicknesses, yet, if they will allow of the raising, the buildings may be raised to ten feet of additional height, but not farther (*d*). And with regard to any building raised, so far as relates to the use thereof by the adjoining owner; if, at any time the owner of any such adjoining building make use of any portion of the part raised of such party wall, the owner of the premises so first raised, may claim, and recover the cost of a proportionate part of the portion which shall be so used, together with the cost of such parts of the chimney-stacks as belong thereto (*e*).

(*b*) See schedule C., Part VII., tit. "Insulated Buildings," *post*, Append. See also tit. "Toll Houses," at the end, and schedule E., tit. "Projections from Insulated Buildings."

(*c*) Section 18, *post*, Append.

(*d*) Then follows a provision respecting chimnies. See 7 C. & P. 22, Wells *v.* Ody. But it is observable, that the surveyor must now receive notice of *every* work done under the statute, which will include the *raising* of a wall. See section 20.

(*e*) Sect. 31. See the section, *post*, Append.

Raising Walls.

There is nothing, however, in this clause to take away the common law right of any individual to bring an action against the building owner, if such owner should invade any existing right. As, for instance, if the builder should raise a wall and thereby obstruct an ancient window. It is true that the surveyor and official referees will be careful not to allow the introduction of fresh windows into party walls where none already exist, but unless a party should be willing to surrender his right, whatever it may be, it must not be encroached upon, unless, indeed, the enjoyment of it were to be in violation of the express provisions of the act.

The following case seems to apply to *old windows*, and although decided under the late act, would probably be authority should a similar dispute arise. The plaintiff and defendant had land contiguous to each other. Until 1803, a wall of brick and mortar standing wholly on the plaintiff's land divided the properties. Thirty-four years before the action, the plaintiff had erected a workshop for the purposes of his trade which required a full light, and the windows fronted the defendant's land. After some time the wall was condemned by the surveyor as ruinous, and a party wall was erected by the plaintiff in lieu of it, half on the land of the plaintiff, and half on that of the defendant, and at their joint expense. The plaintiff, upon his half of the wall, made another frame containing windows similar to those he had before. Whilst the old wall stood, the defendant had used it by erecting against it on his land a shed which did not rise higher than the wall. But now he carried up an additional height of perpendicular wall upon his half of the new party wall, and built up his shed to the same height, so as to obstruct the plaintiff's windows, and render the place unfit for the plaintiff's trade. Upon this, the

Raising Walls.

plaintiff brought his action on the case, and had a verdict, subject to the question whether the windows in the plaintiff's house were not a nuisance, being inserted in the party walls, and so prohibited by the Building Act. It was contended for the defendant; first, that the Building Act forbade all lateral lights; and secondly, that the plaintiff had deserted his ancient rights by erecting the new frame-work, that he was bound, in fact, to raise no edifice but such as, in a new site, would be conformable to the act. For the plaintiff it was said, that as no conviction had taken place within three months under section 60, the building, that is to say, the new frame-work in which the windows were inserted, could not be called a nuisance. The defendant might have carried up his wall if the plaintiff had not previously enjoyed lights, but the maxim, *sic utere tuo ut alienum non lædas*, would be applicable upon this occasion. Sections 14, 26, 27, 42, 43, 60, 62, and 63, were cited on either side. The Court gave judgment for the plaintiff. The question as to the plaintiff's right to raise the wall in the manner he had done by erecting the frame-work would not arise in the present case. The action was one for obstructing lights, and if the defendant could succeed in doing that with impunity, he might, by the same rule, pull down the house and avoid an action. To be sure, the argument for the plaintiff that the building had become legal, because no conviction had taken place within three months was of no avail, for the 65th section, which orders the demolition or amendment of walls, contains no limitation as to time. But here the defendant had mistaken his mode of proceeding, and the rule, therefore, for setting aside the verdict was discharged (*f*).

(*f*) 5 Taunt. 465, Titterton *v.* Conyers.

Raising Walls. So again, in another case, it appeared that the defendant had raised a party fence wall which divided the premises of the plaintiff and defendant, and had built a workshop and a stable, up to and upon the wall so raised, which had the effect of darkening the plaintiff's windows. An action on the case having been brought, the defendant insisted that he was protected by the Building Act, 14 Geo. 3, c. 78, because a period of six months had elapsed since the time of the act committed. He further insisted that as the building was partly on the plaintiff's land, the action should have been trespass and not case. The first objection was overruled, and it was left to the jury to say whether the plaintiff's enjoyment of light and air was diminished to a greater degree than it would have been if the building had been erected on the defendant's moiety of the wall only. The jury found in the negative (*g*), and a verdict was taken for the plaintiff, with liberty to move to enter a nonsuit. And the Court held, that the case was not within the Building Act. A collateral injury, an eventual damage was not within its purview. So, although the act might enable a party to build against the wall of his neighbour under some circumstances, it did not secure him against an excess of the privilege, and, therefore, trespass, probably, would lie. But as the plaintiff could not have received compensation upon the occasion in trespass, it was natural that he should resort to an action upon the case, and that was the proper remedy. The rule for leave to enter a nonsuit was discharged (*h*).

(*g*) But they found that there had been such a diminution of light and air as made the plaintiff's premises less fit for occupation. 7 C. & P. 412.

(*h*) 1 Mees. & Wels. 452, Wells *v.* Ody, S. P., at N. Prius, 7 C. & P. 410.

Party Walls.

Intermixed Properties, and Buildings over Public Ways.]—There are certain buildings which have stories or even rooms, respectively the property of different persons, or at all events occupied by different persons and so lying intermixed. These intermixed properties are, in several instances, made subject to the laws of party walls. In a great measure, if not entirely, they are within the rule which requires notice to be given to the surveyor before any work can be legally executed. (*i*). They are subject to the clauses concerning the execution of works, consent, and notice, and the more especially, because the notice of an intention *to pull them down and rebuild them* must be given three months at the least (*k*) before the commencement of the work (*l*). The clauses of modification also apply (*m*).

(*i*) See section 13, *post*, Append.

(*k*) According to schedule M., No. 8. Sections 22, 23, *post*, Append.

(*m*) Sections 22, 23, *post*, Append.

(*l*) Sections 20, 21, *post*, Append. Consent, therefore, dispenses with notice. See 5 T. R. 130, Peck *v.* Wood, where it was held, that after the work had been begun, a party taking the lease of the adjoining house was liable to contribution.

The case was this:

The owner of a house, who repaired the wall, sued the defendant for contribution; and a part of the defence was, that the defendant had not received any notice. But it appeared, that one Pateman was the ground landlord of the premises, that he, Pateman, consented to the building, if the tenant would agree, and that the tenant did agree, and that after the pulling down of the old wall, and the partial erection of the new, but, perhaps, a few days before its entire completion, a lease was executed from Pateman to the defendant. The defendant, therefore, it was contended, had no interest in the house when the old party wall was pulled down, and, consequently, he could not have had notice given to him. And of this opinion was the Court. Pateman, in whose situation the defendant stood at the trial, actually knew of the plaintiff's intention to build the party wall, and to a certain degree consented

Party Walls. Intermixed Properties, and Buildings over Public Ways.

In the 24th section, which supplies the want of the consent of adjoining owners, intermixed buildings are particularly noticed. After mentioning, under the third head, the site whereon the party wall should be built, it is added, with regard to intermixed buildings, that the surveyor's certificate must say what party arches may be necessary over or under any rooms of such buildings so intended to be rebuilt. And the section should be applied generally, as far as the subject of intermixed properties is concerned (*n*). Of course, when the alteration in the intermixed property takes place, the division between the structures will become a party wall, and liable accordingly to the laws of party walls (*o*).

Moreover, (and the clause about to be noticed extends likewise to buildings over public ways) (*p*), if a party wall or arch cannot be built without pulling down such buildings, and so laying parts thereof to each other, and if in default of the consent of all proper parties (*q*), the official referees authorize such works, the owner of any of those buildings may execute the same, always provided that such works so done by such owner as last-mentioned be conformable to this act, and the directions of the official referees (*r*).

to it. No further notice, therefore, to him was necessary, and, said Lord Kenyon, "the defendant is not more entitled to notice than Pateman was." (5 T. R. *ut supra*.) And then, Buller, J., added: 'I agree with the plaintiff's counsel, that notice is only necessary in those instances where the party is either ignorant of, or adverse to, the building of the wall." (*Id.* 132. See 2 B. & Adol. 880)

(*n*) Section 24, *post*, Append.

(*o*) See also section 25.

(*p*) See schedule D., Part V., tit. "Buildings over Public Ways.

(*q*) If consent, therefore, be given, notice to the surveyor under the 13th section would seem to be sufficient.

(*r*) Section 34, *post*, Append. See schedule M., "Summary of Notices," and Nos. 11, 12, and 13, in that schedule.

Party Walls. Intermixed Properties, and Buildings over Public Ways.

But the Inns of Court are excepted out of this clause (*s*), so far only, nevertheless, as that they shall not be meddled with or laid together under the former section. But the walls or divisions between the several rooms and chambers in such inns, or other buildings divided into rooms or chambers, offices, or counting-houses, and let out in separate suites or sets, belonging to and communicating with each separate and distinct staircase, shall be deemed to be party walls within the act, and as such must be built in conformity with the regulations and clauses thereof relating to party walls (*t*).

Method of Building the Wall where the Properties are intermixed.]—With regard to the mode of building a wall where properties are intermixed, the schedule (D) (*u*) directs, that as to any building already built, having rooms or floors, the property of different owners, which lie intermixed, without being separated by any party wall, or party arch, or stone floor:

If either of such houses shall be altogether or in part rebuilt, and the extent of one-fourth of the cubical contents thereof, then such intermixed properties must be separated from each other as follows:—

If they adjoin vertically, then so far as they adjoin vertically, they must be separated by a party wall.

If they adjoin horizontally, then so far as they adjoin horizontally, they must be separated by a brick or other floor of proper and sufficient incombustible materials, &c.

(*s*) Section 34, contains the exception.

(*t*) Section 35, *post*, Append.

(*u*) See the schedule, Part IV., *post*, Append.

Party Walls.

Power of Entry.]—We have seen, that, with regard to buildings and works, so far as relates to the entry thereon for the supervision thereof, there may be an entry on the part of the surveyor upon the premises to be viewed, and even a forcible entry if required (x). Now, for the purpose of facilitating and regulating the execution of any works authorized by the act, or by any award, in pursuance thereof, in respect of any party wall or party arch, parting the buildings or grounds belonging to different owners, or in the occupation of different persons, or in respect of intermixed buildings; it is enacted, that if the works in question have been duly authorized, upon the consent of parties, or by the award or certificate of the official referees, the building owner or other person acting on his behalf may go with a peace-officer and enter upon the premises of the adjoining owner, so far as may be necessary for executing such works. The statute goes on to state the circumstances under which the outer door may be broken, and how goods, furniture, &c. may be removed in order to further the work. The work may then be carried on until its completion, and if any owner or other person shall obstruct any workman employed for any of the purposes aforesaid, or wilfully damage or injure the said works, the offender shall forfeit for any such offence a sum not exceeding 10*l.* (y)

Party Walls, Vacant Ground.]—With regard to walls built on vacant ground, at the line of junction of premises belonging to different owners, or in different occupations, it is enacted, that one month before the

(x) *Ante*, p. 20, 40.

(y) Section 36, *post*, Append. See sections 103, 105, 106, *post*, Append.

owner of any piece of vacant ground, or ground not hitherto built upon, shall build any building adjoining to another piece of vacant ground, or ground not hitherto built upon, or build a fence wall for such piece of ground, he must give the owner or occupier of such adjoining vacant ground a notice (z), in writing, and must set forth his desire to build a party wall or party fence wall, and describe the thicknesses or dimensions of such desired party wall or party fence wall: then if such adjoining owner shall signify his consent in writing, (a) the same must be built partly on the ground of one of the said owners or occupiers, and partly on the ground of the other owner, which last mentioned part is to be paid for as is hereinafter directed by such other owner or occupier: but if he do not signify such consent, then it shall be the duty of the building owner to build an external wall for such building, and fence wall for such ground entirely on his own ground (b). The 39th section (c) provides for chimney breasts and other accommodation for the adjoining owner. For, upon consent given as aforesaid, a notice of ten days, (d) at the least, must be given by the building owner to the adjoining owner before beginning the new party wall. If, then, in due time the adjoining owner shall give instructions in writing, or by a plan, the building owner must construct, if practicable, chimney jambs, &c. in such parts of the party wall, as the instructions may require, and leave such recesses in such wall as may be required, but so that they

Party Walls. Vacant Ground.

(z) See the Form, schedule M , No. 16, *post*, Append.

(a) See the Form of Consent, schedule M., No. 17, *post*, Append.

(b) Section 38, *post*, Append. See 2 Sir Wm. Bl. 959, Barlow *v.* Norman.

(c) See the section, *post*, Append.

(d) According to No. 16, in schedule M.

Party Walls.

be conformable with the directions of the act. And, thereupon, the building owner may claim and recover from the adjoining owner all the expenses of constructing such chimney jambs, &c. as is provided by the act in that behalf, that is to say, under the 46th section.

Party Walls, Ruinous.]—The 40th section introduces this point. Its preamble states, that buildings within the limits of the act are often, either from litigated titles thereto, or from the obstinacy, neglect, or poverty of the owners thereof, or of the parties interested therein, or from other causes, in so ruinous a condition that passengers are endangered thereby. It then goes on to enact, that the surveyor, upon receiving information of any building being in a ruinous and dangerous condition, shall forthwith apply to the official referees for a survey thereof (*e*). The overseers of the parish must likewise do the same if they have similar information. Then the official referees shall direct the surveyor to make the survey. And the surveyor shall act in all respects as in the case of a survey of *party walls* (*f*). The surveyor's certificate being received, the official referees shall cause a copy to be transmitted, if the premises be within the City of London, to the Court of Lord Mayor and Aldermen, but if elsewhere, to the overseers of the parish. Proper and sufficient hoards are then to be put up, and notice in writing is to be given to the owner of the

(*e*) It is also a part of the surveyor's duty to inspect "ruinous buildings, and projections in danger, at all times when needful, and to take all necessary measures thereupon." Sect. 68. Walls will come within the term "buildings," and the surveyor must make this inspection, whether with or without information.

(*f*) See section 24, *post*, Append.

Party Walls Ruinous.

ruinous building to repair or pull it down within fourteen days next ensuing. Then, upon default of the owner, a declaration shall be made before the Lord Mayor, or a justice, as the case may be, of such notice having been given, and the ruinous building shall be forthwith repaired or pulled down, or secured, at the expense, in the one case, of the City, and, in the other, of the poor's rate. Provided always, that if the Lord Mayor and aldermen, or the overseers, should appeal against the certificate, the referees may proceed to survey, certify, and award in all respects as in the case of an appeal from the surveyor's certificate with reference to party walls and intermixed buildings. Then, if the referees certify that the premises are ruinous and dangerous, it shall be the duty of the Lord Mayor, or of the overseers, to repair or pull down such buildings as aforesaid (*g*).

The 41st section treats of the disposal of the materials of the ruinous buildings thus pulled down (*h*).

The 42nd section directs how the expenses of putting up the hoard, of repairing, pulling down, and securing the buildings, and selling the materials, beyond the amount which shall have been satisfied by the application thereto of the proceeds of the materials, shall be defrayed (*i*).

So strongly is the necessity of repairing party walls recognised by the act, that parts of party walls which may happen to fall down and do damage are excepted out of the rule which in general requires compensation from the owner of the building from which any chimney-pots,

(*g*) See the section, *post*, Append.
(*h*) See the section, *post*, Append.
(*i*) See the section, *post*, Append.

Party Walls Ruinous.

or other things fall and do injury (*k*). It may be added, that all buildings which are not erected conformably to the provisions of this act are nuisances. Therefore, it is ordained, with regard to any buildings, &c., *party walls*, &c., which shall be *hereafter* built, rebuilt, enlarged, or altered, within the limits of the act, contrary to the provisions thereof, so far as relates to the removal thereof: that if the same be not built, &c., in conformity with the act, or if any person build, or begin to build, &c., or use or cause to be used, any part of any ground or building, &c.; the said building, &c. shall, upon the appearance of a certificate to that effect from the official referees, be deemed a nuisance. Next comes the procedure. The surveyor must summon the builder before any two justices, and the builder must enter into a recognizance in such sum as the justices may appoint, to abate the nuisance within a time to be named by the justices, or otherwise to amend it according to the rules and directions of the act, and to pay the surveyor's costs of the information and conviction, and of compensation for his loss of time. Failing to enter into the recognizance, the builder may be committed till he abate the nuisance, or otherwise amend the irregular building, or till the nuisance be abated by order of the justices, and until the costs, charges, and expenses thereof, and of all operations and proceedings in relation thereto shall have been paid. Further, upon an application to any two or more justices, it shall be their duty to order the surveyor or other person to abate the nuisance, and sell the materials, deducting from the proceeds thereof the reasonable charges of demolishing the nuisance, and all the costs and expenses above-mentioned, and paying the surplus,

(*k*) Section 44, *post*, Append.

Party Walls Ruinous.

(if any) to such owner of the building as the official referees shall determine to be entitled thereto. In case, however, of a deficiency upon such sale, it shall be the duty of the person entitled to the immediate possession of the building, or of the occupier to make good the same, subject to reimbursement as afterwards provided; and if he fail, then he shall be liable to the same remedies for the recovery thereof, as are by this act provided concerning the expense of taking down ruinous buildings, and putting up hoards for the safety of passengers (*l*).

It is to be observed, that a compensation clause in a local act will not apply if a party wall be within the condemnation of the Building Act, unless there be express words. Where a party wall belonging to two houses, one of which had been bought by the Hungerford Market Company, was condemned as being out of repair, it was held that the tenant of the adjoining premises was not entitled to compensation, in consequence of the pulling down of such wall by the Company. The only material damage done was the temporary inconvenience sustained by the pulling down and rebuilding of this wall, such as the expense of removing from and being kept out of the premises while the works were in progress, loss of stock, trade, &c. The Court discharged the rule for a mandamus to the Company, calling upon them to issue their warrant to summon a jury. And the Court thought that even if the Company had not proceeded in strict conformity with the Building Act, it did not, therefore, follow that they were amenable to the compensation clause of the local act (*m*). So where the Company had bought No. 11 in a particular street, but which No. 11

(*l*) Section 18, *post*, Append.

(*m*) 1 Ad. & El. 668, Rex *v.* Hungerford Market Company, *ex parte* Yeates; S. C., 2 Nev. & M. 340.

Party Walls Ruinous.

was not specified in their act, the tenant of No. 12 was held not to be entitled to compensation because the Company had pulled down and rebuilt the party wall between No. 11 and No. 12. No. 10 was particularly specified in the act, and if No. 11 had been specified, they, the Company, would then have had a monopoly as to the frontage of No. 11, and would have been liable to render compensation for any damage done in consequence of their own neglect. The rule for a mandamus was discharged (*n*).

II. External Walls.

External Walls.

Having now brought both old and new party walls before the reader, together with the various descriptions of premises to which such walls may belong, we proceed, in the second place, to the consideration of external walls.

There may be an external wall as well as a party wall appurtenant to a house or building. There may be an external wall where there is no party wall, as in the case where a building owner builds on vacant ground, and does not obtain the consent of the adjoining owner, or where there has never been a party wall, and no occasion has happened to make it necessary to rebuild the premises. There may be an external wall in use as a party fence wall (*o*). There may be an external wall where a building of a higher rate than the adjoining

(*n*) 1 Ad. & El., 676, Rex *v.* Hungerford Market Company, *ex parte* Eyre; S. C., 3 Nev. & M., 622. Nevertheless, perhaps an *action* would have lain, (1 Ad. & El. 684,) but the tenant had suffered the time allowed for such action to elapse.

(*o*) See section 25, *post*, Append.

External Walls.

building is constructed. And the outside of a row of buildings or of an insulated structure would necessarily have an external fence. These external walls need not be always of the same thickness as party walls, although they must be so in the higher rates of building.

Thickness, &c.]—Their thickness is directed as carefully as in the case of party walls (*p*). In schedule (D), which concerns walls of every kind, the foundations and footings, together with the materials and width of such footings, are pointed out (*q*). The height, the depth below ground, and the depth below the lowest floor are likewise prescribed (*r*). The external wall is mentioned separately in schedule (D), with reference to its construction and materials, the height and thickness of parapets, breast-summers, materials to be used in repair and in re-building (*s*). And so necessary is it to keep up the strength of external walls, that if it be sought to treat such an external wall, at any time, as a party wall (*t*), this object cannot be attained unless the external wall correspond in footings, height, and thicknesses, and be built in the manner, and with the materials required for *party walls* of buildings of the highest rate, to which such wall shall adjoin (*u*). Otherwise, a good external

(*p*) See schedule C., Part II., referring to section 5; and the same schedule, Part V., at the end. See the schedule, *post*, Append. And see the "Measurement of Stories," in this schedule. See the "Rule for Ascertaining Thickness," schedule C., Part I., at the end, *post*, Append. And see the same schedule, tit. "Rule for ascertaining Area," in which external walls are included, *post*, Append.

(*q*) See the schedule, Part I., *post*, Append.

(*r*) *Id. ibid.*

(*s*) See the schedule, Part II., *post*, Append.

(*t*) Except in the case of an attached building or office.

(*u*) Schedule D., Part II., at the end, *post*, Append.

External Walls.

wall might become an inferior party wall. This regulation becomes important when buildings of some standing are connected by the introduction of new structures. If the external wall, therefore, be imperfect and not equal to a party wall, and a party wall be not built, a distinct external wall, built according to the rules for external walls, and of the rate of building to which it shall belong, must be added on, so that there will be two external walls instead of one (*x*). But if such external wall to any building already built be at the least thirteen inches in thickness in every part, and be of sound and proper materials, and in good condition, then such wall may be used as a party wall; but if the house, of which such wall forms a part, be rebuilt within five years from the time at which the wall shall have been so first used as a party wall, then such wall must become subject to the provisions of this act in respect of party walls, according to the class and rate to which the said wall did first belong.

And herewith, in principle, agrees a clause in the act, independent of the schedule, which directs, that if the owner of one of the buildings, parted by a party wall, rebuild such building of a higher rate, and do not pull down such party wall, and build a proper wall in lieu thereof, it shall be his duty, and he is required, to build up an external wall against such party wall (*y*). So that there must be a structure of a strength equivalent to a party wall, for the higher rate of building would press unequally on the lower rate of a party wall, and an external wall is, consequently, demanded, in order to make up the difference of solidity.

Even although the act be modified upon the rebuilding of buildings already built, the party walls and the

(*x*) Schedule D., Part II., at the end, *post*, Append.

(*y*) Section 27, *post*, Append.

external walls must be of the required height and thickness (z). External Walls.

It is calculated that this proceeding, of building up an external against a party wall may not be a matter of rare occurrence, and, therefore, the possibility of damage accruing from such an alteration is provided against. It may be necessary to excavate or dig out the ground against the wall of the adjoining building for the purpose of erecting this wall. This the builder may do, but upon condition that he shore and underpin the wall adjoining at his own cost. It may be necessary to cut away part of the footings of the party wall, or part of the chimney shafts, &c. This, likewise, may be done, provided a notice of one month be given to the owner of the adjoining building (*a*), at the expiration of the notice (*b*), and provided also that it be done under the superintendence and to the satisfaction of the surveyor (*c*), who is, under the 13th section, to have a notice given him before any party wall, *external wall*, &c. shall be begun to be built, pulled down, rebuilt, *cut into*, or altered (*d*). Then follows a provision, that if by such cutting away, the party wall be so damaged as to become ruinous or dangerous, the surveyor must survey the wall, and condemn it if he find it dangerous. Whereupon the building owner must pull down and rebuild such party wall. The opinion of the surveyor and official referees must then be

(*z*) Section 12, *post*, Append.

(*a*) See the Form, schedule M., No. 15, *post*, Append.

(*b*) If there be a dispute, the official referees will, probably, settle it under section 81.

(*c*) Section 28, *post*, Append.

(*d*) See the section, *post*, Append. And see likewise section 14, *post*, Append., where the surveyor has jurisdiction given him over irregularities in building, and over *external walls*, amongst other structures.

External Walls.

had (*e*), whether the damage has been occasioned by want of care on the part of the building owner. If so, he must not only rebuild the wall at his own cost, but must likewise bear the costs of the survey and other incidental expenses. And further, if the building owner do not proceed with all due dispatch to pull down and rebuild the party wall and to pay the costs of the survey, the adjoining owner may then do so, and may recover all the costs and expenses in respect thereof from such owner, his heirs, executors, administrators, or assigns (*f*). But supposing that the building owner be not in fault, the inference must be that the parties become liable to repair the wall or a proportion thereof at their own costs respectively, or that, if the adjoining owner should make default, the building owner may proceed under the 20th and following sections (*g*), and the surveyor himself under the clause relating to ruinous buildings, if the building owner should not discharge *his* duty (*h*).

External Walls —Raising.] — The clause regarding the raising of buildings has been already referred to (*i*); it is proposed, therefore, to say no more in this place than that external walls are included within the provisions mentioned (*k*).

(*e*) Unless the building owner should bear the whole charge of rebuilding.

(*f*) Section 29, *post*, Append. This default of the building owner, is excepted out of the "Reimbursement or Contribution Clause, (section 46, *post*, Append.) and is the subject of an action. See Chapter III., and see likewise Section 30, *post*, Append.

(*g*) *Ante*, p. 43, &c.

(*h*) Section 40, *post*, Append. See as to "Buildings and Offices," schedule C., Part VI., *post*, Append.; "Insulated Buildings afterwards divided," *ibid*, *post*, Append.

(*i*) *Ante*, p. 55.

(*k*) Section 31, *post*, Append.

External Walls.

External Walls. Stopping Openings.]—By section 37, for the purpose of protecting the interests of adjoining owners, it is enacted, with regard to external walls adjoining the ground or building of another owner, so far as relates to the making of openings therein: that if without the consent in writing of the owner of such ground or building, any opening be made in any such wall, it shall then be lawful for such owner to require the owner of the premises in which such opening shall be made to stop up the same with brick-work; and that, if within one month after such notice (*l*), such stoppage be not effected, such owner may cause such openings to be stopped, and is entitled to be repaid the costs thereof; and with regard to such costs, so far as relates to the adjustment thereof, if such owner refuse to make payment thereof, or if there be any dispute as to the amount thereof, then on application for the purpose to the official referees by either of the parties concerned, the person by whom such costs have been incurred may refer the matter in dispute to the referees and have their determination thereon. The referees shall then give the applicant a certificate in relation thereto, and if any party liable to pay any sum of money under such certificate fail to do so, the same may then be recovered in the manner hereinafter provided for the recovery of the costs, charges, and expenses of executing any works, in pursuance of this act (*m*).

External Walls—Vacant Ground.]—The subject of building upon vacant ground with reference to walls has already received attention (*n*). We need only add here

(*l*) See the Form of Notice, schedule M., No. 5, *post*, Append.

(*m*) Section 37, *post*, Append. See section 50.

(*n*) *Ante*, p. 62.

External Walls.

the last sentence of the 38th section, in relation to the matter: namely, that if the adjoining owner will not permit the building owner to erect a party wall, or fence wall, such building owner must build an external wall for such building, and fence wall for such ground entirely on his own ground, except as to the footings of any such wall (o).

Nuisance.] — Lastly, external walls are particularly mentioned in the 18th section which declares all buildings to be nuisances which are not erected conformably to the provisions of the act (p).

III. Party Fence Walls.

The provisions of the act concerning party fence walls will not detain us long, the law of party walls having nearly exhausted the subject of fence walls, being in many respects the same. A party fence wall is declared by this statute to be any boundary wall parting the grounds belonging to different owners or occupied by different persons, so far as relates to the reparation and rebuilding and raising thereof (q). Party fence walls are mentioned in the clause which condemns as nuisances all buildings erected otherwise than in conformity with the act (r). In the section already set out concerning the

(o) See the section, *post*, Append.

(p) See the section, *post*, Append. And see section 13, which requires that a certain notice shall be given to the surveyor before any work shall be commenced, *post*, Append. And, likewise, schedule E., *post*, Append., "Rules concerning External Projections," with reference to external walls.

(q) Section 32. See the section, *post*, Append.

(r) Section 18, *post*, Append.

execution of works (*s*), party fence walls are distinctly mentioned. The reparation, rebuilding, and raising of such walls are especially provided for in the section alluded to. The fence wall is again noticed in the next clause, which requires a consent from the adjoining owner or a notice before certain works are commenced (*t*). The modification clause applies to these walls (*u*); and they are further mentioned in the clause for supplying the consent of adjoining owners (*y*). Party Fence Walls.

The section, likewise, which requires a notice to be given to the owner of the ground or building adjoining vacant ground speaks of a party fence wall as well as of a party wall, and the provisions of the clause apply to such a wall (*z*).

Height.]—The height of a fence wall, whether new, or raised, seems to be fixed at a limit of nine feet above the ground (*a*). In the case of insulated buildings, a fence wall not less than of the full height of the building is sometimes necessary. The reader is referred to the schedule (C.) for particulars (*b*).

Party Fence Walls—Repair—Party Wall, &c., used as Party Fence Wall.]—If a party wall or external wall

(*s*) Section 20, *post*, Append.

(*t*) Section 21, *post*, Append.

(*u*) Section 22, *post*, Append.

(*y*) Section 24, *post*, Append. See the respective notices in schedule M., as applicable to this kind of wall, Nos. 8, 9, 10, 11, 12, 13.

(*z*) Section 38, *post*, Append.

(*a*) Section 32, *post*, Append.

(*b*) Schedule C., Part VII., tit. "Insulated Buildings," *post*, Append.

Party Fence Walls.

be used as a party fence wall, and it become defective, or so much out of repair as to render it necessary to pull down or rebuild the same, the building owner first giving notice to the adjoining owner may require a survey, certificate, and award, authorizing the execution of such reparation or rebuilding, according to the provisions hereinbefore contained in that behalf (c).

Repair—Height.]—However, the owner of any of the premises parted thereby, may repair, pull down, and rebuild the wall at any time at his own charge. He may also raise it, if below the height of nine feet from the ground on either side, to that height, or may pull it down and rebuild it to that height, upon condition in all the above cases respectively, that he do give notice of such his intention to the adjoining owner, and that he do pay all the expenses thereof. And if a building be to be erected against such party fence wall, and such wall be not conformable to the requisites prescribed for a party wall for a building of that class and rate, it shall be lawful for the building owner, and he is entitled to pull down such party fence wall; but upon condition that he do pay all the expenses thereof; and also that he do make good every damage which shall accrue to such adjoining premises by such rebuilding. Provided always, with regard to the expense of so pulling down and rebuilding, that if the adjoining owner use the wall for any purpose to which it would not have been applicable had it not been pulled down and rebuilt, the building owner shall be reimbursed to that extent. And there is

(c) See sections 20—25 inclusive, *post*, Append.

another proviso with regard to a fence wall, so far as relates to the limitation of its height, that if any party desire to raise such wall so as to screen from view any offensive object or neighbourhood, he may do so upon application to the official referees, but not so as to obstruct the free circulation of the air to injure the property adjoining to or in the neighbourhood of such wall (*d*).

Party Fence Walls.

IV.—Timber Partitions.

The Legislature is not desirous of encouraging the continuance of timber partitions. By section 33, with regard to the party timber partitions of existing buildings belonging to different owners, so far as relates to the pulling down thereof, and any wall under or over the same, it is enacted, that if one of the buildings be rebuilt, or if one of the fronts of such buildings be taken down to the height of one story, or for a space equal to one-fourth of such front from the level of the second floor upwards, then, without the consent of the adjoining owner, but upon giving the requisite notice, according to the forms (Nos. 11, 12, 13) in the schedule of notices, or to the like effect, the building owner is required to pull down such timber partitions, and the walls under or over the same, and in lieu thereof to build a proper party wall, and that at the expense of the owners of all the premises parted thereby (*e*).

Timber Partitions.

This mode of dealing with timber partitions especially concerns intermixed properties, and it is observable that

(*d*) Section 32, *post*, Append. There must be the usual notice to the surveyor, before any building or alteration of a party fence wall takes place. Section 13, *post*, Append.

(*e*) See the section, *post*, Append., and see section 46.

Timber Partitions.

the consent of adjoining owners is not necessary. But where the properties are not intermixed, the owner of premises where a timber partition exists, seems to be entitled to notice under the express provision of the section concerning the execution of works to which we have had occasion more than once to refer (*f*). The consent clause (*g*), and the clause which supplies the want of consent (*h*) may be said to apply to the latter case, but not to that which is regulated by section 33. The clauses of modification likewise will be available in the second but not in the first case (*i*). Nevertheless, the notice mentioned in section 33 as being requisite, must be sought for in the 21st section, and in the schedule (M) (*k*), although the tenor of this thirty-third section would seem to point out that neither survey, nor certificate, nor award, need be called for, but that the work may be done at the expiration of the notice, upon complying with the customary notice to the surveyor under the 13th section (*l*).

The rules concerning external projections from walls or otherwise, will be found in schedule (E) (*m*).

Reimbursement and Contribution Clauses.

Reimbursement and Contribution Clauses.

We have now gone over the various sections of this act, and more especially those relating to party and other

(*f*) Section 20, *post*, Append.

(*g*) Section 21, *post*, Append.

(*h*) Section 24, *post*, Append.

(*i*) That is to say, where the properties are not intermixed, they will be available. Sections 22, 23, *post*, Append.

(*k*) See the Form, schedule M., No. 14, *post*, Append.

(*l*) See likewise section 18, *post*, Append., as to "Nuisance."

(*m*) See the Schedule, *post*, Append., and section 5, *post*, Append., and likewise section 18, *post*, Append.

Reimbursement and Contribution Clauses.

walls. The party wall, the external wall, the party fence wall, and the timber partition have been respectively noticed. Old and new walls have been considered. The reparation, pulling down, rebuilding, and raising of walls have been examined in conjunction with the appointments of the statute. And the law of walls, as it respects buildings over public ways, or intermixed properties, has also been brought before the reader. Lastly, ruinous buildings, including ruinous walls, have had their share of attention.

It remains that we devote a short space to that part of the act which orders the reimbursement to the building owner of his costs and expenses in respect of any party structure, and a contribution from persons interested, according to their respective properties. In pursuance of this intention, we will give the 46th section at length.

By section 46 (*n*), "For the purpose of reimbursing any building owner for the expense of works incurred in respect of any party structure, it is enacted, with regard to the following works, so far as relates to the reimbursement, by the adjoining owner, of expenses incurred by the building owner, in respect of any party structure, built to part the buildings or premises belonging to other owners from the buildings or premises belonging to himself; that is to say,—

"First, with regard to any party wall hereafter built on the line of junction of any two buildings; and,

"Second, with regard to any party wall hereafter built on the line of junction of any building and any vacant ground, or of vacant premises, belonging to different owners or occupiers: and,

"Third, with regard to a ruinous and defective party wall pulled down and rebuilt, either with the consent of

(*n*) See the section, *post*, Append.

Reimbursement and Contribution Clauses.

the adjoining owner, or in pursuance of the condemnation thereof, according to this act, except a party wall condemned on account of the injury done thereto by any building owner (*o*), and the expenses of which and of other incidental works the official referees shall have awarded to be paid by such building owner, by virtue of the provision in that behalf; and,

"Fourth, with regard to one or more timber partitions between any two or more buildings pulled down, and a party wall built in lieu thereof, and,

"Fifth, with regard to a new party wall or party arch, built in lieu of any party wall or party arch, between intermixed properties pulled down, either with the consent of the adjoining owner, or in pursuance of the condemnation of such party wall or party arch; and,

"Sixth, with regard to any party wall built on the site of a party fence or party fence wall, and used otherwise than as a party fence wall by the person who shall not have built the same; and,

"Seventh, with regard to every other case of reimbursement, in respect of any party structure.

"That if the party structure be built in the manner and of the materials, and of the thicknesses of such structure as required by this act in reference thereto, then it shall be lawful for the building owner at whose expense such work shall have been executed, to claim, and he is hereby entitled to be paid and to recover from the owner of any adjoining building or ground, the following compensations; that is to say,—

"If a new party wall or party arch built on the line of junction by one owner, be made use of, either wholly or partially, by the adjoining owner, then a sum of money proportionate to the value of so much of such party structure so made use of; and,

(*o*) See *ante*, p. 72.

" If chimney-jambs, chimney-breasts, and flues have been set up in any party wall in pursuance of the instructions of the owner of any vacant ground adjoining to the same, then a sum equal to the value thereof; and, Reimbursement and Contribution Clauses.

" If an unsound party wall or other party structure be pulled down and rebuilt, then a sum of money equal to a proper proportion of the value of the new party structure, deduction being made for a due proportion of the old materials, and also a proportionate part of all expenses which shall be necessary for pulling down the old party structure, in lieu of which such new party structure shall be built; and,

" If a party wall be built in lieu of a timber partition or other party structure, and be made use of by the adjoining owner, then a sum of money proportionate to the value of so much of such new party wall as shall be so made use of; and also a proportionate part of all expenses which shall be necessary for pulling down the old timber partition or other party structure; and,

" If a party wall or party arch already built, or hereafter rebuilt, be used by an adjoining owner, then a sum of money proportionate to the value of so much of such party structure as the adjoining owner shall use, deduction being made, where proper, for the value of the old materials;

" And, in every case, the whole of the reasonable expenses of the shoring up the adjoining building, and of removing any goods, furniture, or other things therein, and of pulling down any wainscot or partition thereof;

" And also, such surveyor's fees, and any other fees payable in respect of any acts performed by the official referees: and also, such other costs (if any) as may have been awarded by the official referees as aforesaid, in any of the cases hereby provided for;

Reimbursement and Contribution Clauses.

"And until such expenses shall be so paid, every person at whose expense such party structure shall have been built is hereby entitled to and shall be possessed of the sole property thereof, and of the ground whereon it stands, and the same shall be vested entirely in the person at whose expense such party structure shall have been built."

This is a reimbursement clause,—one of considerable importance. It refers distinctly to new walls,—to vacant ground,—to ruinous buildings,—to timber partitions,—to intermixed properties,—to party walls built in lieu of party fence walls,—and to "every other case of reimbursement in respect of any party structure." Consequently, if a partial want of repair be necessary, and proceedings be taken under the 20th and following sections, this 7th article will reach the case. The wall which is partially repaired is not a ruinous or defective wall within the statute, but it is one which the 20th section, concerning the "reparation" of party walls, will embrace, and the last item of reimbursement just cited will probably take in the point of reimbursement. The words, in the 20th section, "payment of the cost of such works," have a general reference to this comprehensive clause (*o*). The 24th section, which directs that certain expenses of surveys shall be certified and awarded in fixed proportions, may likewise be referred to under this head. And the proceedings under section 25 may likewise come under this 46th clause. So under the general head of reimbursement the raising of buildings under the 31st section may be included. The charges of exchanging a timber partition for a party wall are particularly mentioned in section 46, and the 33rd section may, therefore,

(*o*) That is, section 46.

be quoted as being in close connection with the clause of reimbursement. The same may be said of proceedings in building upon vacant ground, where the adjoining owner has consented to the structure. The clauses concerning ruinous buildings also come within its provisions (*p*). Reimbursement and Contribution Clauses.

The 5th article concerning intermixed properties may be identified with the third head of proportionate compensation.

The mode of reimbursing expenses having been fully set forth by the statute, it becomes necessary to ascertain how these charges are to be recovered, and from what class of persons. It is conceived that the adjoining owner is to have, in the first instance, an account of the sum laid out by the building owner. It seems also, that this adjoining owner must be construed to mean the occupier, where there is an occupier, unless such occupier be merely a "tenant from year to year, or for any less term, or a tenant at will;" (*q*) or if there be not an occupier, then he must be the person entitled to the immediate possession of the premises (*r*).

Then, with respect to all leases and agreements made before the coming into operation of the act, the charge is ultimately to lie upon the person now bound by law, or by any existing contract, to maintain and repair the building. But where the lease or agreement is made after the act begins to work, the occupier is to be liable, but he may deduct the charges out of his rent, in the absence of any covenant or agreement, on his own part, to pay them. The official referees are, in cases of dis-

(*p*) Sections 40 to 44, inclusive, *post*, Append.

(*q*) See section 112.

(*r*) See sections 46, 111, *post*, Append.

Reimbursement and Contribution Clauses.

pute, to determine the demands, in respect of which each owner or occupier shall be liable, and likewise the proportionate contributions which may be required from each. Such contributions not being paid, it becomes a question how the liquidation of them is to be enforced. Formerly, this was done by action under the 41st section of the 14 Geo. 3, c. 78, and the owner of the improved rent was the person selected to make the payment. Who might be this owner of the improved rent was a question so nice that numerous lawsuits sprang from the section, and the assistance of the Courts was frequently invoked in order to settle in some measure, a rule upon the subject (*s*). Now, however, the expenses are to be ascertained by the referees, and the amount being calculated, the party refusing to pay may be summoned before a magistrate, or before two justices where the case is out of the jurisdiction of a police magistrate. Then upon conviction, a warrant of distress may be issued against his goods, and if the distress be insufficient, it shall be lawful for the justice to commit the person in default till he have paid the amount due and the costs (*t*).

First, then, we have the clause which requires an account to be given of the work done, and of any deduction which may be justly allowed on the behalf of the adjoining owner (*u*).

It enacts that, " with regard to the costs of all the works

(*s*) See, amongst other cases, 5 T. R. 130, Peck *v.* Wood. 3 T. R. 458, Southall *v.* Leadbetter. 1 Bos. & Pul. 306, Sangster *v.* Birkhead. 8 T. R. 204, Beardmore *v.* Fox. 6 Taunt. 249, Taylor *v.* Reed. 2 B. & Ald. 467, Lambe *v.* Hemans. 2 B. & Ald. 878, Williams *v.* Pocklington.

(*t*) Section 102, *post*, Append.

(*u*) Section 47, *post*, Append.

Reimbursement and Contribution Clauses.

which shall be executed under this act, incurred, either by an owner or by an occupier, on behalf of the owner of the adjoining premises, or on behalf of the owner of the same premises, so far as relates to the recovery thereof, that, within *twenty-one* days after the completion of the work, it shall be the duty of the person by whom such expense shall have been incurred, to deliver to the adjoining owner of the building or premises, in respect of which such expense shall have been incurred, an account in writing of the expenses of the work, including all preliminary and incidental operations; and also, if the work shall have been executed by the authority of the official referees, by virtue of the power hereby provided for supplying the want of consent of owners, then a copy of such account shall also be delivered to the official referees at their office; and that every such account must contain a true account,—

"First, of the number of rods and parts of rods of brickwork, and of all digging, and of concrete, stonework, and other requisite materials, and the labour required in executing so much of the work as the owner of the adjoining building shall be liable to pay, and of the respective prices thereof: and, secondly, of any deduction which such adjoining owner shall be entitled to make therefrom on account of the old materials of so much of the wall or other structure pulled down, which shall have belonged to him:

"And also a true account of the expenses of all other preliminary and incidental operations;

"And that all such works must be estimated and valued, in every such account, at such rates and prices as shall from time to time be fixed by the official referees;

"And that if within *ten* days from the delivery of such

Reimbursement and Contribution Clauses.

account, any party dissatisfied with the proportion of the amount thereof charged to him, appeal to the official referees, then, upon the receipt thereof, or if, in cases of want of due consent as aforesaid, such account be delivered to the official referees as aforesaid, it shall be the duty of the official referees to examine such account, and to certify whether they approve or disapprove of the items thereof, and whether the rates and prices are duly charged, and whether the proportion of the account charged to the party appealing be duly charged, and also to appoint how and by whom the expenses of such examination are to be borne, and also to appoint the time or times at which the amount of such account, and of such expenses payable by any party, are to be paid; and that if they certify their disapproval, or that the charges are not duly made, or the amount fairly apportioned with regard to the party appealing, then before any demand be made, or any proceedings be taken thereon, the account must be amended, and again examined by the official referees, and certified as aforesaid; and that if the official referees certify their approval, then at the time or times appointed by the said official referees, it shall be lawful for the person entitled to such costs and expenses to demand the amount thereof; and that if within *ten* days after the delivering of such account to the party liable to pay the same, such party do not either appeal against such account or pay the same; or if, within *ten* days after the demand thereof in conformity with the certificate of the official referees, the amount thereof, together with the costs of the examination of the account, as the official referees shall certify, be not paid; then it shall be lawful for the person entitled thereto to recover the same, or so much thereof as shall be then due, by the summary proceeding hereby provided" (x).

Reimbursement and Contribution Clauses.

It is, therefore, competent for the parties to avoid a collision, and thus escape the amending hand of the referees. For, unless the work shall have been executed by their order, which, in many instances, would be the consequence of dissension amongst owners, the party called upon can settle the account thus duly delivered, and retire from any further difficulty. Lord Chief Justice *Gibbs* declared in a case before him, that parties would do wisely by agreeing amongst themselves, without having recourse to an intricate law (y), (meaning the 14 Geo. 3,) and, without imputing any such intricacy to the present statute, yet, as far as the principle of mutual union is concerned, the same perhaps may be said here.

With regard to the account above required, it seems that a formal demand is not necessary as under the old act (z). It is sufficient if proof be made that the accounts have been delivered. But it is imperative to deliver the accounts prescribed by the statute, so that where a plaintiff made default in these particulars, the Court made the rule absolute for entering a nonsuit (a). Then, if the requisites of the statute are complied with in an ordinary sense, it will be sufficient. The Court will not put words into the Act of Parliament which it does not contain, for the purpose of construing it like a penal law. Assumpsit was brought under the 14 Geo. 3, c. 78, for contribution. There was an account of the brick-

(x) Section 47, *post*, Append. This summary proceeding is under section 102, *post*, Append.; and note, that the costs of stopping up openings in external walls, (sect. 37,) are recoverable under the provisions of these sections, 47, and 102.

(y) 2 Marsh, 435, 436, Stuart *v.* Smith; S. C., 7 Taunt. 158.

(z) See 2 Taunt. 66, Philp *v.* Donati.

(a) *Ibid.*

Reimbursement and Contribution Clauses.

work, of the deduction for materials, and of the other expenses, and payment was demanded within the twenty-one days. But when the account came to be examined, it was found that the prices actually paid for the brick-work, and received for the materials, exceeded the rates prescribed by the act, making the whole amount 30*l.* instead of 18*l.*, the sum which would have been due had the statutable duty been charged. The counsel for the defendant would not allow this point to escape, and he contended, first, that this could not be a true account, because of the high price demanded, and then, as the demand would necessarily refer to the account delivered, that there could not have been a good demand. Lord *Tenterden*, however, observed, that the requisites of the statute had been apparently adopted. The act itself fixed the price, and if the quantities were correctly stated, the party charged would have the means of knowing the amount of the claim against him. "There is, therefore," said his Lordship, "no necessity for, and *the act does not require*, any specification of the price; and the account will not be vitiated by the unnecessary insertion of a price which the party cannot be charged with." The Chief Justice added, that with respect to the demand, a demand to pay the account is, in effect, a demand to pay the sum authorized by the statute. Nor need the demand be in terms a demand for the exact sum; for in the same section which empowers the plaintiff to proceed at law, the plaintiff is enabled to recover double costs, if he recover the full sum specified. There was a verdict for the plaintiff (*b*).

Another case occurred likewise under the same act of Geo. 3, with regard to the notice. The plaintiff had built a party wall at a time when no house adjoined,

(*b*) Moo. & M. 71, Reading *v.* Barnard.

Reimbursement and Contribution Clauses.

and it was therefore a maiden wall. Some years afterwards the house of the defendant was attached to the house of the plaintiff, and the plaintiff's party wall was cut into. It became difficult for the plaintiff to ascertain the real owner of the improved rent in order to found an accurate claim, and when he had at length fixed upon the defendant, the latter objected that the statute had not been complied with for the want of the ten days' notice. *Best*, C. J., thought there was no one to whom notice could have been given within the ten days, and, consequently, the words "as soon after as conveniently may be," would apply, and a verdict was found for the plaintiff. The matter was then discussed before the Court, and the two points of notice were brought into question. First, the Chief Justice said, that had the defendant's house been built at the time when the plaintiff's wall was raised, he should have thought that the notice within ten days would have been a condition precedent to a recovery in respect of it. But here there was not any adjoining house when the wall was built, so that the second time for giving notice, that is to say, as soon as convenient, would come to be considered. It would be in the discretion of the Judge to say whether such notice had been given in convenient time, and in the present case the Court held, that it had, for the plaintiff had no means of ascertaining the relation that subsisted between the defendant and one *Guppy* who, it was contended, was the owner of the improved rent, and, said *Best*, C. J., "they were trying for six years to trick him out of his claim." "What shall be a convenient time for notice must fluctuate according to the circumstances of each case." The rule for a new trial was discharged (*c*).

(*c*) 4 Bingh. 551, Collins *v*. Wilson.

Reimbursement and Contribution Clauses.

Now it is plain that this latter case is in a great measure rendered useless by the new statute, because the term of twenty-one days is the present time absolutely fixed, and not "as soon afterwards as conveniently may be," and likewise, because the notice is to be served on the adjoining owner of the building *or premises*, in respect of which the expense shall have been incurred. Still an adjoining owner must be found where there is no occupier, or where the occupier is only a tenant from year to year, or at will, and the case of *Collins* v. *Wilson* may yet serve as a lesson to show the necessity of suing the right owner; for the old act deemed it sufficient to leave the account at the adjoining house or building (*d*). But the present act requires a delivery to the adjoining owner, who, whether owner or occupier, must be duly fixed upon, in order to warrant the further proceedings of the statute.

It may be remarked likewise in this place, that although the course by summary proceeding may appear at first sight to withdraw these various cases from consideration, they are yet of some value. First, inasmuch as the police magistrate and justices would feel themselves bound to pay a certain amount of attention to the ancient decisions of the Courts. And, secondly, because if the new tribunal were to act in opposition to the principle of authorities which might be now applicable, an action might well lie, on the one hand, for an illegal distress and imprisonment, or a mandamus on the other for refusing to do an act apparently in conformity with the new statute and the old cases.

The clause authorizing a summary mode of proceeding is as follows:—"And be it enacted, with regard to every

(*d*) 14 Geo. 3, c. 78, s. 41.

sum of money by this act, or by any award or certificate, or other proceeding, in pursuance of this act, charged upon any person in respect of any work done in pursuance of or in accordance with this act, so far as relates to the recovery of such sum of money, that it shall be lawful for the party claiming the same to proceed in a summary way before any two justices of the peace, or if the matter arise within the district of the metropolitan police, then before any police magistrate having jurisdiction within that district; and that, on proof of such sum of money being still due, it shall be lawful for such justices or such police magistrate, and they respectively are hereby required to issue a warrant to levy the amount thereof, and also the costs of the proceeding, to be levied by distress of the goods and chattels of the person in default; and if such person have no goods and chattels whereon to distrain, or if such goods and chattels be insufficient for that purpose, then it shall be lawful for such justices or police magistrate, or for any other justice or police magistrate, to commit the person in default until the amount of such sum so due, of such costs, shall, and have been fully paid (*f*), or until the party shall be discharged by or in accordance with the provisions of any act for the relief and discharge of insolvent debtors."

Reimbursement and Contribution Clauses.

This clause, it will be observed, is intended to cover all sums of money charged upon persons under the act, all sums due by virtue by any award—or certificate—or any sum charged by any other proceeding in pursuance of the act. Therefore, if a party fail to appeal against a charge with which he is not satisfied, the money may be recovered by this proceeding simply; if he appeal, and a certificate of approval be gained from the referees, the word "certificate," is satisfied; if there be any dispute as

(*f*) Sect. 102. See the section, *post*, Append.

Reimbursement and Contribution Clauses.

to the contribution, the referees may make an award, and the word "award" applies. The same remark will affect other clauses of the act where there has been an award, or a certificate or other proceeding, or where a sum of money become due under any provision.

Having thus given the clauses which shew that reimbursement is necessary, and that, upon the production of an account, a summary proceeding may be had recourse to, we come to the remedies which the law has reserved for those who are, in the first instance, liable, but who, nevertheless, are not ultimately debtors to the building, but may call upon others to contribute a share towards the expense.

First, then, with reference to an indemnity in favour of the occupier, the act directs that,—

With regard to works executed under it, so far as relates to the reimbursement to the occupier of any costs by him paid in respect thereof, unless there be some express agreement to the contrary between the parties, it shall be lawful for such occupier and he is hereby entitled to deduct from the rents due or becoming due from him to his lessor or landlord, the amount of any such costs, charges, and expenses payable by his lessor or landlord, and the costs, charges, and expenses of any distress and sale made on him through the default of his lessor or landlord; and, that the receipt for such payment shall be a sufficient discharge to any occupier for so much money as he shall have so paid, or which shall have been so levied on his goods and chattels in pursuance of this act, and shall be allowed by such lessor or landlord in part or full payment (as the case may be) of the rent due to him by such occupier (*g*).

(*g*) Section 48, *post*, Append.

Reimbursement and Contribution Clauses.

This clause would seem to invite landlords to introduce covenants into their leases for their tenants to pay all expenses attending the execution of the Building Act. For we shall find that, with reference to leases in existence when the act commences, the persons "now liable by law, or by any existing contract, to maintain and repair such buildings in respect of which such costs and expenses shall have been incurred," must submit to this obligation. And, next, we shall see, that with regard to leases made after the operation of the act, except a lease renewable for ever on a fixed fine or other customary payment, the costs and charges are to lie upon the lessor, although the occupier will be liable in the first instance, such occupier having a remedy, "*unless there be some express agreement to the contrary*," against his landlord for the full amount of costs and charges.

But this principle of a contract between landlord and tenant is not a new arrangement with respect to party walls.

The maxim, "*modus et conventio vinciunt legem*," applies in this case, and although it is observable that the new statute requires, *an express agreement to the contrary*, it is possible that the case we are about to cite will be found under the term "nett" to contain such an agreement.

The plaintiff covenanted that he would allow a reasonable share and proportion towards the repair of party walls belonging to the demised premises, and it was likewise mentioned in the lease that the landlord *was to have £60 in net money*, without any deduction, defalcation, or allowance whatever. The plaintiff underlet the property in portions, and it was contended that he was liable, but the Court reverted to the covenant, holding it to be absolute, and so the *postea* went to the defendant the land-

Reimbursement and Contribution Clauses.

lord (*h*). Lord *Kenyon*, however, intimated that the plaintiff's case might have been very different had he not covenanted so expressly to pay *in net money* (*i*).

Now it is observable, that the present statute imposes the contribution "*according to the covenants of the several leases or agreements*," between the parties. It is, therefore, clear that the referees will hereafter make a point of looking into the leases for the purpose of ascertaining whether any liability exists, or where it attaches. The Courts would not probably esteem this party wall payment to be a tax now more than formerly (*k*), but upon an action brought by the builder of the party wall against another, the covenants and agreements of the respective leases will doubtless have been previously examined by the referees.

The act presents the alternative. Should the parties have agreed together, upon default, an action will lie upon the express agreement without further dispute or discussion. Should they not agree, the covenant of the leases will be submitted to the referees, whose decision is to be final, so that the Courts will seem to be relieved entirely from the consideration of these contracts.

Again, if the tenant, independently of legal compulsion, should take upon himself the burthen of repairs which belong to his landlord and others, he will not be in a condition to claim indemnity at the hands of the referees, nor to proceed before the justices, nor to retain the amount of rent as a compensation. The following cases will still, then, be of value. The plaintiff declared against his landlord in an assumpsit for money paid, laid

(*h*) 8 T. R. 602, Barrett *v.* The Duke of Bedford.

(*i*) *Id.* 605.

(*k*) 3 T. R. 361; 8 T. R. 605.

Reimbursement and Contribution Clauses.

out, and expended for the use of the defendant. The defendant pleaded the general issue, and paid 76*l.* 2*s.* into Court. A verdict was found for the plaintiff for 194*l.* 14*s.* 2*d.* beyond the money paid into Court subject to a case. It appeared that the plaintiff's party wall stood in need of repair, and that, after the usual notices, the wall was condemned by the surveyors as ruinous. The owner of the adjoining house then rebuilt the party wall, and brought in a bill to plaintiff of 72*l.* 12*s.* 5*d.*, which was reduced to 70*l.* 9*s.* 6*d.*, and together with 5*l.* 12*s.* 6*d.*, the surveyor's charge, amounted together to 76*l.* 2*s.*, the sum paid into Court. The sum was paid by the plaintiff to the adjoining owner, and the defendant had notice of the payment. But in the course of the work it became necessary to shore up the house of the plaintiff, and to build up some of the wainscots and partitions there. Instead of leaving this to be done by the builder of the party wall, the plaintiff employed workmen of his own, and paid them the sum of 194*l.* 14*s.* 2*d.* for the extra work, and this latter amount his landlord refused to recognise, upon which the action was brought. And Lord *Ellenborough*, who had tried the cause, delivered the judgment of the Court in favour of the defendant. It was certainly competent and proper for the builder of the party wall to shore up the adjoining dwelling, and then to demand reimbursement from his neighbour, but here the plaintiff had thought fit to interpose and do the work himself. He ought to have left the builder to have done this, and having paid the demand, to have deducted the amount from his landlord's rent. Not having complied with the provisions of the statute, he could have no remedy, and accordingly the *postea* was delivered to the defendant (*l*). So where the plaintiff,

(*l*) 10 East, 227, Robinson *v.* Lewis.

Reimbursement and Contribution Clauses.

an assignee, thought fit to give a notice (*m*) in his landlord's name to the adjoining owner that the party wall was out of repair, upon which the two parties rebuilt at their joint expense, and the plaintiff's moiety came to 424*l.*, *Abbott*, C. J., directed a nonsuit in an action of assumpsit brought against the landlord, for the plaintiff had failed to obey the provisions of the statute (*n*). And this is very different from the case of damage done by the owner of the adjoining house, and an action brought, not against the landlord, but against such owner. Thus, where the defendant pulled down a party wall, and damaged the decorations of the house adjoining, upon his rebuilding, without replacing the decorations, it was considered by *Wightman*, J., that the tenant of the house injured might bring an action for this damage. And Mr. Justice *Wightman* distinguished the case from *Robinson* v. *Lewis*, because there the tenant sought to charge his landlord, whereas here he received damage in consequence of the act of a third party. The plaintiff, however, had moved for a writ of mandamus for the purpose of reinstating his dwelling, and the Court would not grant the remedy, but left the plaintiff to his action (*o*).

We come now to the 49th section (*p*), to which reference has been already made. That clause enacts, "That, with regard to the costs, and all other expenses of pulling down, securing, repairing and rebuilding party structures, or other parts of buildings, according to the provisions of this act, so far as relates to the recovery thereof, amongst the several owners of the premises; That when such costs and expenses shall have

(*m*) Under 14 Geo. 3, c. 78, s. 38.

(*n*) Ry. & M. 357, Pizey *v.* Rogers.

(*o*) 3 Dowl. N. S. 116, Reg. *v.* Ponsford.

(*p*) See the section, *post*, Append.

Reimbursement and Contribution Clauses.

been ascertained and paid by the owner upon whom the payment thereof shall have first fallen, then as to any building or tenement held under any lease, or agreement for a lease, or other agreement for the occupation thereof, made before the coming into operation of this act, it shall be lawful for such owner, and he is hereby entitled to recover the same from the persons now bound or liable by law, or by any existing contract to maintain and repair such buildings, in respect of which such costs and expenses shall have been incurred; but if any dispute or difference arise as to the persons so bound or liable, then every such dispute or difference shall be referred to the official referees; and that thereupon such official referees shall ascertain and determine the persons bound or liable to pay such costs and expenses, and also in what proportions such costs and expenses are to be paid by the parties liable to pay the same, and their decision shall be final; and that as to any building or tenement held under any lease or agreement for a lease, or other agreement for the occupation thereof, made after the coming into operation of this act, except a lease renewable for ever, on a fixed fine, or other customary payment, all such costs and expenses shall be charged upon the lessor granting such lease or making such agreement, and not upon any lessee or sub-lessee holding under such lease or agreement; subject, nevertheless, to any express covenant or agreement made between any such lessor and lessee in that behalf; and in case of such excepted lease, such costs and expenses shall be charged upon the lessee instead of the lessor, subject as aforesaid, to any express covenant or agreement in that behalf, between any such lessee and his sub-lessee, holding under such lessee upon other than a

Reimbursement and Contribution Clauses.

fixed fine or customary payment as aforesaid; and that in default of such costs and expenses being duly paid, it shall be lawful for the party to whom the same shall be payable, and he is hereby entitled to receive from the occupier thereof the rents and profits of such building or tenement; and for that purpose to give notice to such occupier to pay over to him such rents and profits; and that thereupon, if such occupier fail to pay such rent and profits accordingly, then it shall be lawful for the person to whom such costs and expenses shall be payable to recover the same, by the summary proceeding hereby provided, in such proportions and at such times as shall be appointed by the award of the said official referees in that behalf; and that after such notice shall be given, and before such costs and expenses shall be paid, it shall not be lawful for any person otherwise entitled to receive such rents and profits and he is hereby disabled to bring any action and from taking any proceeding at law or in equity to recover such rents and profits; provided always, that if on the hearing of the application for the warrant to levy such costs and expenses by distress, according to the provision of this act in that behalf, the occupier, not being an owner, show that he is not bound to pay in respect of such building or tenement any rent or profit, or that the amount of the rent or profit payable by him is not sufficient, then it shall not be lawful to issue such warrant, if there be no rent due or accruing; or, if there be rent due or accruing, then to the extent only of the amount of such rent; and that if such costs and expenses, or any part thereof, remain unpaid, and if the same, or any future occupier, be or become liable to pay rent in respect of such building or tenement, then from time to time, until the same be paid, it shall be lawful to levy the same by distress, according

Reimbursement and Contribution Clauses.

to the provisions of this act in that behalf, upon the same or any such future occupier (*q*).

The intentions of this section are well developed, but there is one difficulty which may, perhaps, receive an easy solution, but which is, nevertheless, deserving of a slight notice. The clause before us, (section 49), speaks of the *owner*, upon whom the payment shall have first fallen. The 47th section directs that an account in writing shall be delivered to the "*adjoining owner.*" This is a general provision. The 20th section says that the "*adjoining owner*" shall be the owner of the adjoining premises. The interpretation clause (*r*) defines "owner" to be the party in possession of the rents, *or* the occupier. Now, the owner mentioned in section 49 as the owner upon whom the payment shall have first fallen, and the adjoining *owner* of the 47th section must be deemed occupiers upon many occasions, and must not be held always to be strictly *owners*, for if otherwise, there will be a variance between this clause and those clauses which charge the person in possession as the debtor in the first instance.

The last section upon this part of our subject is that which relates to proportionate contributions. By section 50 (*s*), "with regard to such costs and expenses of works executed under this act, so far as relates to contribution thereto by persons bound or liable to make contribution, it is enacted, that for the purpose of enabling the party upon whom the payment of such costs and expenses shall fall, either in the first instance or subsequently, to obtain contribution from other persons, being owners according to the meaning of this act, in like degree, it shall be

(*q*) See the section, *post*, Append.
(*r*) See the section, *post*, Append.
(*s*) See the section, *post*, Append.

Reimbursement and Contribution Clauses.

lawful for every such first mentioned person, whether he be freeholder, copyholder, leaseholder, mortgagee in possession, and whatever may be his interest or the nature and extent of such his interest, and whether he hold in his own right, or in right of others, and whatever may be the kinds and degrees of their respective interests, and he is hereby entitled, to a contribution from every other person having as owner an interest in the premises of whatever kind or degree; which contribution is to be computed, according to the amount of his interest, in proportion to that of other persons interested, so far as such persons may be known, or can be reached by process of any Court of law or equity: and that it shall be lawful for any party so interested, and he is hereby entitled to require the official referees to settle and determine the same by their award, and their decision shall be final; and that if the person upon whom the payment of such costs and expenses shall have fallen, have paid, in respect of the interest of another or others, either unknown, or who could not be reached by process of any Court of law or equity, more than his own just proportion, then, on the production of such award, duly made, signed, and sealed, it shall be lawful for such person to have and exercise against other parties against whom such award shall be made, and he is hereby entitled to the like remedies, to compel payment of money, as are hereby given for compelling the first payment of such costs and charges of such expenses."

It was at one time intended that the tenant for years should be liable to this contribution, but the terms of the act preclude the possibility of charging the occupier, except in the first instance, unless he be liable to repair under an existing lease, or enter into a special contract to do this particular kind of repair or work.

Reimbursement and Contribution Clauses.

A tenant at rack rent was not liable to contribution under the old law (*t*). Neither was a tenant liable who had much improved his premises, and thus became possessed of a beneficial interest (*u*). It certainly may be a question whether a beneficial occupier may not be chargeable under the respective expressions "owners according to the meaning of this act," and "whatever may be the kinds and degrees of their respective interests" (*x*). If the party occupying has a beneficial interest, and thus is not a tenant from year to year, nor at will, nor at rack rent, he may, perhaps, be called an owner having an interest in the premises, and the interpretation clause, which allows of an occupier being occasionally called an owner, will then be satisfied.

There is not any pretence for saying that an executor or administrator is not liable. Under the old statute, an administrator who appeared to have no assets beyond the improved rent was held liable, and there is not any expression to exempt such a person in the present statute (*y*). In this case assumpsit had been brought, and after non-assumpsit pleaded, it was further alleged in answer, that before the pulling down of the party wall there had been a judgment recovered against the defendant as administrator of one Newberry, which judgment was still unsatisfied. Replication that the defendant could have paid the expenses of repairing the wall. General demurrer and joinder. The Court held that the portion of rent applicable to the repairs of the wall

(*t*) 3 T. R. 458, Southall *v.* Leadbetter. *Id.* 461, Stone *v.* Greenwell. 8 T. R. 214, Beardmore *v.* Fox.

(*u*) See the above cases, and 2 B. & Ald. 467, Lambe *v.* Hemans.

(*x*) Section 50, of this act.

(*y*) 1 Chit. Rep. 132, Wilcox *v.* Newman. 3 Adol. & El. 142, Thacker *v.* Wilson; S. C., 4 Nev. & M. 659; S. C., 1 Har. & Wol. 131.

Reimbursement and Contribution Clauses.

was not to be considered as assets, and that although the Building Act gave no express lien upon the rent, it was very requisite that these expenses should be considered as such. The act, moreover, it was said, made no difference between an owner in his own right and an owner as executor or administrator (z). These premises continued to be the subject of litigation. Debt for rent was brought against this same defendant, as assignee of the intestate, and he pleaded that the premises were of less value than the rent, part of which he had paid to the plaintiff, and part towards the expenses of a wall under the Building Act. Issue was taken upon this fact of insufficiency of value, and it was shewn that the premises, though out of repair, would produce but a very small rent if re-let, without such repair. But the Court gave judgment against the defendant. If the defendant had not taken to the premises, the case might have been different, but here the defendant should have performed the covenant to repair, and if he had done so, the premises would have been worth, according to the admission, at least as much as the rent. Neither could the defendant, under the present record, claim the sum actually paid towards the wall by way of deduction, and therefore the verdict was allowed to stand for the amount of rent found by the jury (a).

Independently of these clauses concerning contribution and reimbursement, there is likewise a section of this act which declares generally the matters to be settled by the official referees, and amongst these matters, the "expenses to be borne by the respective owners of premises parted by the same party walls, or the proportions thereof," are particularly mentioned (b).

(z) See the above note.

(a) 11 Adol. & El. 645, Hornidge *v.* Wilson.

(b) Section 82, *post*, Append.

CHAPTER III.

Of the Actions and Remedies connected with the Subject of Party Walls, together with the Defences to such Proceedings.

Actions and Remedies.

We propose in this section of our work to mention the actions which are occasionally brought with reference to party walls, as well as the defences commonly employed in answer to such actions. The proceedings and penalties under the Building Act shall likewise form a portion of the inquiry, and we will take care to separate the law which belongs to this statute as far as possible from the ordinary legal process in matters respecting which that act is not called in aid. There are various circumstances which from time to time may influence parties in viewing the condition of their party walls without having recourse to the Building Act. There are circumstances likewise which arise out of the act of building, even although the wall be erected by virtue of the statute, which raise points entirely independent of these provisions. And there are, of course, many incidents which are especially governed by the act alluded to. It is true that there have been disputes which the statutes upon this subject have met, and which can no longer arise by reason of the interposition of the Legislature. But it is likewise correct that persons may proceed in arranging

Actions and Remedies.

their party wall concerns without embarrassing themselves further with the Building Act than satisfying the surveyor by notice of the soundness of their erections. As, for example, to take a case already cited, where the defendant and the plaintiff had dealings together upon the subject of erecting a wall; the plaintiff acquainted the defendant that the cost would be 28*l.* The defendant replied, "Very well, I doubt not I shall pay that which is right and fair." The defendant, however, neglected to fulfil his engagement, upon which assumpsit was brought, and the defendant strove to shelter himself under the Building Act, the requisites of which, he said, had not been observed, and, consequently, there existed no consideration for his promise. But the Court refused to disturb the verdict which was found for the plaintiff, and *Gibbs*, C. J., observed, that perhaps owners of adjoining houses would act more wisely by avoiding that intricate law, the Building Act. The defendant said nothing about the Building Act before, and it would be too late for him to set up that objection now that the cause was tried, and the verdict found against him (*a*).

The burden of repairing a party wall lies upon the owner of it at common law, without the intervention of any statute. It is a charge laid upon the party by common right which by law he is subject to, and therefore it was that the plaintiff in an old case was held to have correctly stated his title by possession instead of prescription. He had a cellar contiguous to the privy of the defendant which was parted by a wall, part of the defendant's house. In want of repair the filth of the privy ran into the cellar of the defendant, and the defendant

(*a*) 7 Taunt. 158, Stuart *v.* Smith; S. C., Marsh. 435; S. C., at Nisi Prius, Holt, 321.

suffered judgment by default, only contending of inquiry executed, that a title by prescripti have been shewn, and, consequently that there be an arrest of judgment. But the Court de position, and the maxim "*sic utere tuo ut alien lædas*," was cited to shew the defendant's omission this occasion (*b*). And *Holt*, C. J. said, that, if a man erects a house and a house of office, and the house of office adjoins to a vacant pieee of ground, which keeps in the filth of the house of office, if the owner of the vacant piece of ground will dig a cellar there, he must make a wall to the house of office (*c*). An action of assumpsit, therefore, is the proper remedy to compel contribution where assent has been given to the repair, and an action upon the case is the better course where damage ensues to the plaintiff in consequence of non-repair.

A wall, however, may be *meddled with* by an adjoining owner, and, in this case, it is desirable to know how far the interest of the other party is affected so as to enable him to bring an aotion. The wall may be raised higher, it may be destroyed, it may be partially pulled down or damaged by an alteration; all these are acts worthy of notice with reference to any remedy which may exist. Indeed, in former days, it was lawful for a neighbour to pull down a wall upon his own land which stood between his house and that adjoining, even though the other wall should fall also, where such a wall was erected by another person upon the adjacent land. For he did not himself build this wall, and he had clearly a dominion over his

(*b*) 1 Salk. 21, Tenant *v.* Golding; S. C., 2 Lord Raym. 1089; S. C., 6 Mod. 311; S. C., Holt's Cases, 500. See Poph. 46, Edwards *v.* Halinder.

(*c*) 2 Lord Raym. 1093.

Actions and Remedies.

own territory (*d*). But the Party Wall Act would now intervene to prevent the destruction of a neighbour's fence or partition wall.

Abatement, or an action of trespass is the usual remedy for parties who have to complain of interference with their properties in this respect, although an action upon the case will lie if the violence complained be the cause of consequential damage (*e*). Suppose the case of a wall standing partly upon the land of A. and partly on that of B. We have seen (*f*), that these persons are not on that account tenants in common of this wall. Add to this, that one proprietor heightens his side of the wall, upon which the other pulls down the new erection. Trespass will lie for this invasion, although the wall might have been erected at the joint expense of the two, for each is severally the owner of his respective land (*g*). Suppose, nevertheless, that there has been a common user of a wall for a considerable time by two neighbouring owners: this would be evidence of a tenancy in common, and as trespass will not in general lie by one tenant in common against another, another remedy must be sought for in cases of annoyance or interference with a wall which come short of the destruction of it. The following case will illustrate this. The plaintiff brought trespass against the defendant who had been pulling down and rebuilding his house, for building against a wall dividing the premises of both, and which last wall the plaintiff claimed as his sole property. There was contradictory evidence, and there were conflicting opinions of surveyors whether there were originally one or

(*d*) Cro. Eliz. 269, Wright *v.* Gill, "Trespass."

(*e*) See the case of Wells *v.* Ody, *ante*, p. 58.

(*f*) *Ante*, p. 2.

(*g*) 5 Taunt. 20, Matts *v.* Hawkins.

Actions and Remedies.

two walls upon these several premises; and, again, whether the wall built against was originally the exterior wall of the plaintiff's premises before the premises of the defendant had been built. The jury were directed to consider whether the wall had been jointly used by the owners of both premises, (it was said, for nearly a century), and whether they were satisfied of there having been originally but one wall. If so, the learned judge declared, that, in his opinion, the action was not maintainable, and he left it to the jury to say whether it was a party wall or not. The jury, considering that it was a party wall, found for the defendant. And, upon the discussion for a new trial, *Matts* v. *Hawkins* was relied on by the plaintiff's counsel. But by the Court: in *Matts* v. *Hawkins*, the quantity of land which each party contributed was known, but here there was no such proof, and the reasonable presumption, from the common use of the wall, was, *primâ facie*, that the wall and the land on which it was built, were the undivided property of both. The verdict, being, therefore, considered right, the rule was discharged (*h*). This last case was relied upon some years afterwards. The plaintiff was the occupier of a cottage and garden as tenant to one D. They had formerly been the property of the father of the plaintiff. The defendant was the owner of premises adjoining those of the plaintiff, and separated from them by a wall. In July 1825, the defendant pulled down a part of this wall, and erected another wall on the site of it of a greater height than the old wall, with a cottage and other buildings against it. The action was brought to try the right to this wall. There was evidence on

(*h*) 8 B. & C. 259, Wiltshire *v.* Sidford, cited there; S. C., 1 Man. & Ry. 403.

Actions and Remedies.

both sides of various acts of user of the wall by the respective owners of the plaintiff's and defendant's premises. *Alexander*, C. B., told the jury, upon this evidence, to find for the defendant, if they thought the wall was his, or if, from the common user of the wall by the respective owners of the plaintiff's and defendant's premises, they believed the plaintiff and defendant had a common property in it. The jury said, "We find this to be a party wall;" upon which the Chief Baron observed, "That is a verdict for the defendant." A rule for a new trial having been obtained, it was said for the plaintiff, that if the two proprietors of the premises had contributed jointly to the expense of building the wall, and the site of the land on which it was built, in equal moieties, there would have been the same common user, and yet they would not have been tenants in common of the wall, nor of the soil on which it was built, and for this, *Matts* v. *Hawkins* was cited. The counsel for the plaintiff then denied that there had been any evidence of a tenancy in common. Secondly, however, they said, that here was a total destruction of the wall, for before the new wall was built the plaintiff was wholly deprived of the use of the wall. It was an expulsion. But the Court deemed these persons to be tenants in common; and the rule was discharged (*i*).

"If the wall was the exclusive property of the plaintiff, then the act done by the defendant was a sufficient ground for the action. If it was entirely the property of the defendant, then he was justified in doing what he did. There was a third view of the case, and that was the view taken of it by the Lord Chief Baron at the trial, viz. that it might be the common property of the

(*i*) 8 B. & C. 257, Cubitt *v.* Porter; S. C., 2 Man. & Ry. 267.

Actions and Remedies.

plaintiff and defendant" (*k*). Then, secondly, here was no destruction: the object of the party was not that there should be no wall there, but that there should be a wall there again as expeditiously as a wall could be made. It had been said, that the defendant had heightened the wall. In that case, supposing that act to have been wrongly done, the plaintiff might have removed the excess. That would have been his only remedy. If there be land belonging to two as tenants in common, and one build a wall on that land, the other cannot bring trespass on the ground of his being excluded from the surface of that ground for a certain period of time, viz. for so long a period as that wall stands (*l*). In fact, if one tenant in common were willing to repair a joint wall, and the other refused, the old writ *de separatione faciendâ* might have applied. And with regard to the destruction of the wall, if it be wholly pulled down, and the materials sold, an action upon the case in the nature of waste might perhaps lie, although the intention might be to make a better wall. It is only when an utter abandonment of the joint property takes place, that trespass can be maintained (*m*).

From hence we gather, that trespass, (in the absence of consequential damage) is the proper remedy for a person whose wall is invaded where there is no pretence for calling him tenant in common with his neighbour (*n*). Indeed, either trespass or case will lie upon many occasions. It is likewise plain, that trespass is the right proceeding where an entire annihilation of the subject matter of the common tenancy accrues without any intention

(*k*) Judgment of Bayley, J., 8 B. & C. 262.
(*l*) 8 B. & C. 265, 266.
(*m*) By Littledale, J., 8 B. & C. 270.
(*n*) As in Matts *v.* Hawkins.

Actions and Remedies.

of restoring it (*o*). As if one should destroy the whole flight of a dove cote, or all the deer in a park (*p*), so, if a partial injury only be done, or if the whole wall be prostrated, trespass will lie, where the wall exists *in severalty*, whether an intention to rebuild it appears or not. Whereas, on the other hand, if we suppose a partial injury to a wall held *in common*, or as above-mentioned, an entire prostration of the building, no such action can be maintained, if there be an intention to restore it; an intent which must, of course, be verified by the consequences. Here, if such intention be absent, an action on the case in the nature of waste is the right remedy (*q*). And lastly, although trespass is certainly good for one whose wall is heightened by the act of the neighbour, there being no *common* but a several ownership, yet, in the case of a tenancy in common, abatement is the only proceeding to be adopted (*r*).

An action upon the case will lie for negligence in pulling down a party wall, for the statute (to which we are about to advert) does not interfere to abolish the rights of individuals. This was the old law (*s*); and the principle was affirmed on a late occasion, where the plaintiff complained, in an action upon the case, of the Mayor and Corporation of London, as Overseers of Christ's Hospital, for damaging his party wall. The matter having been referred to arbitration, it was

(*o*) 8 B. & C. 265.

(*p*) 8 B. & C. 268.

(*q*) 8 B. & C. 270.

(*r*) 8 B. & C. 265. If a party persist in continuing a building on land in respect of which the plaintiff has already recovered, upon fresh notice given, the plaintiff may sustain a fresh action for such continuance of the nuisance. 10 Adol. & El. 503; Holmes *v.* Wilson.

(*s*) See 2 Saund. 400, Smith and Others *v.* Martin.

Actions and Remedies.

found, that in consequence of carelessness in the underpinning of the walls, a serious injury had accrued to the plaintiff. The arbitrator awarded him 500*l.* for this damage. And the Court held, that the defendants had no right to underpin the party wall, either partially or wholly, unless that could be done without injuring the plaintiff's house. It was not clear, indeed, whether the wall was held in severalty or in common, but, in either case, it was the opinion of the Court that this action was maintainable in respect of the injury which resulted from the mode of their dealing with it (*t*). But where both the agents of the plaintiff and defendant were to blame, Lord *Ellenborough* directed a nonsuit. In this case the wall was pulled down under the direction of the joint agents, but for want of properly shoring up the back-front of the plaintiff's house, it was considerably injured, and the learned Lord held, that it was not competent to the plaintiff to attach that blame to the defendant which was the common blame of both. The wall had been taken down by both, and neither could impute blame to the other (*u*). Whereas, if the defendant be primarily in fault, the subsequent falling of timbers independently of the defendant's immediate act will not afford him a ground for resisting an action upon the case for not shoring, because he was the proximate cause of the damage (*x*).

Nevertheless, the plaintiff did not ultimately succeed. Error was brought, and the defendant below urged that

(*t*) 4 Man. & Gr. 714, 734, 761, Bradbee *v.* The Mayor, &c. of London; S. C., 5 Scott, 79; 2 Dowl. N. S., 164.

(*u*) 2 Stark. 377; Hill *v.* Warren.

(*x*) 2 Hodges, 167, Trower *v.* Chadwick. See also 16 East, 215, Roberts *v.* Read and Others, where the wall did not fall till three months after the act, and yet the defendants were held liable in case. Ry. & Moo. 161, Gillon *v.* Boddington.

Actions and Remedies.

the plaintiff's wall was underground, and that he had no notice of that fact, so that he could not possibly help the damage he had occasioned. He had used ordinary caution in pulling down his house, and that was sufficient. To which it was replied that the position of the two houses, being together, was such as to require a a notice to the adjoining owner or occupier. And the Court of Error were with the defendant. They held that the defendant was under no obligation to shore up the plaintiff's vaults, or give notice of his intention to pull down his own. They held, likewise, that as the plaintiff had not given any notice to the defendant of the existence of his wall or vault below ground, the defendant was not bound to use such an amount of precaution as must necessarily have prevented damage to the said vault or wall. Then, general damages having been given upon the whole declaration, it was deemed not competent for the Court to reject the plaintiff's allegation that the defendant had not given him notice of the intention to pull down the wall, and to ascribe the damages to the residue of the count (y). But where the plaintiff complained, not of an omission to give notice, but of acts of carelessness and negligence done by the defendants, so that the plaintiff's windows and other property were broken by the defendants, the arbitrator, who had awarded damages for this misconduct, was held to be justified in so doing, and the Court distinguished the case upon this ground from that of *Chadwick* v. *Trower* (z).

(y) 6 Bing. N. C., 1, Chadwick v. Trower; S. C., 8 Scott, 1.

(z) 4 Man. & Gr. 714, 738, 757, Bradbee v. The Mayor, &c. of London; S. C., 5 Scott, N. R., 79. And the Court cited Dodd v. Holme, 1 Adol. & El. 493; 3 Nev. & M. 739, as in point, where the defendant, by carelessly excavating his ground, caused damage to the adjoining dwelling.

Actions and Remedies.

So, where the defendant had been guilty of carelessness and negligence, he was held liable, although an ordinary amount of caution would have discharged him. The plaintiff complained of an injury occasioned by the act of the defendant in meddling with the foundations and footings of his house by digging downwards to make his own wall. The defendant, by reason of the nature of the soil, had certainly dug to a greater depth than his ancient wall stood on, but he resisted the action on the ground of his having used a due amount of caution, and of his having given notice to the plaintiff of his work. *Tindal*, C. J., was of opinion, that more than ordinary caution was not required in this instance, and he left the question, together with that of the notice, to the jury. The jury found, that the notice had been given to the plaintiff, but they, nevertheless, found for the plaintiff, damages 40*s.*, on the fourth count, which charged the defendant with negligence in performing the work (*z*). After the decision in the Exchequer Chamber, in *Chadwick* v. *Turner*, it is probable that this notice to the plaintiff would not be necessary, but the question as to caution or negligence, will always be one for the especial consideration and decision of the jury.

The points demanding attention for the most part are the questions of negligence, of the antiquity of the house, and of easement. It is clear that a wilful injury done by one man to another is punishable by action, whether the house be ancient or not, whether there be a easement or not. As if A., in repairing his own house, should purposely injure that of his neighbour. It is also agreed that if A., in making his alteration, should injure the ancient dwelling of B. adjoining, B. not having con-

(*z*) 4 Car. & P. 161, Massey *v.* Goyder and others.

Actions and Remedies.

sented to the work, A. is liable in damages (*a*). And if B. had consented, A. would still be liable for carelessness. But if the dwelling of B. be not ancient, and A. becomes desirous of meddling with the foundations or party structures of the house in which he lives, he appears to be irresponsible, (speaking of cases beyond the limits of the Building Act,) if he does his work in a careful and businesslike manner, or even if he does not use great caution, provided he be ignorant of the nature of the adjoining premises, as in the case of a vault underneath. For the duty of B., the adjoining owner, would be to shore up his own house under such circumstances. So that where the defendant dug away land so near to the house of the plaintiff, that the house fell in, it was held, that as the plaintiff's house was not ancient, he could not recover (*b*). It is, therefore, a very dangerous omission to neglect shoring. The omission is not absolutely an answer to an action, but it places the plaintiff in a most perilous position. Upon such an occasion, and under such circumstances, it was shewn for the plaintiff that the defendant had carried on the pulling down of his house in a manner most injurious to the adjoining houses, so as, indeed, to cause the injury complained of. The defendant shewed that the plaintiffs had not shored up their house at all, and there was contradictory evidence as to the neglect of the defendant. The jury found for the defendant. And Lord *Tenterden*, when he summed up, said, "It is now settled that the owner of premises adjoining those pulled down must shore up his own in the inside, and do everything proper to be done upon

(*a*) 1 Ad. & El. 493, *ante*, p. 112. 4 Man. & Gr. 735. See also 1 Sid. 167, Pigott and Surie's case.

(*b*) 3 B. & Adol. 871, Wyatt *v.* Harrison. And see 9 B. & C. 725, Peyton *v.* The Mayor and Commonalty of London, *infra*.

Actions and Remedies.

them for their preservation. That has not been done here; and it seems that if it had been, it would have given security. Still the omission does not necessarily defeat the action; if the pulling down be irregularly and improperly done, and the injury is produced thereby, the person so acting may be liable for it, although the owner of the house destroyed may not have done all that he ought for his own protection. If, therefore, you think that the house of the defendant was pulled down in a wasteful, negligent, and improvident manner, so as to occasion greater risk to the plaintiffs than in the ordinary course of doing the work they would have incurred, then I think the defendant liable to make compensation for the consequences of his want of caution: if you think that fair and proper caution was exercised, then the defendant will be entitled to a verdict." (*c*)

Then, on the other hand, reverse the case, and let A. be the owner of an ancient house, and the builder also. In making his alteration, A. damages the house of B. Here it is B.'s duty to shore up *his* house, or abide the consequences, and A.'s negligence, unless wilful, will make no difference. But suppose that the wall of B. is supported by that of A., so that the repair of one would cause the fall of the other. Here the question of easement arises. Thus the defendant having made an excavation in his own land, in order to make a cellar, caused his own wall to sink, and thereby injured the plaintiff's house. This house had been built in 1803, more than twenty years before, by the permission of a former owner of the defendant's house against the wall of the defendant, and was supported by the defendant's wall. The jury found that the defendant had been guilty of negligence,

(*c*) Moo. & Malk. 362, 364, Walters and others *v.* Pfiel.

Actions and Remedies.

and awarded 50*l.* damages to the plaintiff, and the Court held that the assent of the former owner had conferred an easement upon the plaintiff, and that he was entitled to recover (*d*). However, where no such easement can be claimed, the case is different. The plaintiffs were owners of a house in Cheapside, and the defendants owned the house adjoining. The defendants repaired their house, but did not shore up that of the plaintiffs' either externally or internally, upon which certain supports of the plaintiff's house gave way, and damage was occasioned. It was shewn that if the plaintiffs' house had been properly shored inside, the injury would not have happened. Lord *Tenterden* upon this directed a nonsuit, being of opinion that the plaintiffs ought to have propped up their own house, and a rule was obtained to set aside this nonsuit; first, because the defendants were answerable; and, secondly, because the defendants ought to have given notice to the plaintiffs to prop up their house. The Court, however, discharged the rule. As to the notice, the defective state of both premises was known to both parties, and the operations were carried on by day, so as to have been seen and known by the tenant and occupier of the plaintiffs' house. And as to the general point, it was the duty of the plaintiffs to have supported their houses by shores within, unless, indeed, a grant of a right to the support of the adjoining house could be inferred, but of which grant there was no evidence. (*e*).

An enjoyment of twenty years, it will be recollected likewise, will give a right to a way, or other *easement*,

(*d*) 1 Cr. & Jer. 20, Brown *v.* Windsor.

(*e*) 9 B. & C. 725, Peyton and others *v.* The Mayor and Commonalty of London. See, as to this Notice, 6 Bing. N. C., 1, Trower *v.* Chadwick, *ante;* S. C., 8 Scott, 1. And see also 5 B. & Ald. 837, Jones *v.* Bird.

Actions and Remedies.

under 2 & 3 Wm. 4, c. 71, s. 2, and such a right becomes indefeasible after an enjoyment of forty years, unless some consent or agreement thereto by deed or writing be produced to account for such enjoyment.

Public officers, however, must be careful to give notice where there is immediate danger to property.

Certain Commissioners of Sewers, in the course of their work, caused the fall of a stack of chimnies, and consequent damage to the dwelling of the plaintiff. Upon this he brought his action, and *Abbott*, C. J., told the jury that if the stack of chimnies could not by any shoring up have been prevented from falling, it was the duty of the commissioners, if they thought so, to give specific notice of the danger to the owner, and that, if they did not do so, they were responsible. This direction was confirmed by the Court, and the verdict for the plaintiff was sustained (*f*).

These authorities, beyond the limits of the Building Act, are of course of much value, but they are not to be rejected within those limits, because, as we have said, the Building Act does not take away the common law right to sue for injuries done by one neighbour to another, although it certainly is intended to lessen the probability of such injuries. The notice to surveyors of the commencement of buildings, or of alterations (*g*); the supervision of buildings and repairs (*h*); the clause concerning nuisances (*i*), and the arrangements generally respecting party walls, of which ample mention has been already made, are all provisions of this

(*f*) 5 B. & Adol. 837, Jones *v.* Bird.
(*g*) Under section 13, *post*, Append.
(*h*) See sections 14, &c., *post*, Append.
(*i*) Section 18, *post*, Append.

Actions and Remedies.

character, and calculated to afford an additional protection to neighbouring properties.

Ejectment.]—Ejectment is likewise a remedy for recovering the ownership of a wall (*k*).

Actions and Penalties.

We come now to the actions and penalties prescribed by the Building Act, with reference to party fences and walls, not omitting any other remedial proceedings which may seem to bear upon those matters, and which have not hitherto been particularly noticed.

As far, however, as the penalties are concerned, we need do no more than refer to previous pages for an account of such as may be incurred with reference to party walls under this act. A neglect to give notice of the execution of works (*l*), the user of a building subject to a special supervision without a certificate of satisfaction (*m*), a refusal to allow the surveyor to inspect buildings (*n*), the disobedience of workmen (*o*), and the offence of hindering the legal repair of party walls (*p*), may be referred to upon this head of penalties. The limitation of prosecutions for penalties together with the mode of recovering them has likewise been mentioned in a former place (*q*).

As to the actions which may be brought against persons for matters done under colour of the statute, it is observable that one only seems to be especially mentioned. If a party shall show that he has suffered special damage by reason

(*k*) 5 C. & P. 51, Trotter *v.* Simpson.
(*l*) Section 13, *post*, Append.
(*m*) Sections 15, 16, *post*, Append.
(*n*) Section 17, *post*, Append.
(*o*) Section 19, *post*, Append.
(*p*) Section 36, *post*, Append.
(*q*) See sections 106, 107, 110, *post*, Append.

Actions and Remedies.

of an informality in a distress, although the distress shall not be illegal for want of form, yet an action upon the case will lie to compensate such damage, but no other action whatsoever (*r*). Impliedly, however, actions may probably be brought by virtue of other clauses. As for example, under section 29, which authorizes an adjoining owner to recover all the costs and expenses of rebuilding a party wall and of repairing damages in respect thereof, which wall ought to have been built and repair done by the building owner (*s*). This description of work is excepted out of the reimbursement clause (*t*), and therefore an action of assumpsit, or possibly of debt, will be a remedy likely to be entertained in respect of these charges. So, under the 32d section, it is competent for a party to pull down a fence wall upon condition of his paying all the expenses thereof, and likewise making good every damage which shall accrue to such adjoining premises from such rebuilding. Now if the building owner fail to make good the damage, it seems that an action upon the case will lie. Trespass will hardly be the right remedy, because the act permits the invasion of the fence wall in the first instance, but the fence wall having been unskilfully meddled with, the ordinary proceeding for consequential injury seems to present itself. And, moreover, it may be said generally, that the Building Act does not control the common law right of bringing actions for damages for which it has not provided a remedy. As far as its operations prevail, care must be taken not to embark in litigation unless there be no sufficient remedy in the statute, but there will, probably, be found many occasions when disputes of a

(*r*) Section 100, *post*, Append.

(*s*) See sections 28, 29, *post*, Append.

(*t*) Section 46, *post*, Append.

Actions and Remedies.

character not contemplated by that law may arise, and in those cases the usual actions will naturally be resorted to.

The guards thrown around persons acting, in pursuance of the statute with reference to suits commenced against them have been already set forth in the second chapter (*u*). Whether they be actions of trespass or replevin in respect of goods seized, or on the case for other causes of complaint, the law has enabled persons who have acted *bonâ fide* to defend themselves against oppressive suits, either by tendering amends, or bringing money into Court, or if their proceedings be entirely correct, by giving them full costs of suit and such remedy for recovering the same as any defendant shall legally be entitled to (*x*).

(*u*) See sections 101, 108, 109.

(*x*) Section 108, *post*, Append.

CHAPTER IV.

Of the Pleadings and Evidence, &c.

Pleadings and Evidence.

THE various actions incident to the subject of party walls have been laid before the reader in the last chapter. The pleadings now to be noticed in this place will relate, of course, to walls governed by the statute, and to those which are without its limits. Walls governed by the statute will not be directly productive of many lawsuits, because several proceedings which were formerly carried on in the superior Courts, are now committed to the jurisdiction of magistrates and other officers. And although actions will no doubt be brought collaterally with reference to points connected with the new law, it is not probable that there will be so many new and intricate points for decision in the Courts above as formerly, so that our view of the necessary pleadings and evidence will be compressed into a narrow compass. Thus the action upon the case for special damage under the 100th section, and such actions as may be brought for unskilful workmanship will be in the ordinary form, varying only in the respective statements of the particular injuries. So in assumpsit or debt there is nothing of novelty in the statute to prevent the claims in respect of costs or otherwise, from being set forth in the common form. The special mode of charging the owner of the improved rent has ceased with the repeal of the old act which gave the remedy (*a*).

(*a*) See the old form, 3 Chit. of Pleading, 123.

Pleadings and Evidence.

The following case may, nevertheless, be found useful in this place, as shewing the nature of a plea which may still apply, with the exception of the point regarding the improved rent, where a landlord distrains for rent, and there is good ground for the occupier to retain such rent in his own hands, as a compensation for payments made towards the repairs of a party wall (*b*). The plaintiff had declared in covenant upon a lease made to the defendant's assignor, and he alleged a breach for not repairing the premises. The defendant pleaded performance of the repairs required by his lease, except certain repairs, which after the premises came to the defendant by assignment became necessary for the rebuilding of a party wall under the statute 14 Geo. 3, c. 78, the building and repairing of which said party wall did not become necessary by or in consequence of any act or neglect of the defendant, and in respect of which party wall the sum mentioned in the declaration was expended. The defendant then denied that he had underlet the premises, or that he had derived any benefit therefrom, otherwise than by occupation and possession. He pleaded two other similar pleas, taking care to state that he was not the beneficial owner. To these pleas the plaintiff demurred, and the object of the demurrer was to raise the question whether the lessee's general covenant to repair did or not comprise the rebuilding of a party wall erected according to the direction of 14 Geo. 3, c. 78. The Court gave judgment for the defendant. If it were possible for the landlord to state any facts which would have made the tenant liable, he should have replied them, but it is enough for the tenant to say, that merely protecting himself under the act, these repairs did

(*b*) See sections 48, 49, *post*, Append.

Pleadings and Evidence.

not become necessary by any act or neglect of his. The plaintiff by his demurrer admits that fact, that the repairs did not become necessary by the defendant's default, and, therefore, a sufficient answer had been given to the plaintiff's allegation of non-repair (c).

It may be added here, that it is not common to prefer the action of debt to that of assumpsit, but the usual indebitatus count as upon a simple contract may be resorted to when the occasion will warrant. Debt was brought for the charges of a party wall, but it was omitted to be stated that the wall was within the city of London, and the pleading was held bad upon demurrer (d).

In answer to the charge the defendant usually pleads that he is not guilty. But he sometimes places a special answer on the record, as, for instance, that he is executor, and has fully administered the effects of his testator. The following plea was holden insufficient, and the reader will reject from his attention the matter concerning the improved rent. The defendant being sued for contribution, pleaded first, the general issue, and next, that before the building and finishing of the wall, one R. N. was the owner of the improved rent of the premises; that R. N. died before the said building and finishing, and made the defendant his executor, that the defendant became the owner, accordingly, as executor, but in no other right: and the defendant further said that R. N. in his lifetime entered into certain bonds, and that the defendant had fully administered R. N.'s goods and chattels in discharge thereof, and hath no funds in

(c) 5 Taunt. 90, Moore v. Clark.

(d) Skin. 67, Clerk v. Serle. It was likewise an objection that the defendant in this case had not been said to have built upon the plaintiff's party wall, but the Court would not allow it.

Pleadings and Evidence.

his possession more than 10*l.* The plaintiff demurred, and it was admitted that the plea was defective, for the defendant might have received profits from the premises over and above what would have satisfied the bonds, as far as appeared in his plea. And, besides the plea left the money counts unanswered. Leave, however, was given him to amend upon an affidavit verifying the fact that he had fully administered the testator's effects (*e*).

There may be, nevertheless, many causes of action within the limits of the new act which need not owe their validity to its provisions. Upon such occasions as these the law will often be the same as though the matters in question had happened in any other part of the kingdom. The pleadings, consequently, will be of the same nature.

An action was brought against the defendant for not shoring up vaults. The defendant pleaded that he was not bound by law or otherwise to do this, and, upon demurrer, this mode of pleading was held bad, for, in the first place, it amounted to a traverse of the description of the means, and, secondly, it raised an issue in law (*f*).

Trespass.]—An action of trespass is the remedy often resorted to where the plaintiff conceives that his wall has been improperly meddled with. He charges the breaking and entering his close, and the pulling down and destroying his wall, so that he is hindered in the beneficial enjoyment of his premises, and has been put to expense in endeavouring to rebuild the wall. In order to support his case, he proves the particular facts mentioned in his declaration, according to the circumstances; he shows that his wall stood on the boundary line, and that

(*e*) 1 Chit. Rep. 132, Wilcox *v.* Newman.

(*f*) 2 Hodges, 267, Trower *v.* Chadwick.

Pleadings and Evidence.

he has always performed his own repairs upon it, independently of the adjoining proprietor. To contradict this, the defendant may prove not merely that the wall was built at the joint expense of both, which, of itself, would not be sufficient, but likewise that he and the plaintiff have always used the wall together in common. This makes out a tenancy of that nature, and goes to nonsuit the plaintiff, or destroy his verdict. If the plaintiff should prove an entire destruction of his wall, it seems that this defence of a common user and tenancy will not be available (*g*).

If a wall be not erected conformably to the directions of the statute, trespass may be brought. Perhaps leave and license might be pleaded in bar of such an action. It becomes necessary, upon such an occasion, to make the proof unite with the allegation. Therefore, leave and license to erect and maintain a wall, is not supported by proof of a license to erect one (*h*).

Trespass was brought for throwing down a wall. It was pleaded, first, that the wall was not the plaintiff's wall, and secondly, that the wall was a party wall, standing partly upon the land of the plaintiff, and partly upon that of the defendant. The jury found the wall to be a party wall, upon which a verdict was entered for the defendant. For the plaintiff was bound to prove that the *whole* wall was his. The one-half of the wall was the abuttal of the other half wall, because they are in law two walls, and, therefore, as the plaintiff used terms which properly belonged to the entire wall, he could not recover (*i*). Hence it might be surmised, that if the

(*g*) See 5 Taunt. 20, Matts *v.* Hawkins. 8 B. & C. 257, Cubitt *v.* Porter. *Id.* 259, Wiltshire *v.* Sidford, cited there.

(*h*) 1 Arnold, 337, Alexander *v.* Bonnin.

(*i*) 8 Ad. & El. 138, Murly *v.* McDermott; S. C., 3 Nev. & P. 356; S. C., 2 Jurist, 806.

Pleadings and Evidence.

proof of an entirety of wall could be made out for the plaintiff, a plea of a party wall would be no answer to the declaration (*k*).

The defendant may shew, under the plea of "not guilty," that the wall in question was a party fence wall, and that he was acting under the statute. It was so held in an action of trespass for laying bricks upon the plaintiff's wall (*l*).

And a surveyor, when defendant, was allowed to object to the absence of notice under a plea of "not guilty" (*m*).

(*k*) 8 Ad. & El. 138. 3 Nev. & P. 356.

(*l*) 7 C. & P. 24, Wells *v.* Ody.

(*m*) 2 Cr., M. & R. 128, Wells *v.* Ody. See the Rules, Hilary Term, 4 Wm. 4, 1834, "Pleading in Particular Actions." "IV. In Case."

APPENDIX.

METROPOLITAN BUILDINGS ACT.

CONTENTS.

GENERAL PROVISIONS.

Section

If Amendment be not made within 48 Hours, to inform the Official Referees, who are to proceed according to Circumstances

15.—Provides for the special Supervision of Buildings of the First Rate of the Second Class, and of Buildings of the Third Class; if such Buildings be used before being certified, the Owner or Occupier subject to a Penalty of 200*l.* per Day; but the Justices to consider the Circumstances of such Use

16.—Provides for the special Supervision of exempted Buildings, and that the Use of such Buildings shall incur a Penalty of 100*l.* per Day, but the Justices to consider the Circumstances of such Use

17.—The Surveyor and Official Referees may enter upon Premises where Operations have been commenced, for the Purpose of inspecting the same during working Hours; Parties refusing Entry to be liable to a Penalty of 20*l.*, and forcible Entry may be made

18.—All Buildings not according to the Act to be deemed a Nuisance, and Proceedings to be taken by the Surveyor for the Removal thereof

19.—Workmen and others offending against the Rules and Directions of the Act to forfeit 50*s.* or be imprisoned One Month

Party Walls, Party Fences, and Intermixed Buildings.

20.—What Works may be executed on adjoining Properties by Building Owners and adjoining Owners

21.—If Building Owner do not obtain Consent of adjoining Owner, he must give him Notice before commencing to pull down, &c. .

22.—If the adjoining Owner desire the Modification of the Work to render it suitable to his Premises, Notice thereof to be given, or Application made to Official Referees

23.—Delay of Work for Convenience of adjoining Owner to be obtained in like Manner

24.—Where Consent of adjoining Owner cannot be obtained, Notice to be given to the Surveyor and Official Referees, and Proceedings thereon by the Surveyor

25.—Defective Party Structures to be repaired and rebuilt at joint Expense

26.—Party Walls may be rebuilt at the Expense of the Building Owner on Three Months' Notice

27.—A Building Owner rebuilding of a higher Rate, without pulling down the existing Party Wall, to erect an external Wall against such Party Wall

28.—Damage arising from Erection of such external Wall to be made good by Building Owner; and Footings in Chimneys may be cut into after One Month's Notice, but must be again made good

29.—If Damage appear to adjoining Owner to render the Wall ruinous or dangerous, the Surveyor or Official Referees to survey and determine as to rebuilding thereof

30.—Rebuilding of sound Party Walls under certain Circumstances .

31.—As to the raising of future and existing Buildings and Chimneys, and the Use of any raised Building by the adjoining Owner

32.—Party Fence Walls to be repaired, &c., on giving One Month's Notice, or rebuilt as a Party Wall, on Payment of all Expenses, and for the Damages to adjoining Premises. Reimbursement of Expense, if afterwards used by adjoining Owner;

Section

50.—The Official Referees empowered to determine the proportional Contributions to be paid by Part Owners, and Expenses to be recovered in Terms of the Award.

Drainage of Houses.

51.—Drains to be made according to Schedule (H.); saving the Rights and Powers of the Commissioners of Sewers.

Streets and Alleys.

52.—Width thereof to be according to the Rules in Schedule (I.)

Buildings, Use thereof.

53.—Rooms or Cellars in Buildings of the Dwelling House Class, unless made conformably to Schedule (K.), not to be used or occupied (except as Ware-rooms or Store-rooms), under a Penalty of 20s. per Day.

54.—Business dangerous as to Fire not to be nearer other Buildings than 50 Feet; new Businesses to be 40 Feet from public Ways. Businesses at less Distances prohibited after 20 Years. Penalty 50l. for erecting Buildings, and 50l. per Day for carrying on Businesses, contrary to Act. Imprisonment for Six Months if Penalty not paid.

55.—Businesses dangerous as to Health to be made subject to like Regulations; but to be discontinued after 30 Years.

56.—Justices may ascertain the Means used to mitigate the Noxiousness of Businesses, and to lessen Penalty accordingly; and may suspend Execution if other Means of Mitigation be adopted.

57.—Appeal to Quarter Sessions as to Conviction of Justices in respect of certain Trades not specified.

58.—Trial by Jury and Proceedings at Quarter Sessions.

59.—Appeals to Quarter Sessions for Surrey and Kent in respect to Convictions for carrying on certain Trades.

60.—Common Law and Statutory Remedies in respect of such Trades not affected.

61.—Trades deemed Nuisances removable by Purchase, on Memorial by Two Thirds of Inhabitants, and Order in Council thereon. Trades so purchased not to be carried on after Payment or Tender of Compensation.

62.—Funds for defraying such Compensation.

63.—Public Gas Works, and certain Buildings under the Excise Survey, exempted from the Operation of the above Provisions.

Surveyors, their Districts and Duties.

64.—Lord Mayor and Aldermen of London, and Justices in Quarter Sessions for other Parts, may appoint, &c. Districts for Purposes of Act.

65.—And may appoint Surveyors for such Districts.

66.—Qualifications of Surveyors to be ascertained by Examiners appointed by Commissioners of Works, &c. Certificate of Examination to be produced by Candidates One Week before Election.

67.—Surveyors to hold Office during Pleasure.

68.—Functions generally of Surveyors.

69.—Disqualification of Surveyors.

70.—Present Surveyors continued in Office subject to Act.

APPENDIX.

METROPOLITAN BUILDINGS ACT,

7 & 8 VICT. CAP. LXXXIV.

An Act for regulating the Construction and the Use of Buildings in the Metropolis and its Neighbourhood.

[9th August, 1844.]

WHEREAS by the several acts mentioned in schedule (A.) to this act, annexed provisions are made for regulating the construction of buildings in the Metropolis, and the neighbourhood thereof, within certain limits therein set forth; but forasmuch as buildings have since been extended in nearly continuous lines or streets far beyond such limits, so that they do not now include all the places to which the provisions of such acts, according to the purposes thereof, ought to apply, and moreover such provisions require alteration and amendment, it is expedient to extend such limits, and otherwise to amend such acts: and forasmuch as in many parts of the Metropolis and the neighbourhood thereof the drainage of the houses is so imperfect as to endanger the health of the inhabitants, it is expedient to make provision for facilitating and promoting the improvement of such drainage (*a*): and forasmuch as by reason of the narrowness of streets, lanes, and alleys, and the want of a thoroughfare in many places, the due ventilation of crowded neighbourhoods is often impeded, and the health of the inhabitants thereby endangered, and from the close contiguity of the

Extension of limits, and amendment of law.

Improvement of drainage.

Securing a sufficient width of streets, &c.

(*a*) See section 51, and schedule H.

opposite houses the risk of accident by fire is extended, it is expedient to make provision with regard to the streets and other ways of the Metropolis for securing a sufficient width thereof(*b*): and forasmuch as many buildings and parts of buildings unfit for dwellings are used for that purpose, whereby disease is engendered, fostered, and propagated, it is expedient to discourage and prohibit such use thereof(*c*); and forasmuch as by the carrying on in populous neighbourhoods of certain works, in which materials of an explosive or inflammable kind are used, the risk of accidents arising from such works is much increased, it is expedient to regulate not only the construction of the buildings in which such dangerous works are carried on, but also to provide for the same being carried on in buildings at safe distances from other buildings which are used either for habitation or for trade in populous neighbourhoods (*d*): and forasmuch as by the carrying on of certain works of a noisome kind, or in which deleterious materials are used, or deleterious products are created, the health and comfort of the inhabitants are extensively impaired and endangered, it is expedient to make provision for the adoption of all such expedients as either have been or shall be devised for carrying on such businesses, so as to render them as little noisome or deleterious as possible to the inhabitants of the neighbourhood; and if there be no such expedients, or if such expedients be not available in a sufficient degree, then for the carrying on of such noisome and unwholesome businesses at safer distances from other buildings used for habitation (*e*): and forasmuch as great diversity of practice has obtained among the officers appointed in pursuance of the said acts to superintend the execution thereof in the several districts to which such acts apply, and the means at present provided for determining the numerous matters in question which constantly arise tend to promote such diversity, to increase the

Improper use of buildings.

Regulation of explosive works.

Regulation of deleterious works.

Execution of act, and superintendence thereof.

(*b*) See section 52, and schedule I.
(*c*) Section 53, and schedule K.
(*d*) Section 54.
(*e*) See sections 55 to 63 inclusive.

expense, and to retard the operations of persons engaged in building, it is expedient to make further provision for regulating the office of surveyor of such several districts (*f*), and to provide for the appointment of officers to superintend the execution of this act throughout all the districts to which it is to apply, and also to determine sundry matters in question incident thereto, as well as to exercise in certain cases, and under certain checks and control, a discretion in the relaxation of the fixed rules, where the strict observance thereof is impracticable, or would defeat the object of this act, or would needlessly affect with injury the course and operation of this branch of business (*g*). Now for all the several purposes above-mentioned, and for the purpose of consolidating the provisions of the law relating to the construction and the use of buildings in the Metropolis and its neighbourhood, be it enacted by the Queen's most Excellent Majesty, by and with the advice and consent of the Lords Spiritual and Temporal, and Commons, in this present Parliament assembled, and by the authority of the same, that with regard to this act generally, so far as relates to the operation thereof in reference to time, it shall come into operation at the following times; (that is to say,) as to the districts and the officers to be appointed in pursuance hereof on the first day of September next, and as to the buildings, streets, and other matters on the first day of January, one thousand eight hundred and forty-five; and that on the said first day of January all the acts mentioned in the schedule hereunto annexed, except so far as in the said schedule is provided, shall be and are hereby repealed.

General Provisions.

Operation of act.

Statutes repealed.

II. And be it declared, with regard to this act generally, so far as relates to the construction of certain terms and expressions used therein, that the following terms and expressions are intended to have the meanings hereby assigned to them respectively, so far as such meanings are not excluded by the context, or by the nature of the subject matter; (that is to say,)

Construction of terms.

(*f*) See section 64 to 79 inclusive.

(*g*) Such as the official referees. See sections 79 to 88 inclusive.

Street. The word "street" to include every square, circus, crescent, street, road, place, row, mews, lane, or place along which carriages can pass or are intended to pass, and that whether there be or be not, in addition to the carriageway, a footway, paved or otherwise:

Alley. The word "alley" to include any court, alley, passage, or other public place which can be used as a footway only:

Square. The word "square," as applied to any area of building, to contain one hundred superficial feet:

Floor. The word "floor" to mean the horizontal platform forming the base of any story, and to include the timber or bricks or any other substance constituting such platform:

Story. The word "story" to include the full thickness of such floor, as well as the space between the upper surface of one floor and the under surface of the floor next above it; or if there be no floor then the space between the surface of the ground and the under surface of the floor next above it:

External wall. The term "external wall" to apply to every outer wall of buildings now built or hereafter to be built, which (excepting the footing thereof on one side) shall stand wholly upon ground of the owner of such buildings, and shall not be used or intended to be used as a party wall under the definition herein-after contained, whether the same shall adjoin or not to other outer or to party walls (*h*):

Party wall. The term "party wall" to apply to every wall which shall be used, or be built in order to be used, as a separation of two or more buildings with a view to the occupation thereof by different families, or which shall be actually occupied by different families, and also every wall which shall stand upon ground not wholly belonging to the same owner to a greater extent than the projection of its footing on one side:

Already built. The term "already built," used in reference to buildings,

(*h*) See 2 Adol. & El., N. S. 225, Green *v.* Eales.

to apply to buildings built before the first day of January one thousand eight hundred and forty-five, or commenced before that day, and covered in and rendered fit for use within twelve months thereafter; and, used in reference to streets and alleys, to apply to all streets or alleys made or laid out before that day, and which shall be formed and rendered fit for use within twelve months thereafter: *General Provisions.*

The term "hereafter to be built," used in reference to buildings, to apply to all buildings to be built or commenced after the first day of January, one thousand eight hundred and forty-five, or which, being commenced, shall not be covered in within twelve months thereafter; and, used in reference to streets and alleys, to apply to all streets or alleys not laid out before the said first day of January, or which, being laid out, shall not be rendered fit for use within twelve months thereafter: Hereafter to be built.

The word "parish" to include all parochial districts and extra-parochial places in which separate churchwardens, overseers, or constables are appointed; and where two parishes have been united for ecclesiastical purposes, then to include such united parishes: Parish.

The word "owner," to apply generally to every person in possession or receipt either of the whole or of any part of the rents or profits of any ground or tenement, or in the occupation of such ground or tenement, other than as a tenant from year to year, or for any less term, or a tenant at will: Owner.

The term "official referees" to mean the persons appointed in pursuance of this act to be official referees of Metropolitan buildings: Official referees.

The word "surveyor" to apply to all surveyors to be appointed in pursuance of this act, or whose appointment is confirmed by this act, and also to all deputy or assistant surveyors to be appointed under this act: Surveyor.

The words "the surveyor," used without any addition, to mean the surveyor in whose district the buildings, The surveyor.

General Provisions.

street, or alley, or other subject matter shall be, or any deputy or assistant surveyor duly acting in his behalf:

Month. The word "month" to mean a calendar month:

The commissioners of works and buildings. The expression "the commissioners of works and buildings" to mean the commissioners of her Majesty's woods forests, land revenues, works, and buildings:

Justice of peace. The expression "justice of the peace" to mean a justice of the peace for the county, division, or liberty within which the building or other subject matter, or any part thereof, is situate; unless it be situate within the city of *London*, or the liberties thereof, in reference to which any matter or thing elsewhere required or authorized to be done, either by one or by two or more justices of the peace, may be done, either by the Lord Mayor of the city of *London*, or by any one, two, or more justices of the peace for the said city; or unless the subject matter be situate in the district of any police court of the Metropolis, in reference to which any matter or thing elsewhere required or authorized to be done by two or more justices may be done by one magistrate:

Local officers. And, generally, whensoever the name of an officer having local jurisdiction in respect of his office is referred to, without mention of the locality to which the jurisdiction extends, such reference is to be understood to indicate the officer having jurisdiction in that place within which is situated the building or other subject matter, or any part thereof, to which such reference applies:

Singular and plural. Masculine and feminine. Corporate body. And, subject as aforesaid to the context and to the nature of the subject matter, words importing the singular number are to be understood to apply to a plurality of persons or things, and words importing the masculine gender are to be understood to apply to persons of the feminine gender, and words importing an individual are to be understood to apply to a corporation or company, or other body of persons.

Extent of operation of act in reference to localities. III. And be it enacted, with regard to this act generally, so far as relates to the operation thereof in reference to localities, that the operation of this act shall extend to all places within the following limits; (that is to say,)

General Provisions.

To all such places lying on the north side or left bank of the river *Thames* as are within the exterior boundaries of the parishes of *Fulham, Hammersmith, Kensington, Paddington, Hampstead, Hornsey, Tottenham, Saint Pancras, Islington, Stoke Newington, Hackney, Stratford-le-Bow, Bromley, Poplar,* and *Shadwell:*

And to such part of the parish of *Chelsea* as lies north of the said parish of *Kensington:*

And to all such parts and places lying on the south side or right bank of the said river as are within the exterior boundaries of the parishes of *Woolwich, Charlton, Greenwich, Deptford, Lee, Lewisham, Camberwell, Lambeth, Streatham, Tooting,* and *Wandsworth:*

And to all places lying within two hundred yards from the exterior boundary of the district hereby defined, except the eastern part of the said boundary which is bounded by the river *Lea* (*i*).

Power to extend the limits of act.

IV. And forasmuch as, partly by the rapid increase of population in the neighbourhood of the districts to which this act is to apply, and partly by the tendency of this act to induce building speculation in such neighbourhoods in order to evade the provisions thereof, the evils which have arisen in the districts not now subject to regulations will in all probability arise in such neighbourhoods, it is expedient to make provision for the prevention of such evils, and, if they should arise, for the remedy thereof; now for those purposes be it enacted, with regard to this act generally, so far as relates to the application thereof to other parts and places in the neighbourhood of the districts appointed by this act, whether such districts immediately adjoin such parts or places or not, that if, from the growing increase of the population or otherwise, it shall appear to her Majesty in council to be expedient that the provisions of this act should be extended to any place within twelve miles from *Charing Cross* in the city of *Westminster*, then it shall be lawful for her Majesty in council to direct, by order in council, that at

(*i*) A large extent of jurisdiction beyond the old limits under 14 Geo. 3, c. 78, s. 1.

General Provisions.

or from a time to be named in such order the provisions of this act shall apply to such places; and at or from such time all such provisions, of whatever nature, whether penal or otherwise, so far as they shall be capable of application to such places, shall be and are hereby declared to apply thereto as if such places were expressly named herein; and that notice of the time when it shall please her Majesty to order any such extension to be taken into consideration by her privy council shall be published by royal proclamation in the *London Gazette* one month at the least before such extension shall be so taken into consideration; and that three weeks at the least before such matter shall be so considered it shall be the duty of the official referees, and the overseers of the parishes within which such parts or places are situate, to cause copies of such proclamation to be fixed on the doors of the churches and chapels within such parishes; and that every order in council made in pursuance of this enactment shall be published in the *London Gazette*.

Publication of notice of intention to extend limits of act.

Buildings, new and old.

V. And now generally, for the purpose of regulating the building and the rebuilding upon sites of former buildings, and the enlarging and altering of all buildings of what nature soever, within the limits aforesaid, be it enacted, with regard to every such building hereafter to be built, (except the buildings comprised in schedule (B.) hereto annexed, and except sewers made by or under the direction of any commissioners of sewers,) so far as relates to building the same, and with regard to every such building either already or hereafter built, (except the said buildings comprised in the said schedule (B.), and except the said sewers,) so far as relates to the rebuilding and the enlarging or altering the same, and that whether such buildings be built or rebuilt on old or new foundations, or partly on old and partly on new foundations, that, notwithstanding any thing contained to the contrary in any act of Parliament now in force, every such building shall be built, rebuilt, enlarged, or altered in reference to the walls, whether external or party walls, and to the number and height of the stories or rooms therein, and to the chimneys, and to the roofs, and to the timbers, and to the drains, and to the projections, and to any other

Regulation of buildings.

parts or appendages of every such building, in the manner and of the materials, and in every other respect in conformity with the several particulars, rules, and directions which are specified and set forth in the several schedules (C.), (D.), (E.), (F.), (G.), (H.), (I.), (K.) to this act annexed, according to the classes of buildings, and the rates of such classes to which such buildings are by the schedule (C.) declared to belong; subject nevertheless to any other rules and directions in this act contained in the same behalf; and subject in every case of doubt, difference, or dissatisfaction in respect thereof, either between any parties concerned or between any party concerned and the surveyor of the district (*j*), to the determination of the official referees, upon a reference of the matter in question, according to the provisions of this act in that behalf (*k*).

Rates of buildings, and thicknesses of walls and footings, and rules concerning buildings.

Buildings under supervision of official referees.

VI. And be it enacted, with regard to all buildings of the first rate of the second or warehouse class, and to all buildings of the third or public building class (except the buildings herein-before excepted), so far as relates to the supervision thereof, that, subject to the provisions in schedule (C.) (*l*) and elsewhere in this act made in respect thereof, every such building shall be built under the special supervision of the official referees, according to the provisions of this act in that behalf, as well as under the ordinary supervision of the surveyor; and if any difference arise as to whether any such building be liable to such special supervision, the same shall be determined by the official referees; subject nevertheless to an appeal, at the instance of any party interested, to the commissioners of works and buildings, whose decision in the matter shall be final.

Special supervision of exempted buildings.

VII. And whereas by several acts now in force certain buildings and structures have been exempted from the operation of the act mentioned in the schedule (A.) hereto annexed, for the regulation of buildings and party walls within the cities of *London* and *Westminster*, and the liberties thereof, and other the parishes and places therein men-

(*j*) The fees of the surveyor will be found under schedule L.

(*k*) See 14 Geo. 3, c. 78, ss. 2 to 21 inclusive.

(*l*) Schedule C., Part V.

Buildings, new and old.

tioned; be it enacted, with regard to the buildings hereinbefore exempted and comprised in schedule (B.), so far as relates to the supervision thereof, that, notwithstanding any thing contained to the contrary in any act or acts now in force, every such building or other structure mentioned in the said schedule (B.), Part I. shall be subject to special supervision by the official referees, according to the provisions of this act in that behalf, and every such building or other structure mentioned in the said schedule (B.) Part II. shall be exempt from supervision.

Buildings not within rates.

VIII. Provided always, and be it enacted, with regard to any building of whatever kind which is not hereby expressly assigned to any class or rate of a class, so far as relates to the application of this act thereto, that if any party be desirous of erecting any building which does not come within any one of the said classes, or of any rate of such classes, then such building shall be built in accordance with such class and rate as shall be directed by the surveyor, subject, as in other cases of doubt, difference, or dissatisfaction, to an appeal to the official referees.

Modification of building contracts.

IX. (*m*) Provided always, and be it enacted, with regard to any building of whatever class, so far as relates to the modification of any written contract or agreement now in force

(*m*) This is the first of four modification clauses. It provides for disagreements between parties to a contract or agreement by referring them to the surveyor and official referees. But it will be remarked, that these parties are not obliged to enter upon the expenses alluded to in this section, and, upon very many occasions, persons in general may avoid the expenses entailed by the act, by a timely arrangement amongst themselves, and thus settling their differences without appeal. Lord C. J. Gibbs, in a case under the old act, 14 Geo. 3, c. 78, said: "No doubt parties may proceed on the act, and a person may oblige the owner of the adjoining house to follow the course prescribed by that statute. But it is perfectly clear, that parties may agree between themselves, without having recourse to so intricate a law; and I think they would act wisely in so doing." 2 Marsh. 426. The principle mentioned by the Lord Chief Justice is worthy of observation, although the present act may be found to be far less intricate than the last.

Buildings, new and old.

for erecting or altering such building (other than a contract or agreement in the nature of a building lease), that it shall not be lawful to execute such contract otherwise than in conformity with the provisions of this act; but it shall be lawful for either party, and he is hereby entitled to deviate from such contract so far as any part thereof may remain to be executed after this act shall have come into operation; and the alterations rendered necessary by this act shall be performed as if this act had been in force when such contract was entered into; and that if the parties thereto shall disagree about the difference of the costs and expenses of the works when performed according to the provisions of this act, and the works as stipulated for in such contract, then, upon notice being given in writing by one party to the other, it shall be lawful for either party and he is hereby entitled to refer the matter to the surveyor, who shall determine the same, subject to appeal as aforesaid to the official referees; and the award (*n*) of such official referees shall be final and binding on all the parties, and in all respects as if such award had formed part of the contract; and the costs of the reference shall be borne by all or any or either of the parties in such manner and proportion as the surveyor (*o*), or in case of appeal as the official referees, shall apoint.

Reference to the surveyor, or on appeal to the official referees.

X. Provided always, and be it enacted, with regard to any building, of whatever class, so far as relates to the modification of any existing lease or agreement for a lease, being of the nature of a building lease, whereby any person may be bound to erect buildings, that, notwithstanding any thing herein contained, if it be made to appear to the official referees that any rules by this act prescribed will prevent the due observance of or be at variance with any such lease or agreement, and that the objects of this act may be

Modification of building leases.

(*n*) "Award," see section 83.

(*o*) A fee of 2*l*., or less, if the official referees shall think fit, is payable to the surveyor. Schedule L. The official referees are paid by salary, but their fees of office, and the attendance of witnesses, and any other incidental charges, must be added to the amount of costs. As to the mode of recovering fees, see sect. 77. The mode of recovering costs, see sect. 102.

Buildings, new and old.

obtained by modifying such rules, either entirely or partially, in conformity with such lease or agreement, then it shall be lawful for the said official referees by their award to authorize such modification, subject, nevertheless, to the approbation of the commissioners of works and buildings; and, subject to such modification, or in default thereof, it shall be the duty of such person so bound to erect buildings and he is hereby required to erect every building agreed to be built by such lease or agreement according to the conditions rendered necessary by this act, in the same or like manner as if this act had been passed and in operation at the time of making such lease or agreement; and that on the completion of such works, either according to the provisions of this act or according to such modification aforesaid, and on giving to the lessor and other owners of such building fourteen days' notice of his intention to apply to the official referees on this behalf, it shall be lawful for the lessee or tenant and he is hereby entitled to require the official referees to ascertain what loss, present and perspective, has been occasioned by the observance of the provisions of this act, and, having regard to the respective terms and interests of the lessee or tenant, the lessor, and other owners of such building, and having regard to any profit, benefit, or advantage which may have accrued to such lessee or tenant since the execution of such lease or agreement, and which may appear to the said official referees not to have been in the contemplation of the parties to such lease or agreement at the time of such execution thereof as aforesaid, to determine whether he is entitled to any and what compensation, whether by payment of money or reduction of rent, or both, or otherwise; and that on the receipt of such requisition, and on proof of due notice thereof having been given to the lessor and other owners of such building, it shall be the duty of such official referees and they are hereby required to proceed to ascertain if any and what loss has been so occasioned, and, having regard as aforesaid to such terms and interest as aforesaid, and to such profit, benefit, or advantage as aforesaid, to determine if any and what compensation as aforesaid is to be paid in respect thereof, and by whom the same is to be paid, and in

Application to official referees.

Proceedings thereon.

what proportions, and their decision in the matter shall be final (*p*). *Buildings, new and old.*

XI. And for the purpose of preventing the express provisions of this act from hindering the adoption of improvements, and of providing for the adoption of expedients either better or equally well adapted to accomplish the purposes thereof, be it enacted, with regard to every building of whatever class, so far as relates to the modification of any rules hereby prescribed, that if in the opinion of the official referees the rules by this act imposed shall be inapplicable, or will defeat the objects of this act, and that by the adoption of any modification of such rules such objects will be attained either better or as effectually, it shall be the duty of such official referees to report their opinion thereon, stating the grounds of such their opinion to the commissioners of works and buildings; and that if on the investigation thereof it shall appear to the said commissioners that such opinion is well founded, then it shall be lawful for the said commissioners or any two of them to direct that such modification may be made in such rules as will in their opinion give effect to the purposes of this act; and that although such official referees shall be of opinion that such modifications are not requisite or admissible, yet if any party interested present to the official referees a representation, setting forth the grounds whereon such modification is claimed, it shall be

Commissioners of works and buildings empowered to modify rules generally.

Report of official referees.

Extent of modification.

Representation by parties.

(*p*) The surveyor is not called into action in the section. Supposing a party to have entered into a covenant to build, or repair, or the like, without sufficiently foreseeing the provisions of the 53rd section, concerning cellarage; or the 54th section, concerning dangerous businesses; or that he has entered into arrangements incompatible with the building regulations provided by this act and its schedules: in such, and similar, cases, the official referees, if applied to, are to be the arbiters of any loss which may accrue on either side by complying with the new provisions. It will be, of course, impracticable to disobey the act, so that if the original plans be neither agreeable to the act, nor to the clauses of modification, they must be withdrawn, or made subservient to the new law; and then, if parties cannot agree, the official referees stand as the umpires.

Buildings, new and old.

Order thereupon.

the duty of the official referees and they are hereby required to report such representation, as well as their opinion thereon, to the said commissioners, with the grounds of such their report and opinion; and that thereupon, if the said commissioners think fit, it shall be lawful for them or any two of them to direct the official referees to make such order in the matter as may appear to them to be requisite (*q*).

Power to modify provisions of this act as to existing buildings to be rebuilt.

XII. And be it enacted with regard to buildings already built, so far as relates to the rebuilding thereof in conformity with this act in respect of the required area, or in any other respect than the required height and thickness of walls, that if a full compliance with the provisions of this act be attended by great loss and inconvenience, then, subject to the report of the official referees, and to the consent of the commissioners of works and buildings, and to such terms as the said commissioners may impose in that behalf, it shall be lawful for the parties concerned to rebuild such buildings on the site of the old buildings as near as may be practicable, but so that nevertheless both the party walls and the external walls be of the required height and thickness.

Builders.

Works to be executed.

Notice to surveyors.

XIII. And be it enacted, with regard to the works to be executed in pursuance of this act, so far as relates to the supervision thereof by the surveyors, that two days (*r*) before the following acts or events, that is to say,—

Before any building shall be begun to be built; and also

Before any addition or alteration, which by this act is placed under the supervision of the surveyor, shall be made to any building; and also

Before any party wall, external wall, chimney stack, or flues shall be begun to be built, pulled down, rebuilt, cut into, or altered; and also

(*q*) Here the commissioners of works and buildings are constituted the tribunal to revise the opinion of the official referees.

(*r*) The giving of the notice is, when given, an act done. Therefore, although it may not be amiss to allow two clear days to elapse before the work is begun, it seems that if notice be given on Monday, the work may be commenced on Wednesday. See 3 T. R. 623, Castle *v.* Burditt and others. Dougl. 462, Rex *v.* Adderley.

Builders.

Before any opening shall be made in any party wall (*s*); and also

Before any other matter or thing shall be done which by this act is placed under the supervision of the surveyor, except as herein-after is provided;

It shall be the duty of the builder (by which term is to be understood, both in this provision and elsewhere throughout this act, the master builder or other person employed to execute any work, or if there be no master builder or other person so employed, then the owner of the building or other person for whom or by whose order such work is to be done,) and he is hereby required to give to the surveyor, at his office, notice in the terms specified in the form (No. 1.) contained in the schedule of notices annexed to this act, or to the like effect; and that if any builder neglect to give such notice, or begin to build, or to do any of the things aforesaid, before such notice, or before the expiration of such period of two days, then in every such case the party offending shall for every such default forfeit and pay to such surveyor treble the amount of the fees which such surveyor would have been entitled to receive for his trouble in inspecting the same, and shall also forfeit for every such default a sum not exceeding twenty pounds (*t*); and that if for any period exceeding three months any builder, having duly begun any building requiring compliance with the provisions of this act, suspend the progress of such building, and again go on with the same, or if during the progress thereof the builder be changed, then, two days before such builder shall enter upon the performance of the work, it shall be the duty of such builder to give notice to the surveyor,

20*l*. penalty for neglect to give notice, &c.

20*l*. penalty for not giving fresh notices.

(*s*) Openings in party walls. Schedule (C.) Part IV. Schedule (D.) Part III.

(*t*) The distinction betwixt penalties and forfeitures incurred generally under the act, and penalties and forfeiture incurred for any default in not complying with the provisions of the act must be noted. In the first case, the limitation of time in proceedings is six months, in the case of default, three months. See sections 106, 110. This is a case of default. See sections 110, and 103, 104, 105.

Builders.

and such notices must be in the terms specified in the forms (Nos. 2 and 3) contained in the schedule of notices annexed to this act, or to the like effect, and must be given to the surveyor, or left at the surveyor's office, in like manner as is required upon beginning any new building, and that if any builder make default or neglect to give or leave such notice he shall forfeit for every such offence a sum not exceeding twenty pounds (*u*); and that if any such building, chimney, or wall be begun to be built, pulled down, rebuilt, cut into, or altered as aforesaid, or be proceeded with after any suspension of the progress thereof before such notice has been given; or if such surveyor or the official referees be refused admittance to inspect the same premises, then such building or work shall be liable to be abated as a nuisance under the provisions herein contained: provided always, that if by reason of any emergency any act, matter, or thing placed under the supervision of the surveyor be required to be done immediately, or before notice can be given to the surveyor, then it shall be lawful for the builder or any person to do such act, matter, or thing so requisite, but upon this condition, that within forty-eight hours after beginning to execute such work notice thereof be given to the surveyor (*x*).

Penalty for beginning without notice; or refusal to admit surveyor. Emergency.

Buildings generally.

Supervision of works.

XIV. And be it enacted, with regard to such buildings and works, so far as relates to the supervision thereof, that if in building, pulling down, rebuilding, cutting into or altering any part of any building, or party wall or external wall, or chimney stack or flue, drains, cesspools, or any work or other thing be done contrary to or not conformably with the rules and directions of this act, then forthwith it shall be the duty of the surveyor, and he is hereby required to give forty-eight hours' notice, according to the form (No. 4) in the schedules of notices, or to the like effect, to the builder,

Notice of irregularities to builders and others.

(*u*) Section 110, and 103, 104, 105.

(*x*) So that if the builder were to neglect the forty-eight hours' notice, he would be liable to a penalty under the previous provisions. As the clause stands, however, it might be made a question, whether he could be so punished, or only proceeded against by indictment for disobedience to the act of Parliament.

Buildings generally.

foreman, or principal workman on the premises, to amend any such irregularity which he shall deem to have been committed, and forthwith after the expiration of such notice to proceed to inspect the work (*y*); and that if the work be so far advanced that he cannot ascertain whether the irregularity has been committed or not, or exists or not, then it shall be lawful for him, and he is hereby empowered to order any work to be cut into, laid open, or pulled down, which shall, in his opinion prevent his ascertaining whether any such irregularity exists or not; and that if within forty-eight hours the builder to whom any such notice shall have been given refuse or fail to amend any irregular work, or if any such builder, when ordered by the surveyor, refuse to cut into, lay open, or pull down any work which shall in his opinion prevent his ascertaining whether such irregular work exists or not, then, as soon as conveniently shall be, it shall be the duty of the surveyor to give information thereof to the official referees; and that upon the receipt of such information it shall be the duty of such official referees and they are hereby required to proceed to hear the matter, and if any breach of the rules, regulations and directions of this act be found to have been committed, or if there appear good reason to suppose any such breach has been committed and is concealed, then it shall be lawful for the official referees, and they are hereby authorized, to direct by their award (*z*), that such building, party wall, external wall, chimney stack, flue, or other thing, or such part thereof as they shall deem necessary, shall be amended, removed, cut into, laid open, or pulled down; and that all the costs, charges, and expenses of the said work, and of the said application to the official referees, shall be borne by such party or parties as the official referees shall determine.

To cut into works.

Amendment of works.

Proceeding thereon by official referees.

Costs.

XV. And now, for the purpose of making provision for the supervision of buildings of the first rate of the second or warehouse class, and of all buildings of the third or public

Special supervision of first-rate buildings, of second class and of buildings of third class.

(*y*) For which a fee not exceeding 2*l*. seems to be payable. See Schedule L. See section 77.

(*z*) See section 83.

Buildings generally.

building class (except the buildings herein-before excepted), be it enacted, with regard to every such building, so far as relates to the special supervision thereof, that when all the walls of any such building shall have been built to their full height, and all the timbers of the floors, roofs, and partitions shall have been fixed, it shall be the duty of the architect or builder and he is hereby required to give notice thereof to the official referees, according to the form (No. 6) in the schedule of notices, or to the like effect; and if the official referees be of opinion that such building is subject to the special supervision herein provided, then within seven days after such notice it shall be their duty to survey the said building; and that if they approve of the same, then within seven days after such survey to certify such approval, under their hands, to the architect or builder; or that if any part of the walls, timbers, roof, or internal supports appear to such official referees defective, insufficient, or insecure, then within the said seven days after such survey they are hereby required to give to such architect or builder notice of such parts as shall so appear to them defective, insufficient, or insecure, which notice must be in writing; and that upon the receipt of such notice it shall be the duty of the said architect or builder and he is hereby required to amend and strengthen such defective, insufficient, or insecure parts; and that during or within a period of seven days after notice has been given to the official referees that such works have been amended or strengthened as aforesaid, it shall be the duty of the official referees and they are hereby required to inspect the same, or in default thereof the said parts may be covered up; and that upon completion of every such building it shall be the duty of the architect or builder to give fresh notice to the official referees, according to the form (No. 7) in the schedule of notices, or to the like effect; and that thereupon, or within seven days after such notice, it shall be the duty of the official referees to survey the same; and that if upon such survey it shall appear that such building has been built sufficiently strong, and is sufficiently set to be safe, then within fourteen days after such survey it shall be their duty and they are hereby required to certify

Notice to official referees.

Survey.

Approval.

Disapproval.

Amendment of defects.

Notice of completion.

New survey.

Certificate.

Buildings generally.

accordingly, which certificate must be under their hands and the seal of office of registrar of Metropolitan buildings; and that, until such certificate shall have been made, or until fourteen days after such survey shall have elapsed without the official referees having given notice in writing that they are not satisfied, it shall not be lawful to use such building for any purpose whatever without the express authority in writing of the official referees under their hands and the seal of office of the registrar of Metropolitan buildings; and that if before the certificate of satisfaction shall have been made, or if (*a*) such further fourteen days as aforesaid shall have elapsed without due notice being given in writing as aforesaid, any such building subject to special supervision shall be used for any purpose without such express authority in writing, then, on conviction thereof before two justices of the peace, the occupier of such building, or other the person by whom such building shall be so used, shall forfeit for such offence a sum not exceeding two hundred pounds for every day during which such building shall be so used without having obtained such certificate of satisfaction, or such express authority as aforesaid (*b*); and that, in determining the amount of any such penalty, it shall be the duty of the justices and they are hereby directed to have regard to the size and character of the building, and to the nature and extent of danger involved in the use of such building, and to the amount of profit which might be derived from such use thereof.

Prohibition of use.

Penalty.

Justices to consider circumstances.

XVI. And be it enacted, with regard to the buildings comprised in schedule (B.) part I. to this act annexed, so far as relates to the supervision thereof, that before the builder begin to build the same it shall be the duty of the architect or the builder and he is hereby required to give notice thereof to the official referees, and also, at the same time, to transmit for their inspection the plans, elevations, and other drawings which have been made for the same; and that

Special supervision of buildings in schedule (B.) Part I.

Survey by official referees.

(*a*) Here the word "until" has been omitted.

(*b*) See sections 110, and 103, 104, 105.

Buildings generally.

forthwith thereupon it shall be the duty of the official referees and they are hereby required to proceed to survey the situation of the intended building with a view to ascertain whether such building can be erected on such situation with due regard to the security of the public; and that, from time to time during the progress of such building, it shall be the duty of such official referees and they are hereby directed to inspect the same with a view to ascertain the sufficiency thereof; and that if such building or any part thereof appear to such official referees defective, insufficient, or insecure, then they are hereby required to give to such architect or builder notice of such parts as shall so appear to them defective, insufficient, or insecure, which notice must be in writing: and that upon the receipt of such notice it shall be the duty of the said architect or builder and he is hereby required to amend and strengthen such defective, insufficient, or insecure parts; and that during or within a period of seven days after notice has been given to the official referees that such works have been amended or strengthened as aforesaid, it shall be the duty of the official referees and they are hereby required to inspect the same, or in default thereof the said parts may be covered up; and that upon completion of every such building it shall be the duty of the architect or builder to give fresh notice to the official referees; and that thereupon, or within seven days after such notice, it shall be the duty of the official referees to survey the same; and that if upon such survey it shall appear that such building has been built sufficiently strong, then it shall be their duty to certify accordingly, which certificate must be under their hands and the seal of office of registrar of Metropolitan buildings; and that until such certificate shall have been made, or until fourteen days after such survey shall have elapsed without the official referees having given notice in writing that they are not satisfied, it shall not be lawful to use such building for any purpose whatever without the express authority in writing of the official referees under their hands and the seal of office of the registrar of Metropolitan buildings; and that if before the certificate of

Occasional inspection.

Notice of deficiencies.

Amendment of defects.

Approval by official referees.

Notice of completion.

New survey

Certificate.

Prohibition of use.

Penalty.

Buildings generally.

satisfaction shall have been made, or if (*c*) such fourteen days as aforesaid shall have elapsed without due notice in writing being given as aforesaid, any such building subject to special supervision shall be used for any purpose without such express authority in writing, then, on conviction thereof before two justices of the peace, the occupier of such building, or other the person by whom such building shall be so used, shall forfeit for such offence a sum not exceeding one hundred pounds for every day during which such building shall be so used without having obtained such certificate of satisfaction, or such express authority as aforesaid (*d*); and that, in determining the amount of any such penalty, it shall be the duty of the justices and they are hereby directed to have regard to the nature and extent of danger involved in the use of such building, and to the amount of profit which might be derived from such use thereof.

Justices to consider circumstances.

XVII. And be it enacted, with regard to buildings and works, so far as relates to the entry thereon for the supervision thereof, that at all times during the progress of any operations in respect thereof within the meaning of this act, it shall be lawful for the surveyor and for the official referees, and they are hereby respectively authorized, to enter upon the premises upon which such operations have been commenced; and that if at any time whilst any building is in course of construction, demolition, alteration, or re-construction, any person refuse to admit the surveyor, or the official referees authorized under this act, during the customary working hours, to inspect such building, or any person refuse or neglect to afford such surveyor or official referee every assistance which may be reasonably required in and about such inspection, then in every such case on conviction thereof the party offending shall forfeit for every such offence a sum not exceeding twenty pounds (*e*); and that if at any time during such customary working hours the surveyor or the official referees be refused admittance to make inspection of

Entry on premises.

Refusal to permit inspection.

Forcible entry.

(*c*) Here the word "before" seems to be left out.

(*d*) See sections 110, and 103, 104, 105.

(*e*) See sections 106, 107, and 103, 104, 105.

Buildings generally.

any work, then for that purpose it shall be lawful for such surveyor or for such official referees, and they are hereby empowered, accompanied by a peace officer, to enter upon the ground, building, and premises where the same shall be.

All buildings not according to this act declared a nuisance.

XVIII. And for the purpose of more effectually enforcing the observance of the provisions of this act, be it enacted, with regard to any buildings, drains, timber buildings, chimneys and flues, party walls, party fence walls, external walls and projections, and every other part of every building of every class, or rate of any class, which shall be hereafter built, rebuilt, enlarged, or altered, within the limits of this act, contrary to the provisions hereof, so far as relates to the removal thereof, that if the same be not built, rebuilt, enlarged, or altered in the manner and of the materials, and in every other respect according to and in conformity with the several rules and directions which are in this act particularly specified, and if any person build or begin to build, or cause the building or beginning to build, or alter or cause to be altered, or use or cause to be used, any part of any ground or building, projection, drain, or other thing contrary thereunto, and if in either of such cases it so appear by the certificate of the official referees, then the said building, projection, drain, or other thing, or such part thereof so irregularly built or begun to be built, or so irregularly altered or begun to be altered or so used, shall be deemed a nuisance; and that thereupon it shall be the duty of the surveyor and he is hereby directed to summon the builder before any two justices of the peace; and that if at the time and place appointed on such summons such builder fail to appear, then it shall be lawful for the said justices and they are hereby authorized to issue a warrant under their hands and seals to compel such builder to appear before such justices or any other two justices; and that thereupon it shall be the duty of such builder and he is hereby required to enter into a recognizance, in such sum as the said justices shall appoint, for abating and taking down the same within such convenient time as the said justices shall respectively appoint, or otherwise for amending the same according to such rules and directions as are herein contained, and also

Summons before justices.

Compulsory appearance.

Recognizances to pull down and amend.

Buildings generally.

for paying the costs, charges, and expenses incurred by the surveyor in laying the information and obtaining the conviction, including such compensation for the surveyor's loss of time as the said justices shall think fit; and that if the party so required fail to enter into such recognizance, then it shall be lawful for either of such justices or any justice, and they are hereby required, to commit such builder to the common gaol of the city, county, or liberty where the offence shall be committed, there to remain without bail or mainprize until he shall have entered into such recognizance as aforesaid, or until such irregular building shall have been abated or demolished or otherwise amended, or such nuisance shall be abated or demolished by order of such justices respectively (which order the said justices are hereby empowered to make), and until the costs, charges, and expenses thereof, and of all operations and proceedings in relation thereto, shall have been paid; and further, that if application be made to any two or more justices, then thereupon it shall be their duty, and they are hereby empowered, to order the surveyor or any other person to abate or demolish such nuisance, and to order the persons authorized by them so to abate or demolish the same to sell and dispose of the materials thereof, and out of the moneys arising by such sale to pay to themselves, and all persons by them employed for such purpose, the reasonable charges for abating or demolishing such nuisance, and also such costs and expenses as aforesaid, and to pay the surplus moneys arising by such sale (if any) to such owner of the building as the official referees shall determine to be entitled thereto; and that if the moneys arising by such sale be not sufficient to pay such charges, then it shall be the duty of the person entitled to the immediate possession of such building (*f*), or the occupier, to make good the deficiency, subject to reimbursement as hereinafter provided (*g*); and if he fail, then he shall be

Imprisonment.

Removal of buildings declared nuisances.

Expenses.

(*f*) See section 111.

(*g*) Perhaps it would have been better to have named the clauses of reimbursement in the margin. See sections 46, 49, 50. If the *whole* building be abated as a nuisance, it does not seem that any clause of reimbursement applies.

Buildings generally.

liable to the same remedies for the recovery thereof as are by this act provided concerning the expense of taking down ruinous buildings, and putting up hoards for the safety of passengers (*h*).

Fifty shillings penalty on workmen offending.

XIX. And be it enacted, with regard to any building or work, so far as relates to the non-observance of the provisions of this act in that behalf by workmen and others, that if any workman, labourer, servant, or other person employed in any building, or in the alteration, fitting up, or decoration of any building, wilfully, and without the direction, privity, or consent of the person causing such work to be done, do any thing in or about such building contrary to the rules and directions of this act, then upon conviction thereof before any two justices of the peace, upon the oath of one or more credible witness or witnesses (which oath the said justices are hereby empowered and required to administer), every such offender shall be liable to forfeit for every such offence a sum not exceeding fifty shillings; and that if upon or immediately after such conviction any such forfeiture be not paid, then it shall be the duty of any two justices of the peace to whom application shall be made to commit the offenders, by warrant under the hand and seal of such justices, to the common gaol for any term not exceeding one month, at the discretion of such justices (*i*).

Imprisonment.

Adjoining properties.

Party walls. Party fences. Intermixed buildings.

XX. And forasmuch as from time to time occasion hath arisen and will hereafter arise to execute the following works in relation to adjoining buildings and premises parted by the same party wall or party fence wall, but belonging to different owners or occupied by different persons, or to build-

(*h*) Section 42.

(*i*) The proceeding must be in the usual manner, by summons and information. And two justices will mean one police magistrate, where the case applies, under the interpretation clause, (sec. 2). However nothing is said about costs, and the 103rd section will hardly cure this defect, because the procedure there is entirely different from that of section 19. And the 103rd section provides for cases where no other proceeding has been directed by the act. The 105th section, however, gives an appeal, and the 106th limits the time for proceeding to recover such penalty to six months.

ings intermixed belonging to different owners or occupied by different persons; namely,

Execution of works.

The reparation of the party walls by which such premises shall be parted:

The pulling down and rebuilding of such party walls:

The raising of such party walls:

The reparation of party fence walls:

The rebuilding of such party fence walls:

The raising of such party fence walls:

The pulling down of timber partitions which part buildings the property of different owners or occupied by different persons, and building in lieu thereof proper party walls:

The pulling down of buildings built over public ways, or having rooms or stories the property of different persons, or occupied by different persons, lying intermixed, for the purpose of building proper party walls or party arches:

And generally the performance of other necessary works incident to the connexion of such party walls or party fence walls with the premises adjoining; it is expedient to make provision, as well for facilitating the execution of such works by any such owner desirous to execute the same (who is herein denominated the "building owner"), as for protecting the interests of the owner of the adjoining premises (who is herein denominated the "adjoining owner"); now for that purpose be it enacted, with regard to all premises parted by a party wall or party fence wall, or parted by timber partitions, and with regard to all intermixed properties not so parted, so far as relates to the execution of any such works by any owner of any such premises, that if the adjoining owner shall have consented thereto, or if, without such consent, the required notice of such work shall have been given by or on the part of the building owner to such adjoining owner, then, subject to such modification as shall be made by virtue of the provision in that behalf, and subject to the provision for supplying the want of consent of the owners, and subject moreover to the respective conditions hereby prescribed with regard to such works respectively, as well as to the payment of the

Party Walls. Party Fences. Intermixed Buildings.

costs of such works, and to the sanction or to the award of the surveyors or of the official referees, as hereby prescribed in reference thereto, it shall be lawful for every such building owner and he is hereby authorized or required to execute such works.

Consent of or notice to adjoining owner.

XXI. And be it enacted, with regard to such works, so far as relates to the notice thereof, that, unless the adjoining owner consent thereto, it shall not be lawful for the "building owner" to execute such works until he have given notice thereof to such "adjoining owner;" and every such notice with regard to the pulling down, rebuilding, or repairing of party walls or party fence walls must be given three months at the least before the work is to be commenced; and every such notice with regard to the pulling down and rebuilding intermixed walls and timber partitions must be given three months at the least before such work is to be commenced; and every such notice must be in the form or to the effect of the notice (No. 8) for that purpose contained in the schedule of notices hereunto annexed (*k*).

Modification of work to suit adjoining owner.

XXII. And be it enacted, with regard to every such work, so far as relates to the modification thereof, in order to render it suitable to the premises of the adjoining owner or his tenant, that if the adjoining owner, at any time within two months after the receipt of the said notice from the building owner, give notice of his desire that any modification be made in the work, so as to render it suitable to his premises, according to the form (No. 18) in the schedule of notices, or to the like effect, then within seven days after the receipt of such notice it shall be the duty of the building owner, and he is hereby required, to signify his consent to or dissent from such modification or delay; and that if the building owner dissent from, or do not within such seven days signify his consent to such modification, then it shall be lawful for the adjoining owner and he is hereby entitled to require the building owner not to commence the work until the official referees shall have determined thereon; and that if within

Modification of operations.

(*k*) Nevertheless, if there should be immediate danger, the provisions of the 40th section should be consulted.

seven days thereafter application be made in writing to the official referees, according to the form (No. 19) in the schedule of notices, or to the like effect, and notice thereof be given to the building owner, according to the other form (No. 20), then within ten days after such application it shall be the duty of the official referees to signify their decision thereon, and it shall be the duty of the building owner not to commence the work till the decision of such official referees shall have been given; and that if within the period of three (*l*) months from the date of the first notice (*m*) such adjoining owner do not make any objection or any requisition in conformity with this enactment, then, subject to the provisions of this act with regard to such works, it shall be lawful for the building owner and he is hereby authorized to proceed to execute the same.

Application to official referees.

Authority to build.

XXIII. And be it enacted, with regard to every such work, so far as relates to the modification thereof, in order to render it suitable to the premises, or to the convenience of the adjoining owner or his tenant, that if the adjoining owner, at any time within three months after the receipt of the said notice from the building owner, give notice of his desire that the work be delayed, so as to cause it to be executed at a more seasonable or a more convenient time in reference to the business or to the family or domestic arrangements of such adjoining owner or his tenants, according to the form (No. 18) in the schedule of notices, or to the like effect, then within seven days after the receipt of the notice thereof it shall be the duty of the building owner and he is hereby required to signify his consent to or dissent from such modification or delay; and that if the building owner do not within such seven days signify his consent to such modification or delay, then it shall be lawful for the adjoining owner and he is hereby entitled to require the building owner to delay the work until the official referees shall have determined thereon;

Delay of work to suit adjoining owner.

Delay of operations.

(*l*) Two months are allowed for the modification, and, it seems, three months for any other objection.

(*m*) That is, the notice of three months under section 21.

Application to official referees.

and that if within seven days thereafter application be made in writing to the official referees, according to the form (No. 19) in the schedule of notices, or to the like effect, and notice thereof be given to the building owner, according to the other form (No. 20), then within ten days after such application it shall be the duty of the official referees to signify their decision thereon, and it shall be the duty of the building owner to delay the same till the decision of such official referees shall have been given; and that if within the period of three months from the date of the first notice such adjoining owner do not make any objection or any requisition in conformity with this enactment, then, subject to the provisions of this act with regard to such works, it shall be lawful for the building owner and he is hereby authorized to proceed to execute the same.

Authority to build.

Supplying want of consent of adjoining owners.

XXIV. And be it enacted, with regard to any such works hereby authorized to be done in relation to party walls, party arches, party fence walls, or other such structures belonging to the owners of adjoining buildings or parting adjoining premises, so far as relates to supplying the want of consent of the adjoining owners, that if the adjoining premises be unoccupied, or if the owner thereof cannot be found, or if the owner although found cannot, by reason of legal disability or otherwise, consent to the work, or if the owner will not consent thereto, or if differences arise amongst the parties concerned, then the notice required to be given in respect of such work must be served both on the surveyor and on the official referees, in addition to such other parties entitled to notice under this act upon whom such notice can be served, which must be according to the form (No. 9) in the schedule of notices, or to the like effect; and that forthwith on the receipt of such notice it shall be the duty of the surveyor and he is hereby required to give notice to the parties by whom such work is to be executed, and to any one or more surveyors or other agents by them appointed, as to the day and hour when he will view the premises, according to the form (No. 10) in the schedule of notices, or to the like effect; and at such time it

Notice of inspection by surveyor.

Party Walls. Party Fences. Intermixed Buildings.

shall be the duty of the surveyor of the district and he is hereby authorized to proceed to inspect such premises accordingly (*n*), and to certify to the official referees.

First, whether such work ought to be done or not; and

Secondly, if the same ought to be done, whether it ought to done in the proposed manner; and

Thirdly, the site whereon the party wall should be built; and, with regard to intermixed buildings, what party arches may be necessary over or under any rooms of such buildings so intended to be rebuilt; and

Fourthly, the quantity of soil or ground or other parts of the premises (if any) necessary to be laid to or taken from the house of the person desirous to rebuild to the house of the person permitting him to erect a party wall or party arch; and

Fifthly, the compensation (if any) which should be made and paid by either the building owner or the adjoining owner to the other in lieu of the lessening either of the said buildings by such party wall or party arch, or as a satisfaction for such other injury (if any) as shall be done or occasioned thereby to any of the said parties;

Notice to parties.

And that upon the receipt of such certificate it shall be the duty of the official referees, and they are hereby required, to cause notice thereof to be given to the parties or to such of them as are known; and that if within seven days after such notice to the parties the certificate be not appealed against, and if the official referees be of opinion that the work is proper to be done, and the compensation is fair, then it shall be lawful for the official referees to confirm such certificate, and to authorize the building owner to proceed with the works as if the consent of the adjoining owner had been obtained; and that if any party concerned shall appeal against the certificate of the surveyor as to the work to be done, or as to the compensation, or as to any other matter referred to in such certificate in pursuance of the above provisions, then it shall be the duty of the official referees, and they are hereby required, to appoint one of their number to survey

Confirmation by official referees.

Proceedings on appeal against certificate.

Notice by official referees.

(*n*) The fee for which would seem, under schedule L. to be 2*l*.

Party Walls. Party Fences. Intermixed Buildings.

the building in question; and that for that purpose it shall be the duty of the official referee so appointed, and he is hereby required, to give notice to the parties, and to any one or more surveyors or other agents by them appointed, as to the time when he will view the premises; and that at such time it shall be the duty of such referee and he is hereby authorized to view such premises accordingly, and to inquire into the matters appealed against, and to certify to the official referees his opinion thereon; and that upon such certificate being made it shall be lawful for the official referees to make their award (*p*), thereby either confirming or reversing or modifying, as to them the case may seem to require, the certificate of the surveyor, and appointing by whom and in what proportions the expenses of the surveys and of the reports thereon are to be paid, and such award shall be final and conclusive; and with regard to any works by such award authorized, so far as relates to the proceedings of the building owner, that if upon the making of the award the periods of the notices by this act prescribed with regard to works of that nature have elapsed, then immediately upon the making of the award, but if such periods have not elapsed then as soon after the making of the award as such periods shall have elapsed, it shall be lawful for the building owner, his agents, servants, and workmen, to proceed to execute the works.

Survey. Award. Works authorized.

Reparation and rebuilding at joint expense.

XXV. And be it enacted, with regard to any party wall, party arch, or external wall used wholly or in part as a party fence wall, so far as relates to the reparation and rebuilding thereof at the joint expense of the owners of the buildings parted thereby, that if such party structure be so defective or so far out of repair as to render it necessary to pull down and rebuild the same, or any part thereof, then on notice being given by the owner of one of the buildings to the adjoining owner, according to the form (No. 8) in the schedule of notices, or to the like effect, it shall be lawful for the building owner to require a survey, certificate, and award (*q*), authorizing the execution of such reparation or rebuilding, ac-

(*p*) See sect. 83.

(*q*) Section 83.

cording to the provisions hereinbefore contained in that behalf (*r*).

Rebuilding of party walls.

XXVI. And be it enacted, with regard to sound party walls, so far as relates to the rebuilding thereof at the expense of the building owner, that if the owner of one of the buildings desire to rebuild such party wall, then, on giving to the adjoining owner the required notice of three months, according to the form (No. 14) in the schedule of notices, or to the like effect, it shall be lawful for such building owner and he is hereby entitled to pull down and rebuild such party wall, but upon condition that he do reinstate and make good all the internal finishings and decorations of the adjoining premises, and pay all the costs and charges thereof, and also all the expenses incidental to the execution of the work, including therein the fees and expenses of the survey, and the fees of the surveyors, and any fees in respect of any services performed by the official referees, and also such reasonable compensation as to the said official referees may seem proper for any loss which the adjoining owner shall have incurred by reason of such work (*s*).

Rebuilding a party wall.

Building of an external wall against a party wall.

XXVII. And be it enacted, with regard to any party wall, so far as the rebuilding thereof, that if the owner of one of the buildings parted by such party wall rebuild such building of a higher rate, and do not pull down such party wall and build a proper wall in lieu thereof, then it shall be his duty and he is thereby required to build up an external wall against such party wall (*t*).

Damage arising from erection of external wall against a party wall.

XXVIII. And be it enacted, with regard to an external wall built against a party wall, so far as relates to the operations incident thereto, and to the making good any damage occasioned thereby, that if it be necessary to excavate or dig out the ground against the wall of any adjoining building for the purpose of erecting a wall thereon, or

(*r*) That is, under section 24.

(*s*) See sections 77, 102.

(*t*) Otherwise his building may be treated as a nuisance, under section 18, or he may be indicted for disobedience to the act of Parliament.

Party Walls. Party Fences. Intermixed Buildings.

for any other purpose, then it shall be lawful for the building owner and he is hereby entitled so to do, but upon condition that the said building owner do at his own costs shore up and underpin such wall, or such part thereof, to its full thickness and to the full depth of such excavation, with good sound stock bricks and tiles or slates bedded in cement, or with other proper and sufficient materials, such underpinning to be done in a workmanlike and substantial manner; and that if for the purpose of erecting such external wall it be necessary to cut away part of the footings of such party wall on the side next to the wall so to be built, and any part of the chimney breasts and chimney shafts belonging to the building about to be rebuilt as shall project beyond the perpendicular face of such party wall in the lowest floor thereof, then, on giving notice of such intention in writing to the owner of the adjoining building at least one month before commencing operations, according to the form (No. 15) in the schedule of notices, or to the like effect, and on the expiration of such notice, it shall be lawful for the building owner and he is hereby authorized to cut away such portions of the footings, breasts, and chimney shafts aforesaid, but so that the same be done, and the brick-work where cut be again made good in cement, under the superintendence and to the satisfaction of the surveyor (*t*).

Cutting into footings and chimneys.

Making good such damage.

XXIX. Provided always, and be it enacted, with regard to such party wall, so far as relates to the making good of any such damage, that if it be so damaged and injured by such cutting away as in the opinion of the adjoining owner or occupier to be ruinous or dangerous, then upon application for that purpose it shall be the duty of the surveyor and he is hereby required to survey such wall; and if upon the survey thereof it be found ruinous or dangerous, then to condemn it (*u*); and that thereupon it shall be the duty of the building owner to pull down and rebuild such party wall; and that if in the opinion of the surveyor or of the official referees such damage or injury shall have been occasioned

Survey.

Damage from carelessness.

(*t*) See the fee under schedule L., "Fees for Special Duties."

(*u*) See Schedule L., as to the fee.

by want of due care on the part of the building owner, then it shall be the duty of such building owner and he is hereby required to pull down and rebuild such party wall, and that at his own costs and charges, including therein all the costs and expenses incident to such survey, and the pulling down and rebuilding of such party wall, and the reinstating and making good all the internal finishings and decorations damaged thereby; and that if the owner of the building to be rebuilt do not proceed with all due dispatch to pull down and rebuild such party wall, and to reinstate and make good all the internal finishings and decorations of the adjoining premises, and to pay the costs and charges and expenses of the survey, then it shall be lawful for the adjoining owner so to do, and he is hereby entitled to recover all the costs and expenses in respect thereof from such owner, his heirs, executors, administrators, or assigns (v)

Party Walls. Party Fences. Intermixed Buildings.

Rebuilding.

XXX. And be it enacted, with regard to any sound party wall against which an external wall shall have been built, and which shall have been suffered to remain, so far as relates to the rebuilding thereof, that if, while such party wall continues sound, the adjoining building be pulled down or rebuilt, and such party wall be pulled down, then the owner of such adjoining building shall not be entitled to more than his just proportion of the materials thereof, nor to more than his just proportion of the ground on which such party wall was built, nor shall he build on more than his just proportion of the said ground, unless he shall have agreed with and satisfied the owner of the building so previously rebuilt for his half thereof; and that if the said owners cannot agree concerning the division of such materials, or of such ground, or of the building thereon, or concerning the reimbursement of the party first rebuilding as aforesaid, then the price and all matters in difference, including the sale and purchase of the ground in question, shall be settled by a reference to the official referees, whose award (x) shall be final.

Rebuilding of sound party walls.

Reference to official referees.

XXXI. And be it enacted, with regard to every building

Raising of future buildings.

(v) See section 102. (x) See section 83.

Party Walls. Party Fences. Intermixed Buildings.

hereafter built, so far as relates to the raising thereof, that it shall be lawful to raise any building, but so that nevertheless the party and external walls and chimneys thereof, when so raised, be of the materials and of the several heights and thicknesses hereinbefore described for party and external walls and chimneys of the rate such building shall be of when so raised (*y*), and with regard to buildings already built, so far as relates to the raising thereof, that although the walls of such buildings be not of the thicknesses prescribed by this act, if, in the opinion of the surveyor, such walls be sufficiently secure to allow of the raising thereof, then it shall be lawful to raise any such building already built to an additional height not exceeding ten feet; and with regard to any building adjoining one which shall be raised, so far as relates to the raising of the chimneys thereof, that if any building be raised it shall be the duty of the owner of such building and he is hereby required to build up, at his own expense, the party walls between his own and any adjoining building, and all flues and chimney stacks belonging thereto; and with regard to any building raised, so far as relates to the use thereof by the adjoining owner, that if at any time the owner of any such adjoining building make use of any portion of the part raised of such party wall by building against it or otherwise, it shall be lawful for the owner of the premises so first raised to claim, and he is hereby entitled to recover, the cost of a proportionate part of the portion which shall be so used, together with the cost of such parts of the chimney stacks as belong thereto. (*z*)

Existing buildings.

Chimneys of adjoining buildings.

Use of raised buildings.

Repairing and rebuilding of party fence walls.

XXXII. And be it enacted, with regard to party fence walls, by which term is to be understood any boundary wall, parting the grounds belonging to different owners or occupied by different persons, so far as relates to the reparation and rebuilding and raising thereof, that if the owner of any of the premises parted thereby give one month's notice of his intention to the adjoining owner to repair, pull down, and rebuild the same, it shall be lawful for him so to do; and if

(*y*) See section 5, and the schedules therein mentioned.

(*z*) Section 102.

Party Walls. Party Fences. Intermixed Buildings.

the wall be below the height of nine feet from the ground on either side, then either to raise it to that height, or to pull it down and to rebuild it to that height, but upon condition that he do pay all the expenses thereof; and that if a building be to be erected against such party fence wall, and such wall be not conformable to the requisites prescribed for a proper party wall for a building of that class and rate, then it shall be lawful for the building owner and he is hereby entitled to pull down such party fence wall, but upon condition that he do pay all the expenses thereof, and also that he do make good every damage which shall accrue to such adjoining premises by such rebuilding: provided always, with regard to the expense of so pulling down such party fence wall, and rebuilding the same, that if thereafter the adjoining owner use such party fence wall for any purpose to which, if it had not been pulled down and rebuilt, it would not have been applicable, then to such extent as such adjoining owner shall so use such wall the building owner shall be entitled to be reimbursed the expenses of so pulling down and rebuilding such wall (*a*); provided also, with regard to any such party fence wall, so far as relates to the limitation of the height thereof, that if any party desire to raise such wall so as to screen from view any offensive object or neighbourhood, then on application to the official referees it shall be lawful for them to authorise such work, but not so as to obstruct the free circulation of the air, or to injure the property adjoining to or in the neighbourhood of such wall.

Deficient party fence wall.

Reimbursement of expense of operations.

Limitation of height of screen walls.

XXXIII. And be it enacted, with regard to the party timber partitions of existing buildings belonging to different owners, so far as relates to the pulling down thereof, and any wall under or over the same, that if one of the buildings be rebuilt, or if one of the fronts of any such building be taken down to the height of one story, or for a space equal to one-fourth of such front from the level of the second floor upwards, then without the consent of the adjoining owner, but upon giving the requisite notice, according to the forms (Nos. 11, 12, 13) in the schedule of notices, or to the like

Pulling down party timber partitions.

(*a*) See sections 46, 47, 48, 49, 50, 102.

Party Walls. Party Fences. Intermixed Buildings.

effect, it shall be the duty of the building owner and he is hereby required to pull down such timber partitions, and the walls under or over the same, and in lieu thereof to build a proper party wall, and that at the expense of the owners of all the premises parted thereby (*b*).

Pulling down intermixed building.

XXXIV. And be it enacted, with regard to buildings built over public ways, or having rooms or stories, the property of different persons, lying intermixed (except Inns of Court hereinafter provided for) so far as relates to the pulling down and laying the parts thereof to each other, that if a party wall or party arch cannot be built without pulling down such buildings, and so laying parts thereof to each other, and if in default of the consent of all proper parties the official referees authorize such works, then it shall be lawful for the owner of either of the said buildings to execute the same, but so that the party walls or party arches be conformable to the provisions of this act, and the directions of the said official referees in their award made in that behalf (*c*).

Inns of Court, chambers, &c.

XXXV. And be it enacted, with regard to the rooms or chambers in the Inns of Court, (that is to say,) in *Serjeants' Inn, Chancery Lane*, or in any of the Four Inns of Court, or in any of the Inns of Chancery, or any other Inns set apart for the study or the practice of the law, and with regard to other buildings divided into rooms or chambers, offices, or counting houses, let out or to be let in separate suites or sets, so far as relates to the building of party walls, that the walls or divisions between the several rooms and chambers in such inns, or such buildings, belonging to and communicating with each separate and distinct staircase, shall be deemed to be party walls within the meaning of this act, and as such must be built in conformity with the regulations and clauses herein contained relating to party walls (*d*).

Power of entry on premises to effect works.

XXXVI. And for the purpose of facilitating and regu-

(*b*) See sections 46 to 50, and 102. "Fees to Surveyors," schedule L., and section 77.

(*c*) See sections 46 to 50, and 102. Schedule D. "Fees to Surveyors," Parts IV. and V., schedule L., and section 77.

(*d*) See section 20, *et seq.*

lating the execution of any works authorized by this act, or by any award in pursuance thereof, in respect of any party wall or party arch parting the buildings or grounds belonging to different owners, or in the occupation of different persons, or in respect of intermixed buildings, be it enacted, with regard to any such works, so far as relates to the power to enter the adjoining premises in order to execute the same, that if such work have been duly authorized, either by the consent of the parties competent to give such consent, or by the award or certificate of the official referees, then, at any time between the hours of six in the morning and seven in the afternoon, (Sundays excepted), it shall be lawful for the building owner, or any other person acting in his behalf, accompanied by a constable or other officer of the peace, and they are hereby respectively empowered, to enter on the premises of the adjoining owner, so far as may be necessary for executing such work; and that if the outer door of such building be shut, and being thereunto required the person therein refuse to open the same, or if such building be empty and unoccupied, then it shall be lawful to break open such outer door; and if any fixtures, goods, furniture, or other thing obstruct the building of such intended party wall or party arch, or the pulling down any wall, partition, or other thing necessary to be pulled down and removed in order to the building such intended party wall or party arch, then to remove such fixtures, goods, furniture, and things to some other part of the same premises, or if there be no room on the premises sufficient for that purpose, to remove them to some other place of safe custody; and that from and after such entry, and at all usual times of working, it shall be lawful for the builder employed to erect such intended party wall or party arch, and for his servants and all others employed by him, to enter into and upon the premises, and abide therein the usual times of working, as well for the shoring up of the said building so broken into and entered upon, and for taking down and removing any party wall, partition, wainscot, or other things necessary to be taken down and removed for the purpose aforesaid, as to build

Opening doors and removal of goods, &c.

Continuance of entry.

Penalty for hindrance.

such intended party wall or party arch; and that if in any manner any such owner or other person hinder or obstruct any workman employed for any of the purposes aforesaid, or wilfully damage or injure the said works, then every such person so offending shall forfeit for every such offence a sum not exceeding ten pounds (*e*).

Stopping of openings in external walls abutting on other premises.

XXXVII. And now, for the purpose of further protecting the interests of adjoining owners, be it enacted, with regard to external walls adjoining the ground or building of another owner, so far as relates to the making of openings therein, that if, without the consent in writing of the owner of such ground or building, any opening be made in any such wall, then it shall be lawful for such owner and he is hereby entitled to require the owner of the premises in which such opening shall be made to stop up the same with brick or stone work, as the case may be, according to the form (No. 5) in the schedule of notices, or to the like effect; and that if within one month after such notice such stoppage be not effected, then it shall be lawful for such owner and he is hereby entitled, either by himself or his workmen, with tools, implements, and materials, to cause such openings so to be stopped, and he is also hereby entitled to be repaid the costs thereof; and with regard to such costs, so far as relates to the adjustment thereof, that if such owner refuse to make payment thereof, or if there be any dispute as to the amount thereof, then, on application for the purpose to the official referees, by either of the parties concerned, it shall be lawful for the person by whom they have been incurred and he is hereby entitled to refer the matter of such dispute to the official referees, and to have their determination thereon; and that it shall be the duty of such official referees to give to the applicant a certificate in relation thereto; and that if any party liable to pay any sum of money under such certificate fail to do so, then it shall be lawful for the party entitled to such costs to recover the same in the manner herein-after provided for the recovery of the costs, charges,

Stoppage thereof.

Costs of stopping up.

Certificate of official referees.

Recovery of costs.

(*e*) See sections 106, 107, and 103, 104, 105.

and expenses of executing any works in pursuance of this act. (*f*)

XXXVIII. And be it enacted, with regard to walls, so far as it relates to the building thereof on vacant ground at the line of junction of premises belonging to different owners or in different occupations, that one month before the owner of any piece of vacant ground, or ground not hitherto built upon, shall build any building adjoining to another piece of vacant ground, or ground not hitherto built upon, or build a fence wall for such piece of ground, it shall be his duty and he is hereby required to give to the owner or occupier of such adjoining vacant ground a notice, which must be in writing, and must set forth his desire to build a party wall or party fence wall, and describe the thicknesses and dimensions of such desired party wall or party fence wall, according to the form (No. 16) in the schedule of notices, or to the like effect; and that if within such period of one month such adjoining owner shall signify his consent in writing, then the same must be built partly on the ground of one of the said owners or occupiers, and partly on the ground of the other owner, and such last-mentioned part is to be paid for as is herein after directed by such other owner or occupier; but if he do not signify such consent, then it shall be the duty of the building owner to build an external wall for such building, and fence wall for such ground, entirely upon his own ground, except as to the footings of any such wall.

Building of party walls next vacant ground.

Consent of adjoining owner.

XXXIX. And be it enacted, with regard to any new party wall built on the line of junction of premises belonging to different owners, so far as relates to the providing of chimney breasts and other accommodation for the adjoining owner, that when the owner of any piece of vacant ground shall have obtained the consent of the adjoining owner to build a party wall on the line of junction of their respective premises, then, ten days at the least before beginning to build such party wall, it shall be the duty of the building owner to give the adjoining owner notice thereof, according to the form

Building of chimney breasts, &c., in new party wall for adjoining owner.

(*f*) See sections 49, 102. "Fees to Surveyors," schedule L., and section 77.

(No. 16) in the schedule of notices, or to the like effect; and that if in due time the adjoining owner shall give instructions in writing, or by a plan and elevations or other sufficient drawings, then it shall be the duty of the building owner to construct, if practicable, such and so many chimney jambs, breasts, and flues of chimneys in all such parts of such party wall as shall be by such instructions required, and to leave such recesses in every such wall as may be so required, but so that they be conformable with the directions of this act concerning party walls and chimneys; and that thereupon it shall be lawful for the building owner to claim and he is hereby entitled to recover from the adjoining owner all the expenses of constructing such chimney jambs, breasts, and flues of chimneys, and recesses, as provided by this act in that behalf (*g*).

Instructions by adjoining owner.

Reimbursement of expenses.

Ruinous Buildings.

XL. And whereas buildings within the limits of this act are often, either from litigated titles thereto, or from the obstinacy, neglect, or poverty of the owners thereof or of the parties interested therein, or from other causes, in so ruinous a condition that passengers are endangered thereby; now, for the purpose of making provision in that behalf, be it enacted, with regard to ruinous buildings or parts of buildings (*h*), so far as relates to repairing or pulling down the same, that upon receiving information of any building being in a ruinous and dangerous condition it shall be the duty of the surveyor and of the overseers for the time being of the parish or place in which the same shall be, and they are hereby respectively required, to apply forthwith to the official referees to authorize a survey to be made thereof; and that thereupon it shall be lawful for the official referees to direct the surveyor to make such survey; and that thereupon it shall be the duty of such surveyor to act in all respects as in the case of a survey of party wall (*i*), and that upon the receipt of the certificate of the surveyor it shall be

Repairing and rebuilding.

Application to official referees.

Survey.

Notice to Lord Mayor, &c., and to overseers.

(*g*) See sections 46 to 50, and 102. "Fees to Surveyors," schedule L., and section 77.

(*h*) Which will include party and other walls.

(*i*) See section 24.

Ruinous Buildings.

lawful for the official referees and they are hereby required to cause a copy thereof to be transmitted, if the premises be within the city of *London*, then to the Court of Lord Mayor and Aldermen, and if they be elsewhere, then to the overseers of the poor of the parish or place in which such premises shall be; and that thereupon it shall be the duty of such Mayor and Court of Aldermen, and overseers, to cause with all convenient speed any such ruinous building to be securely shored, or a proper and sufficient hoard (*k*) to be

Shoring and erection of hoards, and notice to parties.

(*k*) There has been an immemorial custom in the city of London to put up hoards for the safety of passengers. A person who carried on a business in the city complained of the Mayor and commonalty of London for erecting a hoard, and continuing it for an unreasonable time, by which means the footway remained in a state of obstruction, and the approach to the plaintiff's messuage and business was materially hindered. The Mayor pleaded an immemorial custom to set up a hoarding so as to obstruct or inclose any part of a public way during the erection or pulling down of any building within the city, provided the party so making the hoard had first obtained the license of the Lord Mayor. The plea then stated that such license had been obtained upon condition of first getting a license from the surveyor of pavements. And the plea then went on to say that the last mentioned license had been obtained. The plaintiff taking the custom by protestation, replied *de injuriâ absque residuo causæ*. The case was left to arbitration, and one of the grounds of objection to the award was, that the arbitrator had not expressed any opinion upon the validity of the custom. But the Court would not set aside the award, which on this issue was found for the defendants. And they discharged a rule which the plaintiff had obtained for entering a judgment in his favour generally, *non obstante veredicto*, on the ground of the invalidity of the custom. The Court held the custom good, and said that the Mayor was the fit judge of the time during which the hoarding should be continued. Consequently, as the plea of the custom was pleaded generally by the defendants as to the keeping and continuing of the hoarding, certain sums awarded by the arbitrator as damages for the maintenance for the hoarding beyond a certain period, and likewise for otherwise delaying and retarding the work, were disallowed by the Court. (*a*)

(*a*) 4 Man. & Gr. 714, 756, 764. Bradbee *v.* Mayor &c., of London.

Ruinous Buildings.

put up for the safety of all passengers, and to cause notice in writing to be given to the owner of such building to repair or pull down the same or any part thereof, as the case may require, within fourteen days then next ensuing; and that if within the said fourteen days the repair or demolition thereof be not begun, and be not completed as soon as the nature of the case will admit, then, on a declaration being made before the said Lord Mayor or a justice of the peace of such notice having been so given (which declaration the said Lord Mayor and justice are hereby respectively empowered and required to receive), it shall be lawful for the said Lord Mayor and Court of Aldermen, and they are hereby authorized and required, out of the cash in the Chamber of *London*, and also for every such overseer of the poor by and out of the money in his hands, and they are hereby severally authorized and required, with all convenient speed, to order and cause such building, or such part thereof so certified to be in a ruinous and dangerous condition as shall be necessary for the safety of the passengers, to be repaired or pulled down, or secured in such manner as shall from time to time be requisite: provided always, that if such Lord Mayor and Aldermen, or such overseers, appeal against such certificate, it shall be the duty of the official referees to proceed to survey, to certify, and to award in all respects as in the case of an appeal from the certificate of the surveyor with reference to party walls or intermixed buildings (*l*); and that if such official referees certify that the said premises are ruinous and dangerous, it shall be the duty of the said Lord Mayor

Repairs.

Appeal against survey.

Demolition.

(*l*) See section 24.

S. C., 5 Scott. N. R. 79. It was said by counsel *arguendo* in this case that Morley *v.* The Goldsmiths' Company (a case tried before Tindal, C. J., but not reported) did not apply, because there the jury had found that the hoard had not been continued for an unreasonable time, 4 Man. & Gr. 753. In the case of Bradbee *v.* Mayor of London, the license was for a hoard to contain in front sixty-four feet, projecting from the same four feet, and to continue four weeks, and the license from the surveyor was to erect and continue four hoards in manner and for the time above mentioned.

or the said overseers to repair or pull down such building as aforesaid.

Ruinous Buildings.

Disposal of materials to pay costs.

XLI. And be it enacted, with regard to any such ruinous building so pulled down, so far as relates to the disposal of the materials thereof, and to the application of the proceeds, that it shall be lawful for the said Lord Mayor and Court of Aldermen, or the said overseers, to sell and dispose of such of the materials as they shall judge necessary, and out of the monies arising from the sale thereof to reimburse to themselves, the surveyors and official referees, and every person by them respectively employed for the purposes aforesaid, all the charges of the survey and appeal, and of putting up every such hoard, and of repairing, pulling down, and securing such premises, and of making good the pavement, and of selling the said materials as aforesaid, or so much thereof as the monies arising by such sale will extend to; and that if there be any surplus after payment of all expenses, then, upon demand thereof made by such owner, it shall be the duty of the said Lord Mayor, or of the said overseers, to account for and pay such surplus of the monies arising by such sale to the owner of such building; or if there be any question as to the person entitled to such surplus, or as to the priority of title to such sum of such persons, so entitled, or as to the proportions to which such persons are so entitled, then it shall be lawful, either for the Lord Mayor or the overseers, or for any person claiming to be so entitled, to refer the matter to the determination of the official referees, and their decision shall be final; and that if no such demand be made then such surplus shall, as regards places within the city of *London* and the liberties thereof, be paid to the chamberlain of the city, and as regards all other places such surplus shall be paid to the overseers, and added to the monies raised as rates for the relief of the poor of the parish or place, and accounted for accordingly; provided nevertheless, that at any time within six years from the deposit of such surplus, it shall be lawful for any such owner, his executors or administrators, to claim and he and they are hereby entitled to recover such surplus; and the said Lord Mayor and aldermen of the city of *London*, as regards the

Payment of surplus on demand.

If no demand.

City of London or overseers to refund within six years.

Ruinous Buildings.

said city and liberties thereof, are hereby required to pay such surplus out of the cash in the chamber of *London;* and every overseer, as regards places not within the said city or the liberties thereof, is hereby required to pay such surplus out of any monies raised or to be raised by any rate for the relief of the poor.

If a deficiency, to be paid by the owner;

XLII. And be it enacted, with regard to such ruinous buildings, so far as relates to the expenses of any such survey and appeal, putting up such hoard, repairing, pulling down, and securing such buildings, and selling the materials, beyond the amount thereof which shall have been satisfied by the application thereto of the proceeds of the materials, that if the monies arising from such sale be insufficient to repay all such expenses, then from time to time such deficiency shall be paid by the owner of every such building, being the person entitled to the immediate possession thereof, if known;

or levied by warrant of distress;

and that if, on demand thereof, such owner fail to pay such deficiency, then it shall be lawful for the Lord Mayor for the time being, if such ruinous building in question be within the city of *London* or the liberties thereof, or if elsewhere, for two or more justices of the peace, to levy the amount thereof by warrant under their hands and seals, by distress and sale of the goods and chattels of such owner, if any such can be found;

or occupier to pay and deduct from rent;

and that if no such owner can be met with, or, being met with, shall not, on demand, pay the said deficiency, and no sufficient distress of the goods and chattels of such owner can be found, then it shall be lawful for the person who shall at any time thereafter occupy any such building, or the ground where the same stood, and he is hereby authorized and required, to pay and deduct the same out of the rent thereof;

or by distress on occupier.

and that if he neglect or refuse to pay such deficiency, then it shall be lawful for the said Lord Mayor, or two or more such justices of the peace, and they are hereby empowered and required, to cause the same to be levied by distress and sale of the goods and chattels of any occupier of the premises, together with the costs of every such distress and sale;

Payment of money to chamberlain or to the overseers.

and that if the premises be situate within the city of *London* and its liberties it shall be the duty of the person by whom the same shall be received, and he is hereby required, to pay the amount to the chamberlain, to be by him from time to time placed to the credit of the cash of the said city of *London*, and if the premises in respect of which such money shall be received or recovered be not situate within the said city of *London* and the liberties thereof, then to pay the amount received to the overseers of the poor for the time being of the parish or place where the premises shall be situate, to be by them placed to the account of the said parish, in aid of the poor rate of the parish or place. *Ruinous Buildings.*

XLIII. And be it enacted, with regard to ruinous chimneys, roofs, and projections, so far as relates to the repairing thereof, that if a chimney shaft, chimney pot or other thing thereon, or the eaves, or parapet or coping, or slates or tiles on the roof, or any projection from the front walls of any building, be in danger of falling, then it shall be the duty of such surveyor and he is hereby required to require the occupier of such building, or if there be no occupier then the owner thereof, to take down or secure the same within thirty-six hours after notice thereof shall have been given; and that if within the time specified such occupier, or some other person interested in such building, do not begin to take down or secure the same, and as soon as the nature of the case will admit, complete such taking down or securing of the same, then it shall be the duty of such surveyor to give information thereof to a justice of the peace, and thereupon it shall be the duty of such justice of the peace to proceed to cause such chimney shaft, chimney pot or other thing thereon, or the eaves, or parapet or coping, or slates or tiles on the roof, or projection from the front or side wall of such building as shall be considered by such surveyor in danger of falling, to be forthwith taken down or secured; and that if there be no occupier or known owner then it shall be lawful for such justice to direct that the reasonable expenses, to be certified by the official referees, be paid by the overseers of the parish or place in which such building shall be situated; and that if thereafter the owner of such building become known, or if the building become occupied, then it shall be lawful for the overseers of the poor and they are hereby entitled to recover

Repair of ruinous chimneys, &c.

Notice.

Repairs.

Certification of expenses.

Recovery from owner or occupier.

Ruinous Buildings.

the amount of such expenses from such owner or from such occupier as in the case of ruinous buildings herein-before provided for (*m*); and that if within the time limited the occupier, or some other person interested in such building, do not take down or secure the same, then for every day during which the same shall so remain unrepaired or not sufficiently secured, such occupier, or the owner if there be no occupier, shall forfeit and pay a sum not exceeding five pounds (*n*); and that such occupier or owner shall also pay the surveyor's fees, and all other costs, charges, and expenses attendant upon any such taking down or securing the building (*o*); and all such surveyor's fees, and other costs, charges, and expenses, may be recovered and levied in the same manner as such penalty; provided always, that if the occupier of such building be not bound by virtue of any lease or other instrument to repair, reinstate, or secure the premises, then such occupier is hereby entitled to retain out of the rent payable in respect of such premises all such penalties, costs, charges, and expenses attendant upon or arising out of the taking down or securing, or the repairing or rebuilding the same, as in the case of any other works the costs of which he is hereby required to pay in the first instance.

Penalty.

Fees and expenses.

Reimbursement of occupier.

XLIV. And be it enacted, with regard to adjoining buildings, so far as relates to the making good any damage arising from the falling down of parts thereof (except any such part of a party wall as shall belong to and be used conjointly by the owners or occupiers of the buildings parted thereby), that if at any time any injury or damage be caused to any part of an adjoining building, or to the internal decorations and furniture, goods, wares, and merchandize in such building, by the falling down from any other building of any chimney shaft, chimney pot, parapet, coping, or other thing, then it shall be the duty of the owner of the building from which such part shall fall, and he is hereby bound and required, to reimburse the expense to which the owner or

Injury by the fall of chimneys, &c.

Compensation.

(*m*) Section 40, *et seq.*

(*n*) A default. See sections 110, and 103, 104, 125.

(*o*) See schedule L., "Fees for Special Services."

occupier may be put in making good such injury or damage, in like manner as herein directed concerning the reimbursement of the expenses of ruinous party walls (*p*); and such costs shall be recoverable in the manner herein-after directed for the recovery of the costs and expenses of executing works in pursuance of this act (*q*).

Ruinous Buildings.

Court of mayor and aldermen.

XLV. And be it enacted, that all the powers and authorities by this act vested in the Mayor and Aldermen of the city of London may be lawfully exercised by the Court of Mayor and Aldermen of the said city to be holden in the outer chamber of the Guildhall of the said city according to the custom of the said city.

Expenses of Works.

Repayment of expenses of works in certain cases.

XLVI. And for the purpose of reimbursing any building owner for the expense of works incurred in respect of any party structure, be it enacted, with regard to the following works, so far as relates to the reimbursement by the adjoining owner of expenses incurred by the building owner in respect of any party structure built to part the buildings or premises belonging to other owners from the buildings or premises belonging to himself, that is to say,

First, with regard to any party wall hereafter built on the line of junction of any two buildings; and,

Second, with regard to any party wall hereafter built on the line of junction of any building and any vacant ground or of vacant premises belonging to different owners or occupiers; and,

Third, with regard to a ruinous and defective party wall pulled down and rebuilt, either with the consent of the adjoining owner, or in pursuance of the condemnation thereof according to this act (*r*), except a party wall condemned on account of the injury done thereto by any building owner, and the expenses of which and of other incidental works the official referees shall have awarded to be paid by such building owner by virtue of the provision in that behalf (*s*); and,

Fourth, with regard to one or more timber partitions be-

(*p*) Section 46, *infra*.
(*q*) Sections 47, 102.
(*r*) Section 40.
(*s*) Section 29.

Expenses of Works.

tween any two or more buildings, pulled down, and a party wall built in lieu thereof; and,

Fifth, with regard to a new party wall or party arch built in lieu of any party wall or party arch between intermixed properties pulled down, either with the consent of the adjoining owner, or in pursuance of the condemnation of such party wall or party arch; and,

Sixth, with regard to any party wall built on the site of a party fence or party fence wall, and used otherwise than as a party fence wall by the person who shall not have built the same; and,

Seventh, with regard to every other case of reimbursement in respect of any party structure.

Recovery of expense from adjoining owners.

That if the party structure be built in the manner, and of the materials, and of the thicknesses of such structure as required by this act in reference thereto, then it shall be lawful for the building owner at whose expense such work shall have been executed to claim and he is hereby entitled to be paid, and to recover from the person who is entitled to the immediate possession of the adjoining building or ground, or who is in the immediate occupation thereof (t), the following compensations: that is to say,

If a new party wall or party arch built on the line of junction by one owner be made use of, either wholly or partially, by the adjoining owner, then the sum of money proportionate to the value of so much of such party structure so made use of; and,

If chimney jambs, chimney breasts and flues, have been set up in any party wall, in pursuance of the instructions of the owner of any vacant ground adjoining the same, then a sum equal to the value thereof; and,

If an unsound party wall or other party structure be pulled down and rebuilt, then a sum of money equal to a proper proportion of the value of the new party structure, deduction being made for a due proportion of the old materials, and also a proportionate part of all expenses which shall be necessary for pulling down the old party

(t) Section 111, and see the note there.

structure in lieu of which such new party structure shall be built; and, *Expenses of Works.*

If a party wall be built in lieu of a timber partition or other party structure, and be made use of by the adjoining owner, then a sum of money proportionate to the value of so much of such new party wall as shall be so made use of, and also a proportionate part of all expenses which shall be necessary for pulling down the old timber partition or other party structure; and,

If a party wall or party arch already built or hereafter rebuilt be used by an adjoining owner, then a sum of money proportionate to the value of so much of such party structure as the adjoining owner shall use, deduction being made, where proper, for the value of old materials;

And in every case the whole of the reasonable expenses of the shoring up the adjoining building, and of removing any goods, furniture, or other things therein, and of pulling down any wainscot or partition thereof;

And also such surveyors' fees and any other fees payable in respect of any act performed by the official referees, and also such other costs (if any) as may have been awarded by the official referees as aforesaid in any of the cases hereby provided for:

Delay of payment. And until such expenses shall be so paid every person at whose expense such party structure shall have been built is hereby entitled to and shall be possessed of the sole property thereof, and of the ground whereon it stands, and the same shall be vested entirely in the person at whose expense such party structure shall have been built.

Recovery of costs of building. XLVII. And be it enacted, with regard to the costs of all the works which shall be executed under this act, incurred either by an owner or by an occupier (*u*), either on behalf of the owners of the same premises or on behalf of the owner of the adjoining premises, so far as relates to the recovery thereof, that within twenty-one days after the completion of the work it shall be the duty of the person by whom such

(*u*) By an occupier, see sections 24, 42, &c.

Expenses of Works.

expense shall have been incurred to deliver to the adjoining owner (v) of the building or premises in respect of which such expense shall have been incurred an account in writing of the expenses of the work, including all preliminary and incidental operations, and also if the work shall have been executed by the authority of the official referees, by virtue of the power hereby provided for supplying the want of consent of owners (x), then a copy of such account shall also be delivered to the official referees at their office; and that every such account must contain a true account,—

Account.

First, of the number of rods and parts of rods of brick-work, and of all digging, and of concrete, stone-work, and other requisite materials, and of the labour required in executing so much of the work as the owner of the adjoining building shall be liable to pay, and of the respective prices thereof; and,

Secondly, of any deduction which such adjoining owner shall be entitled to make therefrom on account of the old materials of so much of the wall or other structure pulled down which shall have belonged to him;

Date of account.

And also a true account of the expenses of all other preliminary and incidental operations; and that all such works must be estimated and valued in every such account at such rates and prices as shall from time to time be fixed by the official referees; and that if within ten days from the delivery of such account any party dissatisfied with the proportion of the amount thereof charged to him appeal to the official referees, then upon the receipt thereof, or if, in cases of want of due consent as aforesaid, such account be delivered to the official referees as aforesaid, it shall be the duty of the official referees to examine such account, and to certify whether they approve or disapprove of the items thereof, and whether the rates and prices are duly charged, and whether the proportion of the account charged to the party appealing be

Examination of accounts by official referees.

(v) This "adjoining owner" may be the occupier, unless such occupier be tenant from year to year, &c. See section 112, and section 2.

(x) Section 24.

duly charged, and also to appoint how and by whom the expenses of such examination are to be borne, and also to appoint the time or times at which the amount of such account and of such expenses payable by any party are to be paid; and that if they certify their disapproval, or that the charges are not duly made, or the amount fairly apportioned with regard to the party appealing, then, before any demand be made or any proceedings be taken thereon, the account must be amended, and again examined by the official referees, and certified as aforesaid; and that if the official referees certify their approval, then at the time or times appointed by the said official referees it shall be lawful for the person entitled to such costs and expenses to demand the amount thereof; and that if, within ten days after the delivering of such account to the party liable to pay the same, such party do not either appeal against such account or pay the same, or if, within ten days after the demand thereof, in conformity with the certificate of the official referees, the amount thereof together with the costs of the examination of the account as the official referees shall certify be not paid, then it shall be lawful for the person entitled thereto to recover the same, or so much thereof as shall be then due, by the summary proceeding hereby provided (*y*).

Expenses of Works.

Disapproval.

Approval and demand of payment.

Recovery of amount.

XLVIII. Provided always, and be it enacted, with regard to works executed under this act, so far as relates to the reimbursement to the occupier of any costs by him paid in respect thereof, that unless there be some covenant or agreement to the contrary between the parties, it shall be lawful for such occupier and he is hereby entitled to deduct from the rents due or becoming due from him to his lessor or landlord the amount of any such costs, charges, and expenses payable by his lessor or landlord, and the costs, charges, and expenses of any distress and sale made on him through the default of his lessor or landlord; and that the receipt for such payment shall be a sufficient discharge to any occupier for so much money as he shall have so paid, or which shall have been so levied on his goods and chattels in pursuance

Reimbursements of costs of works to occupiers.

Discharge and repayment.

(*y*) Section 102.

Expenses of Works.

of this act, and shall be allowed by such lessor or landlord in part or full payment (as the case may be) of the rent due to him by such occupier.

Recovery of expenses of buildings.

XLIX. And be it enacted, with regard to the costs and all other expenses of pulling down, securing, repairing, and rebuilding party structures, or other parts of buildings, according to the provisions of this act, so far as relates to the recovery thereof amongst the several owners of the premises, that when such costs and expenses shall have been ascertained and paid by the owner upon whom the payment thereof shall have first fallen (z), then, as to any building or tenement held under any lease or agreement for a lease, or other agreement for the occupation thereof, made before the coming into operation of this act, it shall be lawful for such owner and he is hereby entitled to recover the same from the persons now bound or liable by law or by any existing contract to maintain and repair such buildings in respect of which such costs and expenses shall have been incurred; but if any dispute or difference arise as to the persons so bound or liable, then every such dispute or difference shall be referred to the official referees; and that thereupon such official referees shall ascertain and determine the persons bound or liable to pay such costs and expenses, and also in what proportions such costs and expenses are to be paid by the parties liable to pay the same and their decision shall be final; and that as to any building or tenement to be held under any lease or agreement for a lease, or other agreement for the occupation thereof, made after the coming into operation of this act, except a lease renewable for ever on a fixed fine or other customary payment (a) all such costs and

Differences.

Determination by official referees.

Charges

(z) Who frequently will be the occupier. (See sections 2, 111.) The occupier cannot recover from himself, therefore this sentence applies where an owner, *quâ owner*, independently of an occupier, has paid the costs alluded to.

(a) But suppose the case of a lease for years, as for ninety-nine years, subject to a covenant for renewal at the end of twenty-one or other number of years: in this case, it would be doubtful whether the lessor ought not to bear this burthen, and yet being under a covenant to renew, he cannot well help himself, because

Expenses of Works.

expenses shall be charged upon the lessor granting such lease or making such agreement (*b*), and not upon any lessee or sub-lessee holding under any such lease or agreement, *subject, nevertheless, to any express covenant or agreement made between any such lessor and lessee in that behalf;* and in case of such excepted lease such costs and expenses shall be charged upon the lessee instead of the lessor, subject as aforesaid, to any express covenant or agreement in that behalf between any such lessee and his sub-lessee holding under such lessee upon other than a fixed fine or customary payment as aforesaid; and that in default of such costs and expenses being duly paid it shall be lawful for the party to whom the same shall be payable and he is hereby entitled to receive from the occupier thereof the rents and profits of such building or tenement, and for that purpose to give notice to such occupier to pay over to him such rents and profits; and that thereupon, if such occupier fail to pay such rent and profits accordingly, then it shall be lawful for the person to whom such costs and expenses shall be payable to recover the same from such occupier by the summary proceeding hereby provided, in such proportions and at such times as shall be appointed by the award of the said official referees in that behalf; and that after such notice shall be given, and before such costs and expenses shall be paid, it shall not be lawful for any person otherwise entitled to receive such rents and profits and he is hereby disabled from bringing any action, and from taking any proceeding at law or in equity to recover such rents and profits: provided always, that if on the hearing of the application for the warrant to levy such costs and expenses by distress, according to the provision of this act in that behalf, the occupier, not being an owner, shew that he is not bound to pay in respect of such building or tenement any rent or profit, or that the amount of the rent or profit payable by him is not

Receipt of rents.

Recovery of rents.

Priority of right.

Limitation of distress.

the tenant would, of course, object to a covenant binding him to the repair of party walls.

(*b*) That is to say, ultimately, because, except in the cases of tenants from year to year, &c., (see section 112,) the occupier is, if there be one, primarily liable.

Expenses of Works.

sufficient, then it shall not be lawful to issue such warrant, if there be no rent due or accruing, or, if there be rent due or accruing then to the extent only of the amount of such rent; and that if such costs and expenses or any part thereof remain unpaid, and if the same or any future occupier be or become liable to pay rent in respect of such building or tenement, then from time to time until the same be paid, it shall be lawful to levy the same by distress, according to the provisions of this act in that behalf, upon the same or any such future occupier

Continuance of distress until payment made.

Official referees to determine contributions.

Proportional contributions.

L. And be it enacted, with regard to such costs and expenses of works executed under this act, so far as relates to contribution thereto by persons bound or liable to make contribution, that for the purpose of enabling the party upon whom the payment of such costs and expenses shall fall, either in the first instance or subsequently, to obtain contribution from other persons, being owners according to the meaning of this act (*c*), in like degree, and so bound or liable to make contribution, it shall be lawful for every such first-mentioned person, whether he be freeholder, copyholder, leaseholder (*d*), mortgagee in possession, and whatever may be his interest, or the nature and extent of such his interest, and whether he hold in his own right or in right of others, and whatever may be the kinds and degrees of their respective interests, and he is hereby entitled to a contribution from every other person having as owner an interest in the premises, of whatever kind or degree, which contribution is to be computed according to the amount of his interest in proportion to that of other persons interested, so far as such persons may be known, or can be reached by process of any court of law or equity; and that it shall be lawful for any party so interested and he is hereby entitled to require the official referees to settle and determine the same by their award, and their decision shall be final; and that if the person upon whom the payment of such costs and expenses

Decision of official referees.

Recovery of excess paid by any contributor.

(*c*) See the word "owner," section 2.

(*d*) Not tenant from year to year, or tenant at will, section 2, tit. "owner."

shall have fallen have paid in respect of the interest of another or others, either unknown or who could not be reached by process of any court of law or equity, more than his own just proportion, then, on the production of such award, duly made, signed, and sealed, it shall be lawful for such person to have and exercise against other parties against whom such award shall be made, and he is hereby entitled to the like remedies to compel payment of money as are hereby given for compelling the first payment of such costs and charges of such expenses (*e*).

Expenses of Works.

(*e*) See Section 102. *Quære* whether "if" should not be "and."

Note to sections 46, 47, 48, 49, and 50.

These are clauses of no inconsiderable importance. They cause a very considerable change in the law of reimbursement with reference to party walls. They have been introduced for the purpose of surmounting many difficulties which existed under the late act, and it is to be hoped that when they come to be candidly considered, they will be found to be free from embarrassment. The intention of the Legislature would seem to have been that as soon as party structures are meddled with, the expense shall rest (if we may so speak) upon the premises, for which purpose the occupier must be applied to, or if there be no occupier, or if the occupier be merely tenant from year to year, &c., then the person whose right it would be, if he thought fit, to enter into possession of the premises, must be sought out. (Sections 46, 47, 111, and 112.) Having satisfied the demand, and not being himself under any legal obligation, as by contract or otherwise, to bear the burthen, the occupier looks out for the owner, who is usually his landlord, and from him the occupier is to reimburse himself, by deducting the full sum laid out from the rent due. (Section 48).

If, however, instead of payment being made by the occupier, an owner of the premises, such as one entitled to the improved rent, should pay the demand, it becomes his turn to seek contribution. And whilst he also may have recourse to section 50 for an award of contribution, where the case will admit of it, he may nevertheless charge the *occupier* with such expenses under leases or agreements *in esse* at the time of the passing of the statute, where the contract is that the occupier shall

Drainage of Houses.

Making of drains according to schedule (H.)

LI. And now, for the purpose of facilitating the improvement of the drainage of houses, be it enacted, with regard to the drains, cesspools, and privies to buildings hereafter

---

repair the premises generally. So he may charge the occupier who holds under future lettings, *provided there be an express contract to repair party structures or other buildings*, but otherwise he must bear his burden alone as far as the tenant is concerned, and must look elsewhere for contribution. (Section 49).

Hitherto, we have spoken of party walls and other such structures in this note, but we now request the reader's attention to the 47th and 48th sections which speak of works generally, and to the 49th which has the words "other parts of buildings," as well as "party structures" in its provisions. Now with respect to the delivering of the account of the work done, it must be given to the adjoining owner "by the party who has incurred the expenses," (section 47).

And these words, "adjoining owner," must mean the occupier, if there be such a person, and herewith agrees the interpretation clause (section 2), and likewise perhaps, (section 20).

Where the terms "owner" and "occupier" are used in an act, it seems desirable to place them in a light so clear as that they cannot easily be confounded or mistaken. Whereas by stating in the interpretation clause that the word "owner," may mean owner or occupier, there may, possibly, be room occasionally for doubt under some of the clauses, as to the word "owner" when it occurs.

The 48th section speaks also of works generally, and seems to confirm the notion thrown out with reference to the 47th section.

The 49th section is also rather general. It partially excludes occupiers, as paymasters, in the first instance, because an occupier, when he is justly charged, cannot recover against himself, although he be the "owner upon whom the payment has first fallen," but it takes in the case of an occupier where the landlord and not the occupier is responsible. The section is devoted to the relation of landlord and tenant under existing or future contracts.

It follows, on the whole, that when the occupier (the person liable to pay at once,) makes his payment, he looks (unless bound himself by contract to the repair,) to his landlord and others for contribution; when the landlord pays, he looks, in his turn, to his tenant and to other parties interested in the premises for contribution likewise.

built, so far as relates to the making thereof, that from the passing of this act all the conditions, regulations, and directions contained in the schedule (H.) to this act annexed shall be duly observed and performed; and that if any person offend in this respect thereof he shall be liable to all the penalties and forfeitures by this act imposed in respect of any buildings either built contrary thereto (*f*), or without due notice to the surveyor appointed in pursuance of this act to inspect such buildings (*g*): Provided always, with regard to such drains, so far as relates to the communication thereof with the sewers under the jurisdiction of the commissioners of sewers, that unless the regulations of such commissioners now or hereafter in force be repugnant to the directions contained in such schedule, and to the extent to which such regulations are not so repugnant, it shall be the duty of every person, and he is hereby required to make such drains to conform to such regulations; and that with regard to such drains, except so far as is hereby otherwise provided, all the rights, powers, jurisdiction, and authority vested in any such commissioners shall be as valid and effectual as if this act had not been passed.

Drainage of Houses.

Penalties.

Communications with sewers.

Saving powers, &c., of commissioners of sewers.

LII. And now, for the purpose of making provision concerning streets and other ways of the Metropolis, be it enacted, with regard to such streets and other ways hereafter formed, so far as relates to securing a sufficient width thereof, that from the passing of this act all the conditions, regulations, and directions contained in the schedule (I.) to this act annexed, shall be duly observed and performed; and that if any person offend in respect thereof, he shall be liable to all the penalties and forfeitures by this act imposed in respect of any buildings, either built contrary thereto (*h*), or without due notice to the surveyor appointed in pursuance of this act to inspect such buildings (*i*).

Streets and Alleys.

Width thereof.

Penalties.

LIII. And now, for the purpose of discouraging and prohibiting the use of buildings unfit for dwellings, be it enacted, with regard to every building of the first or dwelling-house

Buildings, Use thereof.

(*f*) Section 18. (*g*) Section 13.
(*h*) Section 18. (*i*) Section 13.

Occupation of cellars or rooms unfit for dwellings.

class, whether already or hereafter built, so far as relates to the occupation thereof, or to the occupation of any underground room or cellar thereof, that from and after the first day of July one thousand eight hundred and forty-six, it shall not be lawful to let separately to hire as dwelling any such room or cellar not constructed according to the rules specified in the schedule (K) to this act annexed, nor to occupy or suffer it to be occupied as such, nor to let, hire, occupy, or suffer to be occupied any such room or cellar built underground for any purpose (except for a wareroom or storeroom); and that if any person wilfully let or suffer to be occupied in manner aforesaid any underground cellar or room, contrary to the provisions of this act, then, on conviction thereof before two justices of the peace, such person shall be liable to forfeit for every day during which such cellar or room shall be so occupied a sum not exceeding twenty shillings (*k*); and one-half of such penalty shall go to the person who shall sue for the same, and the other half to the poor of the parish in which such unlawfully occupied cellar or room shall be situate; and that on or before the first day of January one thousand eight hundred and forty-five, it shall be the duty of the overseers of the poor, and they are hereby required to report to the official referees the number and situation of the dwellings within their respective parishes of which any underground room or cellar shall be so occupied, and that thereupon it shall be the duty of the official referees, and they are hereby empowered to direct such notice to be given to the owners and occupiers of such dwellings as shall appear to such official referees to be best calculated to give to such owners or occupiers full knowledge of the existence, nature, and consequences of this enactment; and that it shall be the duty of the district surveyors, and they are hereby required to give full effect to the directions of such official referees in this behalf.

Penalty.

Report by overseers of poor as to number and situation of dwellings.

Notice thereon by official referees to owners and occupiers.

District surveyors to observe directions of official referees.

Buildings near dangerous businesses as to fire.

LIV. And now, for the purpose of making provision concerning businesses dangerous in respect of fire or explosion,

(*k*) See sections 106, 107, and 103, 104, 105.

be it enacted, with regard to the following businesses, (that is to say,) the manufacture of gunpowder or of detonating powder, or of matches ignitable by friction or otherwise, or other substances liable to sudden explosion, inflammation, or ignition, or of vitriol, or of turpentine, or of naptha, or of varnish, or of fireworks, or painted table covers, and any other manufacture dangerous on account of the liability of the materials or substances employed therein to cause sudden fire or explosion, so far as relates to the erection of buildings in the neigbourhood of the place where any such business is carried on, and so far as relates to the carrying on of any such business in the neigbourhood of public ways or buildings, that it shall not be lawful hereafter to erect any building of any class nearer than fifty feet from any building which shall be in use for any such dangerous business; but if a building already existing within fifty feet from any such building be hereafter pulled down, burnt, or destroyed by tempest, such building may be rebuilt; and that it shall not be lawful for any person to establish or newly carry on any such business, either in any building or vault, or in the open air, at a less distance than forty feet from any public way, or than fifty feet from any other building, or any vacant ground belonging to any other person than his landlord; and that if any such business be now carried on in any situation within such distances, then from the expiration of the period of twenty years next after the passing of this act it shall not be lawful to continue to carry on such business in such situations; and that if any person erect any building in the neighbourhood of any such business contrary to this act, then, on conviction thereof before two justices, he shall forfeit a sum not exceeding fifty pounds for every day during which such building shall so remain near to such dangerous business; or if any person establish anew any such business, or carry on any such business contrary to this act, then, on conviction thereof before two justices, such person shall be liable to forfeit for every day during which such business shall be so carried on a sum not exceeding fifty pounds, as the said justices shall determine, and that it shall be lawful for the justices also to award to the prosecutor such costs as

Buildings, Use thereof.

Distance from buildings.

New businesses.

Prohibition after twenty years.

Fifty pounds penalty, and costs.

Costs. shall be deemed reasonable; and that if the offender either fail or refuse to pay such penalty and costs immediately after such conviction, then they may be levied by distress of the goods and chattels of the person convicted; or if there be such distress, then such person shall be committed to the common gaol or house of correction for any time not exceeding six months, at the discretion of such justices, and that by warrant under the hands and seals of two or more justices of the peace (*l*).

Distress; or imprisonment.

Buildings near noxious businesses as regards health.

LV. And now, for the purpose of making provision concerning businesses offensive or noxious, be it enacted, with regard to the following businesses, that is to say,

Blood-boiler,	Soap-boiler,
Bone-boiler,	Tallow-melter,
Fellmonger,	Tripe-boiler,

Slaughterer of cattle, sheep, or horses,

and any other like business offensive or noxious, so far as relates to the erection of buildings in the neighbourhood of any such business, and so far as relates to the carrying on of any such business in the neighbourhood of any public way, or of other buildings of the first or dwelling-house class, that it shall not be lawful hereafter to erect any buildings of the first or dwelling-house class nearer to than fifty feet from any building which shall be in use for any such offensive or noxious business; but if a building already existing within fifty feet be hereafter burnt, pulled down, or destroyed by tempest, such building may be rebuilt; and that it shall not be lawful for any person to establish or newly carry on any such business, either in any building or vault or in the open air, at a less distance than forty feet from any public way, or than fifty feet from any other such buildings of the first or dwelling-house class; and that if any such business be now carried on in any situation within such distances, then, from the expiration of the period of thirty years next after the

Distance from buildings.

New businesses.

Prohibition after thirty years.

(*l*) This procedure being special, does not come within section 103. But an appeal lies under the 105th section, and the 106th fixes six months as the limit for proceeding to recover the penalty.

passing of this act, it shall cease to be lawful to continue to carry on such business in such situation, save as is hereinafter provided; and that if any person erect any building in the neighbourhood of any such business contrary to this act, then, on conviction thereof before two justices, he shall forfeit a sum not exceeding fifty pounds for every day during which such building shall remain near to such offensive or noxious business; or if any person establish anew any such business, or carry on any such business contrary to this act, then, on conviction thereof before two justices, such person is hereby made liable to forfeit for every day during which such business shall be carried on, a sum not exceeding fifty pounds, as the said justices shall determine, and that it shall be lawful for the justices also to award to the prosecutor such costs as shall be deemed reasonable; and that if the offender either fail or refuse to pay such penalty and costs immediately after such conviction, then they may be levied by distress of the goods and chattels of the person convicted; or if there be no such distress, then such person shall be committed to the common gaol or house of correction for any time not exceeding six months, at the discretion of such justices, and that by warrant under the hands and seals of two or more justices of the peace (*m*).

Buildings, Use thereof.

Fifty pounds penalty, and costs.

Distress;

or imprisonment.

LVI. Provided always, and be it enacted, with regard to any such offensive or noxious business, whether such business be now carried on at a less distance than forty feet from any public way, or than fifty feet from any other building, or be hereafter carried on at a greater distance, yet so as to cause danger or annoyance, so far as relates to the mitigation of any penalty or punishment for unlawfully carrying on thereof, that every such penalty hereinbefore imposed shall be enforceable only at a special sessions of the peace summoned for that purpose, or on an appeal as hereinafter provided (*n*), or on a trial as hereinafter provided (*o*), and that, notwithstanding

The penalty hereinbefore imposed to be enforceable only at a special sessions.

(*m*) See the last note to section 54, which is applicable to this section also.

(*n*) Section 57.

(*o*) Section 58.

Use of means to mitigate noxiousness of businesses.

the said term of thirty years shall have expired, if any party charged with carrying on such business show that in carrying on such business all the means then known to be available for mitigating the effect of such business in any such respect have been adopted, then it shall be lawful for such justices to receive evidence thereof, and according to such evidence to mitigate the penalty as to them shall seem fit: provided further, with regard to such offensive or noxious business, so far as relates to the adoption of means to mitigate the injurious effects thereof, that, notwithstanding the said period of thirty years shall have expired, if it shall appear to the justices, whether at petty sessions as aforesaid, or on appeal, or on trial by jury, as hereinafter provided, that the party carrying on any such business, shall have made due endeavours to carry on the same with a view to mitigate, so far as possible, the effects of such business, then, although he hath not adopted all or the best means available for the purpose, yet it shall be lawful for such justices assembled and they are hereby empowered to suspend the execution of their order or determination, upon condition that within a reasonable time, to be named, the party convicted do adopt such other or better means as to the said justices shall seem fit, or before passing final sentence, and without consulting the prosecutor, to make such order touching the carrying on of such business as shall be by the said Court thought expedient for preventing the nuisance in future: provided always, that if the matter in respect of which such penalty shall be incurred come before any superior Court (*n*), it shall be lawful for such Court to exercise such power of mitigating such penalty, or of suspending the execution of any judgment, order, or determination in the matter, or to make such order touching the carrying on of such business, as to the Court shall seem fit in the case.

Adoption of means to mitigate after conviction.

Mitigation of penalty by superior Courts.

Conviction and appeal as to certain trades not specified:

LVII. And be it enacted, with regard to any business offensive, noxious, or dangerous, and with regard to any building erected or continued within any such distance as aforesaid from any such business dangerous, noxious, or offensive, so far as relates to a conviction in respect of any

(*n*) By certiorari, indictment, or otherwise.

such business, and to an appeal from such conviction, that if any person be dissatisfied with the decision of such justices, and if, within four days after such decision, notice be given to the party appealed against, by or on behalf of such person, of his intention to appeal, and if he enter into a recognizance, with two sufficient securities, conditioned to try such appeal, and to abide the order of the Court, and pay to the party appealed against such costs (if any) as shall be awarded against him, then it shall be lawful for such party so dissatisfied to appeal against such conviction to the justices of the peace at their general quarter sessions of the peace to be holden within four months after such conviction for the place in which such premises shall be situate; and that if the premises shall be situate within the city of *London* and liberties thereof, then the appeal must be to the quarter sessions thereof, or if the premises be situate in the counties of *Middlesex*, *Kent*, or *Surrey*, or in the city and liberties of *Westminster*, or in the liberties of her Majesty's Tower of *London*, then to the quarter sessions thereof respectively, as the case shall be; and that if within the above-mentioned period such appellant shall have entered into such recognizance as herein required, and if within one month thereafter he give notice of the grounds of such appeal, then it shall be lawful for such justices and they are hereby empowered to proceed to hear and examine on oath into the causes and matters of such appeal (which oath they are hereby empowered to administer), and to determine the same, and to award such costs to be paid by the said parties as they think proper; and the order, judgment, and determination of the said justices in their respective sessions shall be binding and conclusive upon all parties (*o*).

Buildings, Use thereof.

Recognizances.

Sessions.

Proceedings.

LVIII. Provided always, and be it enacted, that if before conviction by two such justices the party complained against desire to have the matter tried by a jury, and enter into a recognizance to try such matter without delay, and to pay all costs of trial if a verdict be found against him, then such matter may be tried at the next practicable Court of quarter

Trial by jury at quarter sessions.

(*o*) But the order of justices is removable by certiorari under section 104, if it comes within the exception there mentioned.

Summoning of a jury.

sessions, or whensoever the Court shall appoint; and that thereupon, or on the application of such party, it shall be lawful for the said Court of quarter sessions and they are hereby authorized and required to issue their warrant or precept to the sheriff or other proper officer (as the case may be), requiring him to return a competent number of persons qualified to serve on juries according to the provisions of an act made in the sixth year of the reign of his late Majesty King George the Fourth, "for consolidating and amending the laws relative to jurors and juries;" and that it shall be lawful for the said Court of quarter sessions and they are hereby authorized and empowered, by precept, from time to time as occasion may require, to call before them respectively every person who shall be thought proper or necessary to be examined as a witness before them on oath concerning the premises; and that if the said Court think fit it shall be lawful for them and they are hereby empowered to authorize the said jury to view the place in question in such manner as they shall direct, and to command the attendance of such jury, and of all such witnesses and parties as shall be necessary or proper, until such affairs for which they are summoned shall be concluded; and that the said jury shall inquire and try, and determine by their verdict, whether the business in question be offensive or noxious, and whether the party in question have done any act whereby the penalty hereby imposed in respect thereof has been incurred; and that, subject to the power hereinbefore conferred of mitigating such penalty, or suspending their judgment, order, or determination thereon, or making such order touching the carrying on of the business aforesaid, the said Court of quarter sessions shall give judgment according to such verdict, and shall award the penalty (if any) incurred by the defendant, and shall and may (if they see fit) award to either of the parties such costs as they may deem reasonable; which verdict, and the judgment, award, order, or determination thereupon, shall be binding and conclusive (*p*).

6 Geo. 4, c. 50.

Witnesses.

View of the premises.

Verdict of jury.

Judgment according to verdict;

and judgment to be binding.

Appeals to quarter sessions for Surrey and Kent:

LIX. And be it enacted, with regard to any appeal in

(*p*) All these proceedings seem to be removable by certiorari under section 104, if they fall within the exception there laid down.

Buildings, Use thereof.

respect of a conviction for carrying on any such dangerous, offensive, or noxious business, so far as relates to the place where such appeal is to be heard, that if the appeal be to the general quarter sessions of the peace for the county of *Surrey* or the county of *Kent*, then the jury (if any) to be empannelled in pursuance of this act, and all parties required to attend the quarter sessions for the said counties pursuant to such application, shall be empannelled and required to attend at some general or special adjournment of the said quarter sessions to be held within six weeks next after the original sessions; and that if the matter relate to the county of *Surrey*, then such adjournment shall be to some convenient place in the borough of *Southwark* in the said county; and that if the matter relate to the county of *Kent*, then such adjournment shall be to some convenient place in the borough of *Greenwich* in the said county; and such times and places shall be appointed by the justices of the said counties respectively assembled at such original sessions; and that from time to time every further meeting of the said sessions, for any thing to be done upon such application, shall be appointed at or within the space of three weeks from the last meeting; and that from time to time it shall be lawful for the justices of the peace for the said counties of *Surrey* and *Kent* respectively, and they respectively are hereby empowered and required, to make such adjournment and hold such sessions as there shall be occasion.

To sessions at Southwark: To sessions at Greenwich. Further meetings. Adjournments.

LX. Provided always, and be it declared, with regard to any business which is contrary to any existing act of Parliament, or otherwise contrary to law, so far as relates to the operation of this act in that behalf, that, notwithstanding any thing in this act contained, this act shall not be deemed to authorize any person to carry on any such business either within such limits or otherwise, or any business which it is unlawful to carry on within any limits or in any manner contrary to any public, local, or private act of Parliament, or otherwise contrary to law; nor to affect, abridge, or restrain the right, the duty, or the power of any person, whether private person or public officer, to prosecute, either civilly or criminally, any person who shall carry on within the

Common law and statutory. Remedies not affected.

Buildings, Use thereof.

limits of this act any offensive, noxious, or dangerous business.

Regulation or removal of trades deemed nuisances by purchase:

LXI. And further, for the regulation or removal of any offensive, noxious, or dangerous business now carried on (*q*), be it enacted, with regard to any such business, so far as relates to the purchase thereof, or of the premises wherein it shall be carried on, that if two-thirds in number of the inhabitant householders of any parish in which such business

Memorial to Queen in council.

shall be carried on present a memorial to her Majesty in council, stating the existence of such offensive, noxious, or dangerous business in such parish or neighbourhood thereof, and praying the removal of such business therefrom, and thereby engaging to provide compensation to the persons carrying on the same, either at the expense of the memorialists, or by means of a rate to be levied on the inhabitants of the said parish, or such part thereof as may be affected by such business, then it shall be lawful for her Majesty to refer the matter to the lords of the committee of privy council for trade to consider the character of such business, whether

Order for removal.

it be offensive, noxious, or dangerous; and if it appear to be so, and that there are no means of rendering it otherwise by the adoption of methods available, without unreasonable sacrifice on the part of the person by whom it is carried on, then it shall be lawful for her Majesty, by order in council, to direct that the removal of such business may be purchased, either at the expense of the memorialists or by means of a

Compensation.

rate as aforesaid, as to her Majesty shall seem fit, and also to direct the sheriff of the county or other proper person in the parish or liberty in which such business is carried on to summon a jury, according to the provisions of an act made and passed in the fourth year of the reign of her present

4 & 5 Vict. c. 12.

Majesty, intituled *an act to enable her Majesty's commissioners of Woods to make a new street from* Coventry Street *to* Long Acre, *and for other improvements in the Metropolis*, to determine what compensation shall be paid to the party

(*q*) This clause is available till the respective periods of twenty years, and thirty years mentioned respectively in sections 54 and 55 have elapsed.

carrying on such business for the removal thereof, and to the owner and occupier of the premises for the restriction of the use of his buildings for such purpose; and that if within three months after the verdict of such jury shall be given, and judgment thereon, the inhabitants of such parish or neighbourhood pay or tender such compensation, then within three months from the paymont or tender of such compensation it shall cease to be lawful for the party carrying on such business to continue the same, and for any owner or occupier thereof either to carry on or to permit to be carried on such business in the same or any part of the same premises.

Buildings. Use thereof.

Unlawful to continue such trades after purchase.

LXII. And be it enacted, with regard to the funds for defraying such compensation, so far as relates to the raising thereof, that if her Majesty shall by such order direct the compensation to be paid by means of a rate, then it shall be lawful for the overseers of the parish to raise such sum as shall be necessary, either as a separate rate in the nature of poor's rate, or as part of the poor's rate, on the inhabitants at large of such parish; or if in pursuance of the memorial of the inhabitants of such part of the said parish as shall be affected by the said business it be appointed by such order in council that such last-mentioned inhabitants do defray such compensation, then it shall be lawful for the said overseers to raise such sum as shall be necessary for that purpose: and that if such rate be so levied either on the inhabitants at large of such parish, or on the inhabitants of such part thereof as aforesaid, then such rate may be levied and recovered as poor's rates are leviable and recoverable.

Funds for defraying compensation.

Levy of rate.

LXIII. Provided always, and be it enacted, with regard to public gas works and other works heretofore established within the limits of this act, so far as relates to the operation of the provisions of this act in reference to businesses dangerous in respect of fire or explosion, or offensive or noxious, that such provisions shall not be deemed to apply to any such public gas works; and that if by any act of Parliament now in force relating to gas companies to which such works belong any extension of such works, or any additional works, or any other works, be authorized to be erected or substi-

Exemption of public gas works.

Extension or substitution of works.

Buildings, Use thereof. tuted, then such provisions shall not be deemed to apply to any such extension, addition, or substitution within the limits of the district now lighted from such first-mentioned works; and that such provisions shall not be deemed to apply to any premises entered or used for the purpose of distillation or the rectification of spirits under the survey of the commissioners of excise or their officers.

Distilleries.

Surveyors, their District and Duties.

LXIV. And now, for the purpose of dividing the district to which this act is to apply into several smaller districts, for the convenient execution therein of this act, and for appointing competent surveyors for superintending the same in each such district, and for regulating the duties of their office, be it enacted, with regard to such districts, so far as relates to the appointment and alteration thereof, that at any time after this act shall come into operation, and from time to time, it shall be lawful for the Lord Mayor and aldermen of the city of *London*, with reference to the city of *London* and the liberties thereof, and for the justices of the peace for the county of *Middlesex*, the county of *Surrey*, the county of *Kent*, the city and liberties of *Westminster*, and the liberty of her Majesty's *Tower of London*, in the general quarter sessions respectively, or any adjournment thereof, with reference to their respective counties, city, and liberties, and they respectively are hereby empowered, but subject, nevertheless, to the consent of one of her Majesty's principal secretaries of state, to appoint the districts to which the respective places within their jurisdiction shall belong for the purposes of this act, and to unite, enlarge, and alter such districts for the more convenient distribution of the business.

Appointment of districts.

Appointment of surveyors.

LXV. And be it enacted, with regard to the surveyors to be assigned to such districts for the purposes of this act, so far as relates to their appointment, that at any time after this act shall come into operation, and from time to time, it shall be lawful for the said Lord Mayor and aldermen of the city of *London*, with reference to the city of *London* and the liberties thereof, and for the said justices of the peace in their general quarter sessions respectively, or any adjournment thereof, with reference to their respective counties, and they are hereby required, but subject, nevertheless, to the consent of one of her Majesty's principal secretaries of state, to nominate and appoint as surveyors such and so many discreet persons, of the full age of thirty years, and properly educated and skilled in the art and practice of building, as they the said Lord Mayor and aldermen and the said justices shall think fit.

District Surveyors.

LXVI. And be it enacted, with regard to such surveyors, to be hereafter appointed under this act, except present district surveyors appointed to new districts, so far as relates to the ensuring the possession of due scientific and practical qualifications, that it shall be lawful for the commissioners of works and buildings and they are hereby empowered to appoint three or more architects, surveyors, or builders to examine, together with the said official referees, any persons who may present themselves to be examined for the purpose of obtaining a certificate of qualification, with the view of becoming candidates for the office of surveyors of Metropolitan buildings of any district within the limits of this act; and that for that purpose it shall be lawful for such examiners from time to time to appoint such times as to them may seem fit, and from time to time to prescribe such course of examination as to them may seem fit, and to make any other rules for the regulation of such examination, and the granting of certificates in respect thereof, subject, nevertheless, to the approval of the commissioners of works and buildings; and that when such rules shall have been registered by the registrar of Metropolitan buildings they shall continue to be in force until they shall be amended, altered, or rescinded by other rules to be made by such examiners and so registered as aforesaid; and that unless, one week before the election of a surveyor for any district created by this act, or for any district in respect of which the office of surveyor may become vacant, there be produced by or on the part of any person being candidate for the said office, a certificate of such examiners, certifying that he has been examined, and that he was thereby found to be duly qualified for such office, to the town clerk of the city of *London*, or to the clerk of the peace for the county, city, or liberty, it shall not be lawful for any

Practical qualifications of surveyors.

Examiners.

Examiners to prescribe rules.

Production of certificates of examination.

District Surveyors.

justices by this act empowered to appoint surveyors to appoint such person to be such surveyor, and that if such person be so appointed his election to such office shall be void.

Tenure of office.

LXVII. And be it enacted, with regard to such surveyors, so far as relates to the tenure of their office, that it shall be lawful for every such surveyor and he is hereby entitled to hold such his office of surveyor during the pleasure only of the said Lord Mayor and aldermen and of the said justices respectively.

Functions generally.

LXVIII. And be it enacted, with regard to such surveyors, so far as relates to their functions generally, that it shall be the duty of every such surveyor, and he is hereby required,—

To see that all the rules and directions of the act are well and truly observed in and throughout his district; and for that purpose,

To proceed from time to time, in due course, upon the receipt of any notice (*r*), or if from ignorance or neglect, or from any other circumstance, notice of any work intended to be done have not been given, then upon such work being observed by or being made known to him, to inspect the works intended to be done, or which shall have been commenced, and to cause all the rules and directions of this act in respect thereof to be strictly observed; and also

To attend and perform every thing required of him by this act, whether with or without notice; and also

To inspect ruinous buildings and projections in danger, at all times when needful, and to take all necessary measures thereupon (*s*); and also

To survey all buildings built, rebuilt, enlarged, or altered by or under the superintendence of a district surveyor within any other district to which he shall be appointed by the official referees for that purpose; and also

To cause a book for registering all notices, informations, and complaints to be at all times kept at his office, and

(*r*) See section 13. (*s*) See section 40.

to enter in such book every notice, information, or complaint which shall be delivered or made to him, and any proceeding thereon by him taken.

District Surveyors.

Disqualifications.

LXIX. And be it enacted, with regard to such surveyors, so far as relates to their disqualifications, that during the time that any such person shall act as a justice of the peace for the county in which his district shall be situated it shall not be lawful for him and he is hereby disqualified from holding the office of a surveyor or of deputy or an assistant surveyor for any district under this act.

Continuance of present surveyors. 14 Geo. 3, c. 78.

LXX. And be it enacted, with regard to the surveyors who at the time of this act coming into operation shall have been appointed under the act of the fourteenth year of the reign of king George the Third, mentioned in the schedule (A.) hereto annexed, so far as relates to their continuance in office, and the application of this act to them, that until they shall be removed it shall be lawful for them and they are hereby entitled to continue to be the surveyors for the purposes of this act, and for the districts assigned to them at the time this act shall come into operation, but subject to such alteration of such districts as may be made by virtue of any power in that behalf, and to act in all respects as if they had been appointed under this act; and that every provision in this act applicable to district surveyors, so far as relates to the exercise of the office of surveyor, and to their remuneration in that behalf, shall apply to them.

Subject to this act.

Declaration of official fidelity.

LXXI. And be it enacted, with regard to every surveyor hereafter appointed, so far as relates to making a declaration of official fidelity, that before any such surveyor shall act in pursuance of this act it shall be his duty and he is hereby required to make a declaration of official fidelity, which must be administered by the said Lord Mayor and aldermen in their Court of aldermen, or by the said justices of the peace in their respective general quarter sessions, and must be in the form or to the effect following; that is to say,

"I A. B., being one of the surveyors appointed in pursuance " of an act made and passed in the eighth year of the reign " of her Majesty Queen Victoria, intituled *An Act for regu-" lating the Construction and the Use of Buildings in the*

District Surveyors.

"*Metropolis and its Neighbourhood*, and commonly called "the Metropolitan Buildings' Act, do solemnly declare, that "I will diligently, faithfully, and impartially perform the "duties of my office, and to the utmost of my power, skill, "and ability endeavour to cause the several provisions of "the said act to be strictly observed, and that without favour "or affection, prejudice or malice, to any person whomso- "ever."

Penalty for acting before declaration made.

And that if before making such declaration any such surveyor act in pursuance of this act, then on conviction thereof he shall be liable to pay, for every day during which he shall so act before making such declaration, the sum of five pounds (*t*).

Regulation of duties:

Offices.

LXXII. And be it enacted, with regard to the surveyors, so far as relates to the regulation of their official duties, that it shall be the duty of every surveyor for the city of *London* and the liberties thereof, and he is hereby required to have an office at his own expense in such public situation as shall be approved by the Lord Mayor and aldermen; and that it shall be the duty of every other surveyor and he is hereby required to have an office at his own expense in some central part of the district to which he shall be appointed, as shall be approved by the justices of the peace in quarter sessions within whose jurisdiction he shall act; and that it shall be the duty of every such surveyor and he is hereby required, by himself or by some other person in his behalf, to attend at his office every day (Sundays, Christmas day, and Good Friday excepted) from ten of the clock in the morning till four of the clock in the afternoon; and that immediately upon his appointment, and from time to time upon every change of his residence or of his place of business, or oftener if required, it shall be the duty of every surveyor and he is hereby required to make a return to the registrar of Metropolitan buildings, and to the overseers of the poor of every parish or place within his district, of his name and place of abode, and the place where such office shall be.

Attendance.

Return of name and residence.

Surveyor pro tempore.

LXXIII. And be it enacted, with regard to such surveyor

(*t*) See sections 110, and 103, 104, 105.

District Surveyors.

so far as relates to the appointment of a deputy or substitute in certain cases, that if any surveyor shall be prevented by illness or any other unavoidable circumstances from attending to the duties of his office, then forthwith it shall be his duty and he is hereby required, but subject to the previous consent and approval of the official referees, to appoint some other surveyor duly qualified as aforesaid as his deputy, to perform all such his duties for so long a time as he shall be so prevented from executing them; and that thereupon, during such time as aforesaid, it shall be the duty of such deputy surveyor and he is hereby required to perform all the duties of such surveyor, and that in all respects as if he were the surveyor appointed or confirmed under this act; and that it shall be lawful for such deputy surveyor and he is hereby entitled to receive the fees (*u*) payable in respect of the services so performed by him in such district.

Duty of deputy.

Fees.

LXXIV. And be it enacted, with regard to such surveyors, so far as relates to the filling up of vacancies, that if any vacancy shall happen through the death or removal of any surveyor, then, within one month thereafter, it shall be the duty of the Lord Mayor and aldermen, or of the justices of the peace in general quarter sessions or any adjournment thereof as aforesaid, and they are hereby respectively required, to appoint a successor as herein directed; and that in the meantime it shall be lawful for the official referees to direct the surveyor of any one or more of the other districts to perform the duties of surveyor for the vacant district, or if no district surveyor can be spared from his own district to appoint some other competent person duly qualified as aforesaid for that purpose; and that every such surveyor is hereby entitled to receive the fees (*v*) payable in respect of the services so performed by him in such vacant district.

Vacancies.

Occasional services.

Fees for services.

LXXV. And be it enacted, with regard to the surveyors, so far as relates to the regulation of their business, that if it shall appear to the official referees that the district appointed for any surveyor is too extensive for the prompt discharge of

Regulation of business.

(*u*) See schedule L.

(*v*) See schedule L.

District Surveyors.

his functions, then it shall be their duty to represent such their opinion to the Lord Mayor and aldermen of the city of *London*, or to the justices of the peace with whom the appointment of a surveyor for that district may rest, and for that purpose to transmit with their letter of representation a transcript of their "register of notices," with the results; and that if at any time it appear to such official referees that on account of the pressure of business in any district, or on any other account, the surveyor of that district cannot discharge his duties promptly as regards the builders and others engaged in building operations, and efficiently as regards the purposes of this act, then it shall be lawful for such official referees and they are hereby empowered to appoint any other district surveyor to assist the surveyor of such district in the performance of his duties, or if no district surveyor can be spared from his own district, then to appoint some other competent person to give such assistance; and that with regard to all buildings surveyed by such assistant surveyor, and all other acts done by him, it shall be the duty of such assistant surveyor to make returns and to act in all respects as if he had been appointed by the said Lord Mayor and aldermen, or by the said justices, to be the surveyor of such district; and that every such person shall be entitled to receive the fees payable in respect of the services so performed by him (*x*).

Assistant surveyors.

Duties of assistants.

Fees.

Superintendence of surveyors.

LXXVI. And be it enacted, with regard to such surveyors, so far as relates to the supervision of buildings built, rebuilt, enlarged, or altered by or under their professional superintendence, that it shall not be lawful for any such surveyor to survey any such building for the purposes of this act, but that such building must be surveyed by another district surveyor, or by another surveyor to be appointed by the official referees for that purpose.

Surveyor's fees.

LXXVII. And be it enacted, with regard to such surveyors, so far as relates to their remuneration, that upon the expiration of one month after the roof of any building erected

(*x*) See schedule L.

District Surveyors.

and surveyed under this act shall have been covered in, and all the walls thereof have been built to their full heights, and the principal timbers and floors shall have been fixed in their places, (*y*) and upon the expiration of fourteen days after the completion of any addition, alteration, and repair, and upon the expiration of fourteen days after each special service shall have been performed, and upon delivering to the owner of the building an account of the fees incurred, and upon tendering a receipt, signed with his Christian and surname, and stating the amount of such account, and the work done, it shall be lawful for the surveyor and he is hereby entitled to receive from the builder, or from the owner or from the occupier of the building, for his time and trouble and expenses in causing the rules, regulations, and directions of this act to be observed, the several fees specified in the schedule of fees (L.) hereunto annexed; and that if on tender of such receipt any builder, owner, or occupier who shall become liable to pay any such fee shall refuse to pay the same, then, upon application to any justice of the peace, it shall be lawful for such justice, and he is hereby required to summon the party complained of in the first instance, and if he do not appear, or if he fail to satisfy the said justices as to the refusal of payment as aforesaid, it shall be lawful for such justice and he is hereby required to issue his warrant to levy the amount of such fee by distress and sale of the goods and chattels of the party so refusing, in like manner as poor's rates are by law recoverable, and if such fee be paid by the occupier he shall be entitled to recover the amount thereof from the owner (*z*). Provided always, that if the work in respect of which such fee shall become payable have not been done in every respect agreeably to the directions of this act, then it shall not be lawful for any surveyor to receive such fee; and that if he shall so receive it, then, upon application to the official referees by any party interested in the building in respect of which such work shall have been executed, and upon its appearing that such fee

Refusal of payment.

Fees to be paid only for work done agreeably to act.

Refunding fees.

(*y*) See section 15.

(*z*) But how he is to recover is not specified.

District Surveyors.

has been received wrongfully, it shall be lawful for such official referees and they are hereby authorized (if they think fit) to order the said surveyor to refund such fees.

Surveyor's returns.

LXXVIII. And be enacted, with regard to such surveyors, so far as relates to a return of the business done by them, and to the inspection thereof, that within seven days after the first day of every month it shall be the duty of every surveyor and he is hereby required to make a return to the registrar of Metropolitan buildings, enumerating therein the number and nature of all the several works executed within the previous month under his supervision, and the fees paid to him for the same, and also a copy of the list, or register of notices served upon him, with the results thereof, and to keep in his office a copy of such return; and that if any person shall apply to inspect the same, then on the payment of one shilling it shall be open for inspection at all reasonable times; and with regard to such return, so far as relates to the authentication and effect thereof, that every such return must be signed by such surveyor and if so signed it shall be deemed to be a certificate that all the works enumerated therein have been done in all respects agreeably to this act, according to the best of his knowledge and belief, and that they have been duly surveyed by him; but no such return shall be any protection from or hindrance to any future proceeding in respect of works not executed according to the provisions of this act, though the same may have been done before the making of such return.

Inspection of returns.

Authentication and effect of returns.

Penalty for extortion, negligence, or unfaithfulness.

LXXIX. And be it enacted, with regard to every surveyor, so far as relates to the discharge of his duties, that if any surveyor demand or wilfully receive any higher fee than he shall be entitled to under this act, or if in his capacity of surveyor he receive a fee for any act or omission in respect of which he is not entitled to receive any remuneration, or if he refuse to refund any fee wrongfully received by him in respect whereof the official referees shall have made an order to that effect, or if at any time he wilfully neglect his duty, or behave himself negligently or unfaithfully in the discharge thereof, then and in every or any such case it shall be lawful

District Surveyors.

for any person to present a complaint in writing under his hand to the Lord Mayor and aldermen of the city of *London*, or the Court of Quarter Sessions having jurisdiction over the district for which such surveyor shall act for the time being, at any sessions of the peace, quarter or general, either original intermediate, or adjourned, and which complaint shall set forth the nature and particulars of the offence charged by the complainant against any such surveyor; and that the said Lord Mayor and aldermen or Court of Sessions, as the case may be, shall by order of Court appoint a time for the hearing of the said complaint, and a copy of which order and of the said complaint shall be served by or for the said complainant on the said surveyor ten days at the least before the time appointed for the hearing of such complaint; and the said surveyor shall appear before the said Lord Mayor and aldermen or Court of Sessions, as the case may be, at the time and place so appointed for hearing the said complaint, to answer the same; and that if, upon the hearing of the complainant and of the surveyor, and the evidence respectively produced by or for them, it shall appear unto the said Lord Mayor and aldermen or Court of Sessions, as the case may be, that such complaint in whole or in part is well founded, then it shall be lawful for the said Lord Mayor and aldermen, or the said Court of Quarter Sessions, as the case may be, and they are hereby respectively required, either to fine such surveyor in such sum of money not exceeding fifty pounds as they shall think fit, or to discharge him forthwith from his said office; and that if for any such cause such surveyor be discharged, he shall be incapable of being again appointed a surveyor for the purposes of this act (*a*).

Complaint to justices.

Proceedings thereon.

Decision.

Incapacitation of surveyor.

Official Referees.

LXXX. And now, for the purpose of providing for the appointment of competent official referees to superintend the

(*a*) If he do not appear, it is presumed that he may be discharged under section 67. If he do not pay the fine, the judgment of the Court, in ordinary cases, would be, that he be imprisoned till such fine be paid, but, perhaps, there may be a difficulty in carrying out such a punishment under the present section.

Appointment of two official referees.

execution of this act throughout all the districts to which it is applicable, and also to determine sundry matters in question incident thereto, as well as to exercise, in certain cases, a discretion in the relaxation of the fixed rules and directions of this act, where the strict observance thereof is impracticable, or would defeat the object of this act, or would needlessly affect with injury the course and operation of [this] branch of business (*b*), be it enacted, with regard to the official referees, so far as relates to their appointment, to their qualifications, and to the tenure of their office, that it shall be lawful for one of her Majesty's principal secretaries of state and he is hereby empowered to appoint two persons being of the profession of an architect or surveyor, to be official referees of Metropolitan buildings, and from time to time, as he shall think proper, to remove such official referees, and in their place to appoint other persons so qualified; and that while any such person shall so hold the office of official referee it shall not be lawful for such person and he is hereby expressly prohibited to act as surveyor, either alone or with any partner or by an agent, or to act as official referee in the case of any building or matter in which he shall act as architect (*c*); and that if an official referee be employed as architect as to any building or matter within the limits of this act, then it shall be the duty of such official referee and he is hereby required to report thereon to the commissioners of works and buildings; and thereupon it shall be the duty of such commissioners of works and buildings and they are hereby required to appoint some other competent person to act in conjunction with the other official referee as to such building or matter.

Tenure of office.

Not to act as surveyors.

Temporary official referee.

Their functions generally.

LXXXI. And be it enacted, with regard to such official referees, so far as relates to their functions generally, that it shall be the duty of such official referees and they are hereby required to superintend the execution of this act by the several district surveyors already existing or hereby authorized

(*c*) And in case of disobedience, the course will be to remove him.

(*b*) See sections 9, 10, 22, 23, &c. *Query*, if the word "this" should not be read "*any*" branch of business.

to be appointed, and to perform the several matters to them respectively assigned by the provisions of this act, and to determine all questions referred to them, whether expressly by this act or at the instance of any one or more of the parties concerned.

Official Referees.

Matters of reference.

LXXXII. And be it enacted with regard to the official referees, so far as relates to their jurisdiction, that if any doubt, difference, or dissatisfaction in respect of any matter within the limits of this act arise between any parties concerned, or between any party and any surveyor, or between any two surveyors, as to any act done or to be done in pursuance of this act, or as to the effect of the provisions thereof in any case, or as to the mode in which the provisions and directions of this act are or ought to be carried into effect, and particularly as to whether the requirements implied in terms of qualification applied to sites, to soils, to materials, or to workmanship, or otherwise (*d*), and denoting good, sound, fire-proof, fit, proper, or sufficient, are fulfilled in certain cases, or as to the district in which any building, matter, or thing is to be deemed to be situate, especially in cases where such building, matter, or thing is partly in one district and partly in another, or as to the expenses to be borne by the respective owners of premises parted by the same party walls, or the proportions thereof, or as to the proportions of the expense to be borne by the occupier or by the owners of premises in respect of any work executed (*e*), or any other matter whatever, then it shall be lawful for any party concerned and he is hereby entitled to require the official referees to determine such matter, but so that such requisition be made in writing, and that it set forth, either generally or otherwise, the matters in respect of which the determination of the official referees is required; and that the determination of such referees, or of one of such referees, with the assent of the registrar of Metropolitan buildings (*f*),

One referee may act.

(*d*) See section 24.

(*e*) See sections 49, 50.

(*f*) This does not mean that the assent of the registrar is necessary upon all occasions, but only when one referee is called upon to act alone. See section 88, *post*.

Official Referees.

as to all or any of the points in difference on which such referees shall make their award, and as to the costs, charges, and expenses of such reference, shall be binding on all parties to such reference.

Award and powers of referees.

LXXXIII. And be it enacted, with regard to the official referees, so far as relates to their authority in respect of any reference to them, and to the effect of their award upon the rights and interests of the owners and occupiers of property, that it shall be lawful for such referees, and they are hereby empowered to exercise all such powers of arbitrators as they would have had in case they had been appointed under an order of her Majesty's Court of Queen's Bench at *Westminster*; and that if such award be given in writing, and be sealed by the official seal of the registrar of Metropolitan buildings, it shall be as effectual as if made under an order of reference by such Court, and shall be enforced by the said Court in all respects as if made under an order of such Court; and that it shall be binding and conclusive against every person, including the Queen's Majesty, her heirs and successors, claiming any estate, right, title, trust, use, or interest in, to, or out of the said premises or any part thereof, either in possession, reversion, remainder, or expectancy, and against every other person whomsoever.

Legal effect of awards.

Effect as to persons.

Revocation of authority of official referee.

LXXIV. And be it enacted, with regard to any reference to the said official referees, so far as relates to the revocation of their authority, that the power and authority of the official referees shall not be revocable by any party to such reference, without the consent of all parties thereto; and that although any party shall not attend upon such reference it shall be lawful for such official referees to proceed with the reference, and to make their award.

Not to affect their award.

Taking of evidence by the official referees.

LXXXV. And be it enacted, with regard to such reference, so far as relates to the evidence of any matter thereof, that it shall be lawful for the official referees and they are hereby empowered, by their summons in writing, sealed with the seal of office of the registrar of Metropolitan buildings, to require the attendance of any person who may be able to give evidence in the matter of any reference to them, and to require by such summons the production of any documents to be mentioned therein; and that if, in addition to the service of such summons, an appointment of the time and place of attendance in obedience thereto, signed by one at least of the official referees before whom the attendance is required, be also served, either together with or after the service of such summons, then, if the party so summoned do not attend in obedience thereto, such party shall be liable to be proceeded against as for a contempt of Court (*g*); and that every person whose attendance shall be required shall be entitled to the like conduct money, and payment of expenses as for and upon attendance at any trial; and that no person shall be compelled to produce under any such summons any writing or other document that he would not be compelled to produce at a trial, or to attend on more than two consecutive days to be named in such summons; and that it shall be lawful for the official referees, and they are hereby respectively authorized and required to administer an oath to such witnesses as may come before them, or, in cases where affirmation is allowed by law instead of an oath, to take their affirmation; and that if upon such oath or affirmation any person making the same wilfully and corruptly give false evidence, then every person so offending shall be deemed to be guilty of perjury.

Appointment of time and place.

Compensation for attendance.

Production of documents.

Administration of oaths.

Penalty for false evidence.

LXXXVI. And be it enacted, with regard to such award, so far as relates to the effect thereof as evidence of the matter thereof, that if on the trial or hearing of any cause or matter in any Court of law or equity, or elsewhere, any copy of an award, signed and sealed with the seal of the said registrar, be produced, then it shall be the duty of all judges,

Effect of awards as evidence.

(*g*) This is intended to mean a contempt out of Court, which is punishable by attachment. The party is taken into custody, and compelled to answer interrogatories, which, if he fail to do satisfactorily, he may be fined, and sometimes imprisoned. No instructions are here given as to the party who is to serve the summons, nor who, in case of default of appearance, is to apprehend the offender. Probably, the officer of the referees or registrar will be charged with this duty, but it would have been better to have expressed it.

Official Referees.

justices, and others, and they are hereby required, to receive the same as *primâ facie* evidence of the matters therein contained (*h*).

Declaration of official fidelity.

LXXXVII. And be it enacted, with regard to the official referees, so far as relates to the declaration of official fidelity, that before any official referee shall act in pursuance of his appointment, it shall be his duty and he is hereby required to make the following declaration, to be administered by the Chief Baron or any other of the Barons of her Majesty's Court of Exchequer; that is to say,

"I A. B., do solemnly declare, that I will diligently, "faithfully, and impartially execute the duties of an official "referee in relation to matters arising under the provisions "of the act made and passed in the eighth year of the reign "of her Majesty Queen Victoria, intituled *An Act for "regulating the Construction and the Use of Buildings in "the Metropolis and its Neighbourhood*, and commonly "called the Metropolitan Buildings Act."

Regulation of business of the official referees.

LXXXVIII. And be it enacted, with regard to such official referees, so far as relates to the regulation of the business of their office, that when any matter is by this act required, directed, or permitted to be done by the official referees the same may be done by either of them, with the assent of the registrar of Metropolitan buildings, unless express provision to the contrary be made, and if done by any one of them with such assent it shall be as valid and effectual as if done by both of them; and that, subject to such restrictions and regulations as may be made in that behalf by the commissioners of works and buildings, it shall be lawful for the official referees to appoint one of their number, under their hands and the seal of the registrar of Metropolitan buildings, to make any inquiry or any survey which shall appear to them either necessary or expedient in order to enable them to determine any matters in reference.

Official referees may delegate powers.

Registrar of Metropolitan Buildings.

LXXXIX. And for the purpose of duly recording relaxations of the requisitions of this act, made in pursuance of the

(*h*) Liable, nevertheless, to be rebutted by opposite testimony.

provisions hereof in that behalf, and of providing for the revision from time to time both of such relaxations and requisitions, and of providing against the partial exercise of the powers of this act, and for the more effectually providing for the due recording of the acts of the official referees, and for exercising a due control thereon, be it enacted, that it shall be lawful for the commissioners of works and buildings, and they are hereby authorized and required, to appoint a registrar of Metropolitan buildings; and that such registrar shall hold his office during the pleasure of the said commissioners; and that, subject to the provisions of this act, it shall be lawful for the said commissioners to make rules for regulating the execution of the duties of the office of the said registrar; and that it shall be the duty of such registrar to keep a seal, and to affix such seal to all documents made by the said official referees, and required to be sealed, and to keep all the documents and records relating to the business of their office, and to register the same: Provided always, with regard to such registrar, so far as relates to the affixing the seal of office to any document, that if it shall appear to the said registrar that any such documents are contrary to law, or not complete in any of the requisite forms, or beyond the competence of the said official referees, either with regard to the provisions of this act, or any rules or regulations prescribed for their guidance by the said commissioners of works and buildings, then it shall be the duty of the said registrar to refuse to affix the seal, and that thereafter, if the said official referees shall so require, it shall be his duty and he is hereby required to report the matter, and the particular grounds and reasons for his refusal, to the said commissioners; and that upon the receipt of such report it shall be lawful for the said commissioners to authorize the said registrar to affix the seal, or to confirm his refusal: Provided always, with regard to such office of registrar, so far as relates to the execution of his duties in certain events, that if such registrar be ill, or otherwise unable to discharge the duties of his said office, or if he be absent, then it shall be lawful for the said commissioners of works and buildings to appoint

Appointment of registrar.

Tenure of office.

Rules of office.

Seal of office.

Use of seal of office.

Report of objections by registrars.

Authority of commissioners of works.

Interim registrar.

Registrar of Metropolitan Buildings.

some other person to act temporarily in his behalf, and to assign to such person such part of the remuneration of the said registrar, or otherwise to remunerate him, as the lords of the treasury shall appoint in that behalf.

Declaration of official fidelity.

XC. And be it enacted, with regard to the registrar, so far as relates to the declaration of official fidelity, that before any registrar shall act in pursuance of his appointment it shall be his duty and he is hereby required to make the following declaration, to be administered by the Chief Baron or any other of the Barons of her Majesty's Court of Exchequer; that is to say,

'I *A. B.*, do solemnly declare, that I will diligently, faithfully, and impartially execute the duties of registrar in relation to matters arising under the provisions of an act made and passed in the eighth year of the reign of her Majesty Queen Victoria, intituled, *An Act for regulating the Construction and the Use of Buildings in the Metropolis and its Neighbourhood*, and commonly called the Metropolitan Buildings Act.'

Custody and inspection of records of official referees.

XCI. And be it enacted, with regard to such awards, certificate, and other records of the said official referees, so far as relates to the custody and the inspection thereof, that all such awards, certificates, and other documents relating to the business of their office shall be kept in the office of the registrar of Metropolitan buildings; and that if, for the purpose of evidence or otherwise, any party require a copy of such award, or certificate, or other document, or to inspect the same, then on payment of the expense thereof, and of such fees as may be appointed in that behalf, it shall be lawful for such party and he is hereby entitled to demand from the registrar an inspection thereof, or a copy thereof or extract therefrom; and that on such payment and demand it shall be the duty of such registrar and he is hereby required to give, under his hand and seal of office, a copy of any such award or any other document to the person so demanding the same.

Copies of awards, certificates, &c.

Authentication of copy, and fees therefore.

Office of registrar, and regulation of businesses.

XCII. And be it enacted, with regard to the registrar of Metropolitan buildings, so far as relates to his office or place of business, and to the regulation of the business thereof, that it shall be lawful for the commissioners of works and buildings, and they are hereby required to appoint, in some central and convenient situation within the city of *London* or the city of *Westminster*, an office for carrying on the business of the registrar of Metropolitan buildings, and registering all documents relating to such business; and in such office it shall be the duty of such registrar, and he is hereby required,— *Registrar of Metropolitan Buildings.*

To keep a register of all matters referred to the official referees, and otherwise of all matters which shall come under their cognisance in pursuance of this act; and also

To keep and preserve all documents connected with the duties of official referees; and also

To receive all notices requiring any act to be done by them, and to file and number them in the order in which they are received.

XCIII. And be it enacted, with regard to all the awards and certificates, and all documents relating to the business of the official referees, so far as relates to the registration thereof, that the same shall be registered, not only chronologically in the order in which they are received, but according to the subject matters thereof, and also according to the order of and in relation to the provisions of this act. Registration of awards, &c.

XCIV. And be it enacted, with regard to such official referees and registrar, so far as relates to their remuneration, that it shall be lawful for her Majesty to grant to each of such official referees and the said registrar a salary not exceeding one thousand pounds by the year, in four equal quarterly payments; and that if any such official referee or such registrar shall be appointed, or shall die, resign, or be removed from office, in the interval between two quarterly days of payment, then he shall be entitled to a proportionate part of the salary for the period of such interval during which he shall hold such appointment. Remuneration of official referees and registrar.

XCV. Provided always, and be it enacted, with regard to Disqualification of official referees and registrar.

the said official referees and registrar, so far as relates to their qualifications, that if any person be or become commissioner, receiver, steward, or agent for or on behalf of any owner of houses within the limits of this act, then such person shall not be eligible to the office either of official referee or of registrar under this act; and that if after having been appointed thereto he shall become such commissioner, receiver, steward, or agent, then he shall cease to be qualified to hold such office of official referee or registrar, and thereupon such office shall be vacant, without prejudice, nevertheless, to any acts done by any such person in his capacity of official referee or registrar, so far as other persons are affected thereby.

Offices vacant.

Funds for defraying expenses of the official referees and registrar.

XCVI. And forasmuch as the services of such official referees and of such registrar will be employed chiefly on behalf of the localities comprised within the limits of this act, it is expedient to provide for the payment of a portion of their salaries by means of a county rate, or by a rate in the nature of a county rate, on such localities, in proportion to the assessed value of inhabited houses and buildings therein, or as near thereto as may be; now, for that purpose, be it enacted, with regard to such official referees and registrar, so far as relates to the payment of a portion of their salaries out of local funds, that it shall be lawful for the Lord Mayor and aldermen of the city of *London*, and they are hereby required to direct the chamberlain of the said city, and for the justices of the peace for the several counties of *Middlesex*, *Surrey*, and *Kent* (*i*), and they are hereby respectively required, to direct the treasurer of such respective counties to pay, by two half-yearly payments in the months of June and December in every year, to or into the hands of the cashier of the commissioners of works and buildings, on account of the said official referees and of the said registrar, the several sums of money herein-after mentioned, as and by way of contribution to such salaries; that is to say,

(*i*) It is to be presumed at quarter sessions, although it is not so said.

The city of *London* and the liberties and the suburbs thereof - -	the sum of	£ 100	*Registrar of Metropolitan Buildings.*
The county of *Middlesex* - -		1,000	
The county of *Surrey* - -		320	
The county of *Kent* - -		80	
		£1,500	

And it shall be lawful for the said justices, and they are hereby empowered and required to cause the same to be levied by a rate upon the several parishes and places within the limits of this act, in such amounts as to such justices may seem proper, having regard to the assessed value of the inhabited houses and the buildings in such places respectively, in addition to the county rate in respect thereof; and that for the purpose of levying such sums they shall be deemed to be part of the county rate, and leviable by all the ways and means by which a county rate is leviable, and subject in all respects to the legal incidents of a county rate.

Nature of levy.

XCVII. And be it enacted, further, with regard to the official referees and registrar, so far as relates to the payment of the balance of their salaries, that such balance shall be payable and paid out of the consolidated fund of the United Kingdom of *Great Britain* and *Ireland*.

Payments of official referees and registrar out of consolidated fund.

XCVIII. And be it enacted, with regard to the fees payable to the registrar, so far as relates to the appointment thereof, and to the application thereof, that from time to time it shall be lawful for the commissioners of the treasury to appoint such fees to be paid in respect of the services to be performed by the said official referees or by the said registrar as shall be deemed requisite to defray the expenses of the said office, or incident to such services, and the salaries or other remuneration of any persons employed under the registrar in the execution of this act, with the sanction of the commissioners of the treasury, and which are not otherwise provided for by this act; and that the balance, if any, shall be carried to the consolidated fund of the United Kingdom, and be paid accordingly into the receipt of her Majesty's

Fees of office, and application thereof.

Balance to consolidated fund.

Regulations as to receipt, custody, and accounts.

List of fees to be hung up.

Exchequer at *Westminster*; and that it shall be lawful for the commissioners of the treasury to regulate the manner in which such fees are to be received, and in which they are to be kept, and in which they are to be accounted for; and that it shall be the duty of the registrar and he is hereby required to cause a list of the fees so appointed by virtue of this act to be fixed up in some conspicuous part of his office.

Officers generally.

Appointments of officers subject to regulation by any future act.

XCIX. Provided always, and be it enacted, with regard to the officers appointed by or by virtue of this act, so far as relates to the functions, appointment, and tenure of office of such officers, that any appointments to such offices which shall be made by virtue of this act shall be made subject to any provision that may be made by this act of Parliament hereafter to be passed for assigning other duties than those to be imposed by virtue of this act; and such officers shall be held not only subject to the pleasure of the officers and justices by whom such appointments shall be made, but also subject to the provisions of any future act of Parliament in relation thereto.

Legal Proceedings.

Informalities in distress.

Action for damages.

C. And now, for the purpose of regulating sundry legal proceedings, be it enacted, with regard to any distress for any sum of money to be recovered by virtue of this act, so far as relates to the remedying of any damage occasioned by any irregularity therein or in reference thereto, that, notwithstanding there be any defect of form in the proceedings relative to any such distress, neither the distress itself shall be deemed unlawful, nor shall the party making the same be deemed a trespasser *ab initio*, but that if any irregularity be committed by any party, then, subject to the conditions in this act prescribed with regard to actions brought for any thing done in pursuance thereof (*k*), it shall be lawful for the person aggrieved by such irregularity and he is hereby entitled to recover full satisfaction for the special damage only, and that by action on the case, and not by any other action whatsoever (*l*).

(*k*) Section 108.

(*l*) Therefore, if he recover less than the money paid into

CI. And be it enacted, with regard to any action for any irregularity or other proceeding, so far as relates to the tender of amends, or payment of money into Court in respect thereof, that if, before such action be brought, the party who committed or cause to be committed any such irregularity or wrongful proceeding make or cause to be made tender of sufficient amends, then the plaintiff shall not be entitled to recover in such action; and that although such tender shall not have been made, yet if at any time before issue joined the Court in which such action shall be depending, or a judge of any of the superior Courts, grant leave, then it shall be lawful for the defendant to pay into Court any sum of money, by way of compensation or amends, in such manner, and under such regulations, as to the payment of costs and the form of pleading, as is and are customary and in force in the said superior Courts (*m*).

Tender of amends.

Payment of compensation into Court.

CII. And be it enacted, with regard to every sum of money by this act, or by any award or certificate or other proceeding in pursuance of or in accordance with this act, charged upon any person in respect of any work done in pursuance of or in accordance with this act, so far as relates to the recovery of such sum of money, that if any party claim any such sum of money, then it shall be lawful for any one justice of the peace to summon the person on whom such sum is alleged to be charged before any two justices, or, if the matter arise within the district of the Metropolitan police, then before any police magistrate having jurisdiction within that district; and if such award or certificate be produced, or if such other proceeding be proved by the oath of the party claiming or of any other credible witness, and if it be proved by the oath of such party or other witness that such

Recovery of money under awards.

Court (if any), or, otherwise, if less than 40*s*., there will, in the first case, be a verdict for the defendant, and in the second, the plaintiff cannot have any costs whatever, unless the judge shall certify that the grievance in question was wilful and malicious. Sect. 108 of this act, and 3 & 4 Vict. c. 24, s. 2.

(*m*) See sections 100 and 108.

Distress. sum of money is still due, then it shall be lawful for such justices or such police magistrate, and they respectively are hereby required to issue a warrant to levy the amount thereof, and also the costs of the proceeding, to be levied by distress of the goods and chattels of the person in default;

Imprisonment. and if such person have no goods and chattels whereon to distrain, or if such goods and chattels be insufficient for that purpose, then it shall be lawful for such justices or police magistrate, or for any other justice or police magistrate, to commit the person in default, until the amount of such sum so due, and of such costs, shall have been fully paid, or until the party shall be discharged by or in accordance with the provisions of any act for the relief and discharge of insolvent debtors.

Prosecution of offences. CIII. And be it enacted, with regard to all offences against the provisions of this act for which no other proceeding is provided, so far as relates to the prosecution

Complaint. thereof, that it shall be lawful to proceed by complaint before any one justice of the peace or before a police magistrate as

Summons. aforesaid; and that it shall be lawful for such justice to summon the party against whom such complaint shall be made;

Compulsory appearance. and that if such party fail to appear in pursuance of such summons, then it shall be lawful for such justice or magistrate, or any other justice or magistrate, to issue a warrant under his hand and seal to compel the appearance of such

Distress. party; and that on conviction of the offender before two justices or before any police magistrate it shall be the duty of such justices or magistrate and they are hereby required to cause the amount of the penalty hereby imposed in respect of such offence, and of the costs of any such proceeding in respect of such offence, to be levied by distress of the goods

Imprisonment. and chattels of the offender; and that if such offender have no goods and chattels whereon to distrain, or if they be insufficient for that purpose, then it shall be lawful for such justices or magistrate, or for any other justice or magistrate, and they are hereby empowered, either on failure of such distress, or in the first instance (*n*), to commit the offender,

(*n*) That would seem to be, if the offender have no goods, but for any period not exceeding three months, or till he shall have paid the full amount of such penalty and such costs.

Legal Proceedings.

Removal of orders, &c., into superior Courts.

CIV. And be it enacted, with regard to every order which shall be made by virtue of or under this act, and to any other proceeding to be had touching the conviction of any offender against this act (except proceedings touching the conviction of any person offending for carrying on a trade or business offensive, noxious, or dangerous, contrary to this act, otherwise than those herein-before specified) (*o*), that it shall not be lawful for any person to remove such order or other proceeding by certiorari, or any other writ or process whatsoever, into any of her Majesty's Courts of Record at *Westminster;* and every such order and other proceeding is hereby declared not to be so removable.

Certiorari.

Appeal from convictions as to penalties.

CV. And be it enacted, with regard to any conviction for any offence in respect of which a penalty is by this act imposed, so far as relates to the appeal from any such conviction in respect thereof, that if any party be dissatisfied with the decision of the justices (*p*) in any case in which such penalty may be proceeded for, and if within four days after such decision notice be given by or on behalf of such party to the party appealed against of his intention to appeal against such decision, and of the grounds of such appeal, and if the appellant enter into a recognizance, with two sufficient sureties, conditioned to prosecute such appeal, and to abide the order of the Court, and to pay to the party appealed against such costs (if any) as shall be awarded against him, then it shall be lawful for such party so dissatisfied to appeal against such conviction to the justices of the peace at their general quarter sessions of the peace to be holden within four months after such conviction; and that if within such period of four days such appellant have entered into such

Proceedings thereon.

the words "in the first instance," are so placed in the sentence as to cause a doubt whether the offender might not be committed in the first instance without a distress. But the prior words of the clause concerning the distress are too strong to be got over.

(*o*) *i. e.* by section 55.

(*p*) Or the Metropolitan magistrate, see section 2.

Legal Proceedings.

recognizance as is herein required, then it shall be lawful for such justices and they are hereby empowered to proceed to hear and examine on oath into the cause and matters of such appeal (which oath they are hereby empowered to administer), and to determine the same, and to award such costs to be paid by either of the said parties as they think proper; and the order, judgment, and determination of the said justices shall be binding and conclusive.

Limitation of actions for penalties.

CVI. And be it enacted, with regard to every penalty or forfeiture incurred under this act, so far as relates to the limitation of proceedings for the recovery thereof, that if within six calendar months next after such penalty or forfeiture shall have been incurred an action or prosecution be not brought or commenced against the person liable in respect thereof, then thereafter it shall not be lawful for any person to bring such action or commence such proceeding in respect of such penalty or forfeiture (*q*).

Recovery of penalties.

CVII. And be it enacted, with regard to every such penalty or forfeiture, so far as relates to the recovery and the appropriation thereof, that it shall be lawful for any party to sue or proceed for the same; and that if such penalty be not otherwise specifically appropriated, then the person so suing or proceeding shall be entitled to receive one-half thereof for his own benefit, and the other half shall be applied to her Majesty's use, and shall be paid to the sheriff of the county, city, or town where the same shall have been imposed; and that all convictions before justices shall be returned to the Court of quarter sessions, under the provisions of an act passed in the third year of the reign of his late Majesty King George the Fourth, intituled *An Act for the more speedy Return and levying of Fines, Penalties, and Forfeitures, and Recognizances estreated*, and shall be paid to the sheriff of the county, city, or town, and shall be duly accounted for by him.

Appropriation.

3 Geo. 4, c. 46.

Regulation of actions against persons acting under this act.

CVIII. And for regulating proceedings against persons acting in pursuance of this act, be it enacted, with regard to any action or suit against any person in respect of any act or

(*q*) See section 110, *post*.

Legal Proceedings.

thing done or intended to be done in pursuance of this act, so far as relates to the limitation thereof, and to the notification thereof to the offending party, and to the venue thereof, and to the pleadings therein, and to the evidence of the matters thereof, and to the verdict therein, and to the judgment of the Court thereon, and to the costs of such action, and to the recovery of such costs, that after the expiration of six months next after the fact committed it shall not be lawful to bring any such action or suit against any person in respect of any such act; and that if, twenty-one days at the least before the commencement of the action or suit, notice in writing of an intention to bring such action or suit, and of the grounds of action, be not given to every person against whom such action or suit shall be brought, then it shall not be lawful for any person to bring any such action or suit against any person in respect of any such act; and that if the cause or matter of any such action or suit arise within the said city of *London* or the liberties thereof then such action or suit must be laid in the city of *London*, and not elsewhere; and that if the cause of any action or suit arise in any part of the limits aforesaid out of the said city of *London* and liberties thereof then it must be laid and tried in the county of *Middlesex*, and not elsewhere; and that in every such action or suit it shall be lawful for the defendant and he is hereby entitled to plead the general issue, and at the trial to be had thereof to give this act and the special matter in evidence, and to prove that the matter or thing for which such action or suit is brought was done in pursuance and by the authority of this act; and that if upon the trial of such action it appear that the said matter or thing has been done by the authority or in pursuance of this act, or if it appear that such action or suit was brought before the expiration of twenty-one days, after such notice given as aforesaid, or if it appear that sufficient satisfaction was made or tendered before such action was brought, or if upon plea of payment of money into Court it shall appear that the plaintiff has not sustained damages to a greater amount than the sum paid into Court, or if any such action or suit be not commenced within the time herein for that purpose limited, or if it be laid in any other county or place than as aforesaid, then and in every such case it shall

Limitation of action.

Notice of action.

Venue in London.

Venue in Middlesex.

Plea and evidence.

Verdict.

Costs.

be the duty of the jury and they are hereby required to find for the defendant; and that if a verdict be found for the defendant, or if the plaintiff in any such action or suit become nonsuited, or discontinue or suffer a discontinuance of any such action or suit, or if judgment be given for the defendant therein, on demurrer, or by default or otherwise, then the defendant shall be entitled to have judgment to recover full costs of suit, and to such remedy for recovering the same as any defendant shall have by law.

Security for costs.

CIX. And further, for the prevention of vexatious litigation, be it enacted, with regard to every action in respect of any matter or thing done or intended to be done in pursuance of this act, so far as relates to the costs of such action, that if the defendant apply to the superior Court at *Westminster* in which such action is pending, or to any judge of any of the said Courts, then it shall be lawful for such Court or any such judge to require the plaintiff to give such security as such Court or such judge shall think fit for the payment of all costs, charges, and expenses incurred or to be incurred in and about the said action, and which shall be or become payable by him on the taxation thereof by the proper officer.

Prosecutions for preventing neglect or evasion of this Act.

CX. And be it enacted, with regard to any penalty or forfeiture incurred by any default in complying with the provisions of this act, so far as relates to proceedings for the recovery thereof, that at any time within three months (*r*) after such penalty or forfeiture shall have been incurred it shall be lawful for any surveyor appointed or confirmed by virtue of this act, and all other persons, and they are hereby entitled, to commence and prosecute proceedings for the recovery thereof, or for the expenses of pulling down or altering of any building, against any owner, occupier, builder, workman, or other person, or for any default made in complying with the provisions of this act: provided always, that if such proceedings be taken by any person except one of the surveyors, or except the official referees, then seven days'

Notice of action.

(*r*) See sect. 106, *ante*, which gives six months as the limit. But then the limitation under section 106, applies to penalties incurred for acts done, whereas the present section respects defaults only.

notice of the intention to commence such proceedings must be given at the office of the surveyor of the district, and at the office of the registrar of Metropolitan buildings.

Legal Proceedings.

Miscellaneous.

Liability of owners and occupiers for expenses, &c., under this act.

CXI. Provided always, and be it enacted, with regard to the owners of any building, fence, ground, land, or tenement, so far as relates to their liabilities in respect of expenses incurred in respect of such premises or otherwise, that in all cases, whatever may be the nature of the interest in any such premises of the person entitled to the immediate possession thereof, or of the occupier thereof, such person entitled to the immediate possession of such premises, or such occupier, shall in the first instance bear all costs and expenses by this act imposed on the owner thereof, and shall perform all duties by this act imposed on such owner; subject, nevertheless, to any right or claim which such person or such occupier may have to be repaid such costs and expenses, and to be indemnified in respect of such duties, according to the provisions of this act, according to the nature and extent of the covenants or agreements under which such person or occupier may hold such premises, as fully and effectually as if such covenants or agreements were herein recited (*s*).

Notifications:

CXII. And be it enacted, with regard to notices by this act required, so far as relates to the service thereof upon the owner or occupier of any building, fence, land, ground, or

(*s*) This is not a very clear clause. It sets out in the first instance with reference to the liabilities of *owners*, and it then goes on to speak of persons entitled to the immediate possession, or of occupiers. If the Legislature intended that the occupier should be liable only when no owner could be found, it might have been better to have said so. For the person entitled to the immediate possession of a building is the *occupier*, and, therefore, the only way, apparently, of putting such a construction upon the section as to agree with the former part of the act, would be to apply the words "entitled to the immediate possession" to cases where there is no occupier, *i. e.* where the premises are vacant, otherwise the occupier to be liable. As the interpretation clause permits that the occupier shall be deemed an owner upon occasion, the difficulty in the early sentence which speak of "owners" may be got over.

tenement, that every such notice must be given as follows; that is to say,

Married females.

If such owner be a married female, other than a cestui que trust in regard to such property, then such notice must be given to the husband of such married female; or,

Infants, idiots, or lunatics.

If such owner be an infant, idiot, or lunatic, or cestui que trust, then such notice must be given to the guardian, trustee, or committee of such infant, idiot, or lunatic, or cestui que trust; or,

Owners unknown.

If such owner, husband, trustee, guardian, or committee is not known, or cannot be found, then such notice must be given to the occupier of such building, fence, land, ground, or tenement to which it shall relate; or

Buildings unoccupied.

If such building, fence, land, ground, or tenement, be unoccupied, then such notice must be affixed to some conspicuous part of such building, fence, land, ground, or tenement, at a height of not more than nine feet from the ground.

Immediate landlord.

And if the person in the occupation of any building, fence, land, ground, or tenement, in respect of which notice is to be given, allege that he is a tenant from year to year (*t*), or for any less term, or a tenant at will, and not the owner thereof, within the intent and meaning of this act, then such notice must be given to the immediate landlord of such occupier; and it shall be the duty of such occupier and he is hereby required to inform any person by whom such notice shall be required to be given, or any other person applying on his behalf, or the name, place of residence, or place of business of such owner or landlord, or of his agent or other person by whom the rent of such building, fence, land, ground, or tenement shall be received; and if such owner or landlord be not in the receipt of the whole of the rents or profits of such building, fence, land, ground, or tenement, and if any notice shall be served upon such owner or landlord, then, immediately upon the receipt thereof, it shall be his duty and he is hereby required to transmit to his immediate land-

Part ownership.

(*t*) The inference from which is, that a tenant under a lease for years may be deemed an owner.

Miscellaneous.

lord or his agent, and also to any other person being part owner in such building, fence, land, ground, or tenement, or in receipt of the rents or profits thereof under the same immediate landlord, or to the agent of such person, a copy of such notice; and so on in turn it shall be the duty of every landlord, agent, or other person by whom such notice shall be received to transmit it to any such landlord, agent, or other person, being part owner of any such building, fence, land, ground, or tenement, to the intent that every person affected by the work or proceeding to which such notice relates may have due notice thereof: provided always, with regard to every such notice, so far as relates to the service thereof upon any such owner, that if it be served upon the immediate landlord of the occupier or upon his agent, by or on behalf of the person by whom it is hereby required to be served in the first instance, then, although it may not be served by such immediate landlord upon any other landlord or owner, such service is to be deemed to be sufficient service; but that nevertheless, if any owner suffer damage by the failure of any other person, being either the occupier or any person holding under such owner, to serve such notice, then such owner shall be entitled to recover the amount thereof against such person by whom such damage shall have been occasioned (*u*), and that every notice served under this clause on any person must contain a copy of the provisions thereof, so far as they require him to transmit the same to his immediate landlord, or the agent of such landlord.

Service of notices.

Damage arising from defective service.

Requisites of notice.

CXIII. And be it enacted, with regard to notices by this act required, so far as relates to the mode of service thereof upon the occupier of any building or ground, that if such notice be intended for the occupier of any building or ground then it must be given either personally or by leaving the same with some inmate at the premises, or it must be affixed as aforesaid.

Mode of service upon occupier.

CXIV. And be it enacted, further, with regard to all such notices, so far as relates to the mode of service thereof upon owners by delivery, that every such notice (except such

Mode of service upon owners by delivery.

(*u*) By Action on the case.

Miscellaneous.

notice as may according to the provision in that behalf be sent by post) (*x*) must be given either personally or by leaving the same with some inmate at the usual place of abode of such party, or if that be not known then at his last known place of abode; and that every such notice, when so given to such persons respectively as aforesaid, or left at the last known place of their respective abodes, or when so affixed as aforesaid, according to the cases herein-before mentioned, shall have the same effects and consequences as if given to the actual owner.

Effect of notice.

Mode of service upon owners by transmission.

CXV. And be it enacted, further, with regard to notices, so far as relates to the mode of service thereof by transmission, that if any owner upon whom the same is required to be served be not within the limits of this act, or have not within the limits of this act any agent acting in his behalf in the matter of the premises to which the notice refers, then it shall be lawful to give notice by post letter, duly registered according to the practice for the time being adopted with regard to letters transmitted by post, but so that nevertheless such letter be posted in such time as will afford to the person addressed, after the receipt of such letter, the full period of notice required in the case.

Notices for surveyors and official referees.

CXVI. And be it enacted, with regard to notices, so far as relates to the service thereof upon the surveyors and upon the official referees, that if the notice relate to the surveyor then such notice must be served at the office of the surveyor; and that if the notice relate to the official referees or any of them, then such notice must be left at the office of the registrar of Metropolitan buildings.

Consents by incapacitated persons.

CXVII. And be it enacted, with regard to consents by this act required to be given by the owner or occupier of any building or ground, so far as relates to the making thereof on behalf of incapacitated persons, that if such owner or occupier be a married female, not being a cestui que trust in regard to the property to which such consent relates, then such consent must be given by the husband of such married female; or that if such owner or occupier be an infant, idiot,

(*x*) See the next section.

or lunatic, or cestui que trust, then such consent must be given by the guardian, trustee, or committee of such infant, idiot, or lunatic, or cestui que trust; or that if such owner or occupier, husband, trustee, guardian, or committee, be not known or cannot be found, then with a view to protect the interests of such parties, as well as to facilitate the purposes of this act, it shall be lawful for the official referees and they are hereby authorized, by writing duly sealed by the registrar of Metropolitan buildings, to give such consent as may be requisite, upon such terms and subject to such conditions as may seem fit to them, having regard alike to the nature and purpose of the subject matter in respect of which such consent is to be given, and to the fair claims of the parties on whose behalf such consent is to be given. *Miscellaneous.*

CXVIII. And be it enacted, with regard to the following documents, so far as relates to the payment of stamp duty in respect thereof, that every certificate and every award required to be made or signed by the surveyor or the official referees shall be and is hereby exempted from stamp duty. Exemption from stamp duty.

CXIX. And be it enacted, that this act shall be deemed to be a public act, and shall be judicially taken notice of as such by all judges, justices, and other persons whomsoever, without specially pleading the same. Public Act.

CXX. And be it enacted, that this act may be amended or repealed by any act to be passed in this present session of Parliament. Amendment of Act.

SCHEDULES to which the foregoing Act refers.

SCHEDULE (A).—(*See* § 1.)

Containing a Description of the ACTS and PARTS of ACTS repealed by this Act.

Date of Act.	Title of Act.	Extent of Repeal.
1st.—14 Geo. III. c. 78. (1774).	An Act for the further and better Regulation of Buildings and Party Walls, and for the more effectually preventing Mischiefs by Fire, within the Cities of London and Westminster and the liberties thereof, and other the parishes, precincts, and places within the weekly bills of mortality, the parishes of Saint Mary-le-bon, Paddington, Saint Pancras, and Saint Luke at Chelsea, in the county of Middlesex; and for indemnifying, under certain conditions, builders and other persons against the penalties to which they are or may be liable for erecting buildings within the limits aforesaid contrary to law.	Wholly; except so far as any such Act may repeal any other Act, either wholly or partly; and except as to offences committed, penalties incurred, and fees payable, and any proceedings taken or commenced, or which might be taken or commenced under the said Act, on or before the said first day of January, one thousand eight hundred and forty-five; and except the whole of the several sections of the said Act which relate to the keeping of fire engines and ladders and firecocks (§ 74, 75), and to the fees or rewards to turncocks and engine keepers (§ 76), and to the payment of such rewards or fees (§ 77, 78), and to the providing of engines by parishes (§ 80, 81), and to the payment of the expenses and rewards out of the poor rates (§ 81), and to the exemption of Watermen and others from impressment, or the liability to serve either as mariners or as soldiers (§ 82), and to the application of insurance money on houses burnt (§ 83), and to the punishment of servants for carelessly firing a house (§ 84), and to the attendance of peace and parish officers at fires (§ 85), and to legal proceedings in respect of accidental fires (§ 86); and any other part of the said Act, so far as it is necessary for giving full effect to the respective purposes of such several unrepealed sections.
2d.—50 Geo. III. c. 75. (1810.)	An Act to amend an Act of the Fourteenth Year of his present Majesty, for the better Regulation of Buildings and Party Walls, and for the more effectually preventing Mischiefs by Fire, within the Cities of London and Westminster, by permitting John's patent tessera to be used in covering of houses and buildings within the places therein mentioned.	Wholly (*a*.)
3d.—3 & 4 Vict. c. 85. (1840.)	An Act for the Regulation of Chimney Sweepers and Chimneys.	So much thereof as relates to the construction and regulation of chimneys and flues within the limits of this Act.

(*a*) See 1 Phillips, Rep. 306. Viscount Canterbury *v.* The Attorney General.

SCHEDULE (B.)—(*See* § 5 & 7.)

PART I.

LIST of BUILDINGS, of whatever Class, placed under special Supervision.

Bridges, embankment walls, retaining walls, and wharf and quay walls:

And her Majesty's royal palaces, and any building being in the possession of her Majesty, her heirs and successors, or employed for her Majesty's use or service:

And any common gaols, prisons, houses of correction, and places of confinement under the inspection of the inspectors of prisons, and Bethlem Hospital and the House of Occupations adjoining:

And the Mansion House, Guildhall, and the Royal Exchange of the City of London:

And the offices and buildings of the Governor and Company of the Bank of England already erected, and which now form the edifice called "The Bank of England," and any offices and buildings hereafter to be erected for the use of the said governor and company either on the site of or in addition to and in connexion with the said edifice: 39 & 40 Geo. 3, c. lxxxix.

And the buildings of the British Museum already erected or to be erected for the like purposes:

And the erections and buildings authorized by an act passed in the ninth year of the reign of his late Majesty King George the Fourth, for the purposes of a market in Covent Garden: 9 Geo. 4, c. cxiii.

And the warehouses of or belonging to the Saint Katharine Dock Company, commonly called the New Street and Cutler Street warehouses, and the Haydon Square warehouses, purchased by the said Company from the East India Company:

And all other buildings exempted by any act of Parliament from the operation of the act passed in the fourteenth year of his late Majesty King George the Third, and by this act repealed, except buildings included in the second part of this schedule.

Part II.

List of Buildings, of whatever Class, exempted from Supervision.

6 Geo. 4, c. cv. And the warehouses of or belonging to the Saint Katharine Dock Company, and situate in the parish of Saint Botolph-without-Aldgate, and in the precinct of Saint Katharine, near the Tower of London, in the county of Middlesex:

9 Geo. 4, c. cxvi. s. 99. And the warehouses and buildings of or belonging to the London Dock Company, comprehended within the wall of the said Company, as set forth in an act passed in the ninth year of the reign of his late Majesty King George the Fourth:

1 & 2 Vict. c. ix. And the several warehouses and buildings of or belonging to the East and West India Dock Company, established by an act made in the first year of the reign of her present Majesty:

3 & 4 Wm. 4, c. xxxvi., and 5 & 6 Wm. 4, c. lvi. s. 126. And the buildings erected or to be erected by the London and Birmingham Railway Company, established and incorporated by an act passed in the third year of the reign of his late Majesty King William the Fourth, within and in connexion with the works of their Railway, by virtue of the several acts relating thereto:

And the buildings and structures belonging to any other dock or railway authorized to be executed by any act of Parliament.

SCHEDULE (C.)—Part I.—(*See* § 5.)

Rules for determining the Classes and Rates to which buildings are to be deemed to belong for the purposes of this act, and the thicknesses of the walls of buildings of such rates.

Classes of Buildings.

For the purposes of this act, all buildings of whatever kind, subject to the provisions thereof, are to be deemed to belong to one or other of the following three classes; that is to say,

First Class.

If a building be built originally as a dwelling-house, or be occupied or intended to be occupied as such, then it is to be deemed to belong to the first or dwelling-house class.

Second Class.

If a building be built originally as a warehouse, storehouse, granary, brewery, distillery, manufactory, workshop, or stable, or be occupied or intended to be occupied as such, or for a similar purpose, then it is to be deemed to belong to the second or warehouse class.

Third Class.

If a building be built originally as a church, chapel, or other place of public worship, college, hall, hospital, theatre, public concert room, public ball room, public lecture room, public exhibition room, or occupied or intended to be occupied as such, or for a similar purpose, or otherwise used or intended to be used, either temporarily or permanently, for the assemblage of persons in large numbers, whether for public worship, business, instruction, debate, diversion, or resort, then it is to be deemed to belong to the third or public building class.

Alteration of Class.

And if any room, whether constructed within any other building or not, and whether included in the aforesaid classes or not, be used at any time for the public or general congregation of persons, then the building containing such room is to be deemed a building of the third or public building class.

Or if a building originally built, or subsequently altered so as to bring it within any one class, be subsequently converted into or used as a building of another class, then it is to be deemed to belong to such other class; and as to it all the conditions prescribed with regard to buildings of the same rate of such other class must be fulfilled as if it had been originally built of such class, subject nevertheless to such modifications as shall be sanctioned by the official referees on a special supervision thereof.

Or if a building be used partly as a dwelling-house and partly for any purpose which would bring it within the second or warehouse class, then it is to be deemed to belong to the said second or warehouse class; and as to all the conditions prescribed with regard to buildings of the same rate of such class must be fulfilled as if it had been originally built of such class, subject nevertheless to such modifications as shall be sanctioned by the official referees on a special supervision thereof.

Rates of Buildings.

And the buildings included in the said classes are to be deemed to belong to the rates of those classes, according to the conditions of height, area, and number of stories set forth in the following Tables; which conditions are to be determined according to the following rules:—

Rule for ascertaining Height.

The height of every building is to be ascertained by measuring from the surface of the lowest floor of the building up to the under side of the ceiling of the topmost story at the highest part thereof, whether such story be within the roof or not.

And if there be no ceiling made or intended to be made to the topmost story, then by measuring from the surface of such lowest floor of the building up to the under side of any tie-beam, collar-beam, or other substitute for a tie-beam, to or within the roof of the building, and to the highest part of such roof; and the level of the under side of such tie-beam, or such substitute for a tie-beam, is in such case to be taken to mean the ceiling of the topmost story.

And if there be no tie-beam, collar-beam, or other substitute for a tie-beam to or within the roof of any building, then up to a level three feet below the level of the under side of the ridge-piece, or substitute for a ridge-piece, to the roof of such building.

Rule for ascertaining Area.

And the area of every building is to be determined by the number of squares contained in the surface of any floor which shall contain the greatest number of squares at or above the principal entrance to such building, including in such surface the area of all the external walls, and such portions of the party walls as belong to such building, but excluding from such surface the area of any attached building or office, area, balcony, or open portico.

Rule for ascertaining the Capacity of any Building of the Second Class.

And the capacity or cubical contents of any such building is to be ascertained by measuring according to the rule for ascertaining area, and from the surface of the lowest floor up to the under surface of the roof covering of such building.

Rule for ascertaining Number of Stories.

And the stories of every building are to be counted from the foundation upwards.

And if the space in height between the top of the footings and the level of the lowest floor do not exceed five feet, then the story nearest the foundation is to be considered the lowest or first story; but if such space exceed five feet, then such space is to be considered to contain the lowest or first story; and in that case nine inches above the top of the footing is to be considered the level of the lowest floor.

Rule for ascertaining Thickness of Walls.

And the thickness or width of every wall, and of the footing thereof, is to be ascertained by measuring only the thickness or width of which such walls or footings shall have been originally built.

SCHEDULE (C).—PART II.—(*See* § 5).

CONDITIONS for determining the Rates to which Buildings of the First or Dwelling House Class are to be deemed to belong, and the Thickness of the external Walls and of the Party Walls thereof.

In reference to Height.	In reference to Area.	In reference to Stories.	Rate of Building.	Requisite Thickness of External Walls of each Rate of the First Class.	Requisite Thickness of Party Walls of each Rate of the First Class.
1. If the building be in height more than 70 feet and not more than 85 feet.	If the building cover more than 10 squares, and not more than 14 squares.	If the building contain 7 stories.	It is to be of the first rate of this class.	And the thickness of the external walls must be at the least 21½ inches from the top of the footing up to the under side of the floor next but three below the topmost floor; and at the least 17½ inches from the under side of the floor next but three below the topmost floor up to the under side of the floor next below the topmost floor; and at the least 13 inches from the under side of the floor next below the topmost floor up to the top of the wall.	And the thickness of the party walls must be at the least 21½ inches from the top of the footing up to the under side of the floor next but three below the topmost floor; and at the least 17½ inches from the under side of the floor next but three below the topmost floor up to the under side of the floor next below the topmost floor; and at the least 13 inches from the under side of the floor next below the topmost floor up to the top of the wall.
But if it be in height more than 85 feet.	Or if it cover more than 14 squares.	Or if it contain more than seven stories.	It is to be an extra first rate of this class.	And the thickness of the external walls must be at the least 21½ inches from the top of the footing up to the under side of the floor next but two below the topmost floor, and at the least 17½ inches from the under side of the floor next but two below the topmost floor up to the top of the wall.	And the thickness of the party walls must be at the least 21½ inches from the top of the footing up to the under side of the floor next but three below the topmost floor; and at the least 17½ inches from the under side of the floor next but three below the topmost floor up to the under side of the topmost floor; and at the least 13 inches from the under side of the topmost floor up to the top of the wall.

SCHEDULE (C).—PART II.—(*See* § 5).—*continued.*

CONDITIONS for determining the Rates to which Buildings of the First or Dwelling House Class are to be deemed to belong, and the Thickness of the external Walls and of the Party Walls thereof.

In reference to Height.	In reference to Area.	In reference to Stories.	Rate of Building.	Requisite Thickness of External Walls of each Rate of the First Class.	Requisite Thickness of Party Walls of each Rate of the First Class.
2. If more than 52 feet, and not more than 79 feet.	Or if it cover more than 6 squares, and not more than 10 squares.	Or if it contain 6 stories.	It is to be of the second rate of this class.	And the thickness of the external walls must be at the least 17½ inches from the top of the footing up to the under side of the floor next but one below the topmost floor; and at the least 13 inches from the under side of the floor next but one below the topmost floor up to the top of the wall.	And the thickness of the party walls must be at the least 17½ inches from the top of the footing up to the under side of the floor next but one below the topmost floor; and at the least 13 inches from the under side of the floor next but one below the topmost floor up to the top of the wall.
3. If more than 38 feet, and not more than 52 feet.	Or if it cover more than 4 squares, and not more than 6 squares.	Or if it contain 5 stories.	It is to be of the third rate of this class.	And the thickness of the external walls must be at the least 17½ inches from the top of the footing up to the under side of the floor next but two below the topmost floor; and at the least 13 inches from the under side of the floor next but two below the topmost floor up to the top of the wall.	And the thickness of the party walls must be at the least 17½ inches from the top of the footing up to the under side of the floor next but two below the topmost floor; and at the least 13 inches from the under side of the floor next but two below the topmost floor up to the under side of the topmost floor; and at the least 8½ inches from the under side of the topmost floor up to the top of the wall.
4. If not more than 38 feet.	Or if it do not cover more than 4 squares.	Or if it do not contain more than 4 stories.	It is to be of the fourth rate of this class.	And the thickness of the external walls must be at the least 13 inches from the top of the footing up to the under side of the floor next below the topmost floor; and at the least 8½ inches from the under side of the floor next below the topmost floor up to the top of the wall.	And the thickness of the party walls must be at the least 13 inches from the top of the footing up to the under side of the floor next but one below the topmost floor; and at the least 8½ inches from the under side of the floor next but one below the topmost floor up to the top of the wall.

SCHEDULE (C.)—PART III.—(*See* § 5.)

CONDITIONS for determining the Rates to which Buildings of the Second or Warehouse Class are to be deemed to belong, and the Thickness of the External Walls and of the Party Walls thereof.

In reference to Height.	Rate of Building.	Requisite Thickness of the External Walls of each Rate of the Second Class.	Requisite Thickness of the Party Wall of each Rate of the Second Class.
1. If the building be in height more than 66 feet.	It is to be of the first rate of this class.	And the thickness of the external walls must be at the least 26 inches from the top of the footing up to the level of 76 feet below the topmost ceiling; and at the least 21½ inches from the level of 76 feet below the topmost ceiling up to the level of 36 feet below the topmost ceiling; and at the least 17½ inches from the level of 36 feet below the topmost ceiling up to the top of the wall.	And the thickness of the party walls must be at the least 26 inches from the top of the footing to the level of 76 feet below the topmost ceiling; and at the least 21½ inches from the level of 76 feet below the topmost ceiling up to the level of 36 feet below the topmost ceiling; and at the least 17½ inches from the level of 36 feet below the topmost ceiling up to the level of the topmost ceiling; and at the least 13 inches from the level of the topmost ceiling up to the top of the wall.
2. If more than 44 feet and not more than 66 feet.	It is to be of the second rate of this class.	And the thickness of the external walls must be at the least 21½ inches from the top of the footing up to the level of 58 feet below the topmost ceiling; and at the least 17½ inches from the level of 58 feet below the topmost ceiling up to the level of 22 feet below the topmost ceiling; and at the least 13 inches from the level of 22 feet below the topmost ceiling up to the top of the wall.	And the thickness of the party walls must be at the least 21½ inches from the top of the footing up to the level of 58 feet below the topmost ceiling; and at the least 17½ inches from the level of 58 feet below the topmost ceiling up to the level of 22 feet below the topmost ceiling; and at the least 13 inches from the level of 22 feet below the topmost ceiling up to the top of the wall.
3. If more than 22 feet and not more than 44 feet.	It is to be of the third rate of this class.	And the thickness of the external walls must be at the least 17½ inches from the top of the footing up to the level of 28 feet below the topmost ceiling; and at the least 13 inches from the level of 28 feet below the topmost ceiling up to the top of the wall.	And the thickness of the party walls must be at the least 17½ inches from the top of the footing up to the level of 28 feet below the topmost ceiling; and at the least 13 inches from the level of 28 feet below the topmost ceiling up to the level of the topmost ceiling; and at the least 8½ inches from the level of the topmost ceiling up to the top of the wall.
4. If not more than 22 feet.	It is to be of the fourth rate of this class.	And the thickness of the external wall must be at the least 13 inches from the top of the footing up to the level of 9 feet below the topmost ceiling; and at the least 8½ inches from the level of 9 feet below the topmost ceiling up to the top of the wall.	And the thickness of the party walls must be at the least 13 inches from the top of the footing up to the level of 16 feet below the topmost ceiling; and at the least 8½ inches from the level of 16 feet below the topmost ceiling up to the top of the wall.

TRANSVERSE S LING-HOUSE CLASS,
accordin DULE (C.)—PART II.

FIRST RAT

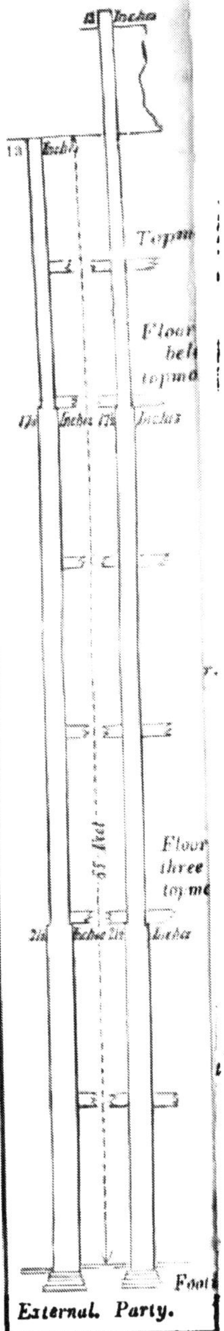

FOURTH RATE.

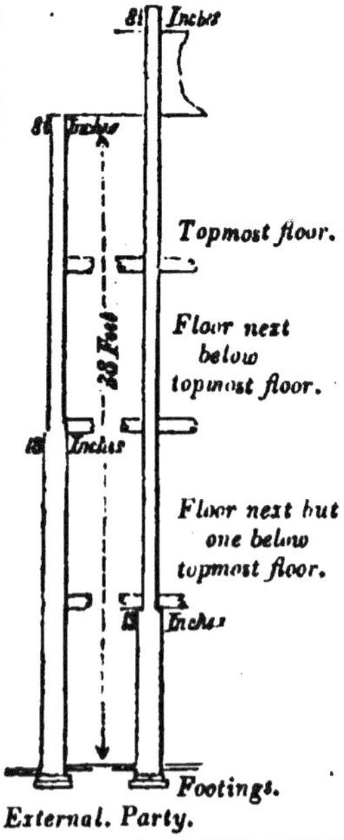

COND or WAREHOUSE CLASS,
sses in Schedule (C.)—Part III.

THIRD RATE.

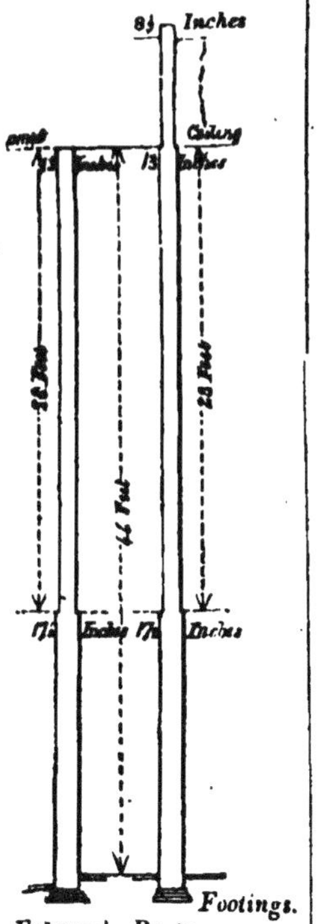

External. Party.

FOURTH RATE.

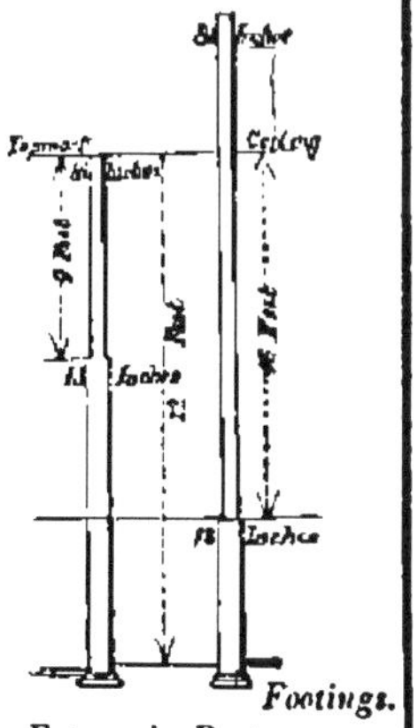

External. Party.

SCHEDULE (C.)—PART IV.

RULES concerning BUILDINGS of the SECOND or WAREHOUSE CLASS.

Warehouses, &c.

With regard to any building of the second class hereafter built or rebuilt, in reference to the capacity or contents thereof within the same inclosing walls,—

If such building contain more than 200,000 cubic feet, then such building must be divided by party walls, so as that there be not in any one part of such building more than 200,000 cubic feet without party walls.

Openings in Party Walls.

And with regard to buildings of the second class, in reference to openings through party walls,—

Such openings must not be made wider than six feet, nor higher than eight feet, unless in each case, and upon special evidence of necessity for convenience or otherwise, the official referees shall previously authorize larger openings.

And the floor, and the jambs, and the head of every such opening must be composed of brick or stone or iron work throughout the whole thickness of the wall.

And every such opening must have a strong wrought-iron door on each side of the party wall, fitted and hung to such opening without wood-work of any kind; and such doors must be not less than one-fourth of an inch thick in the panels thereof.

And each of such doors must be distant from the other not less than the full thickness of the party wall.

Roofs.

And with regard to the roofs of buildings of the second class, in order to prevent the formation of curbed roofs to such buildings, the plane of the surface of the roof of every such building must not incline from the external or party walls upwards at a greater angle than 40 degrees with the horizon.

SCHEDULE (C.)—Part V.

Requisites for determining the Rate to which any Building of the Third or Public Building Class is to be deemed to belong.

If any building of the third or public building class correspond in form or structure or disposition with a dwelling-house, then the rate thereof is to be determined by the same rules as the rates of the first or dwelling-house class; and the thicknesses of the external and party walls, and the width of the footings thereof, are to be at the least four inches more than is hereby required for the external and party walls, and the footings thereof, of buildings of the same rate of the first or dwelling-house class, unless the official referees, on special supervision in each case, shall otherwise appoint.

But if it correspond in form or structure, or disposition with a warehouse, or any building of the second class, then the rate thereof is to be determined by the same rules as the rates of the second or warehouse class; and the thickness of the external and party walls, and the width of the footings thereof, are to be at the least four inches more than is hereby required for the external and party walls, and the footings thereof, of buildings of the same rate of the second or warehouse class, unless the official referees, on special supervision in each case, shall otherwise appoint.

But if it do not correspond in form and structure, or in either, with buildings of the first or second classes, or any of them, then such building is to be subject, as to its walls or other construction, to the special approval of the official referees.

SCHEDULE (C.)—Part VI.

Rule concerning Fire-proof Accesses and Stairs to Buildings of the First and Third Classes.

With regard to buildings of the first class, whereof the internal stairs are of stone or other incombustible substance, such stairs must be set in, or be fixed to, and be wholly upborne by, fire-proof constructions, and must be connected internally by landings, the floors of which are fire-proof, and wholly upborne and supported by fire-proof constructions, and must be connected with the exterior entrance by passages, the floors of which are fire-proof, and wholly upborne and supported by fire-proof constructions.

And with regard to buildings of the third class, the floors of the halls, vestibules, lobbies, corridors, passages, and the stairs and landings, and all other ways of ingress and egress within the building to and from all rooms or apartments used for public congregation, and to and from all galleries being part of, or being connected with, any such room or apartment, must be wholly supported, constructed, formed, made, and finished fire-proof.

SCHEDULE (C.)—Part VII.

Rules concerning attached and detached and insulated buildings, as to the rates and walls thereof.

Attached Buildings and Offices.

With regard to buildings or offices now built or hereafter to be built (except greenhouses, vineries, aviaries, or such like buildings), and that whether such buildings or offices be attached to, or detached from, the buildings to which they belong,—

Every such building is to be deemed, in respect of the walls thereof, and all other requisites, as a building of the rate to which it would belong if it had been built separately.

Insulated Buildings.

And with regard to buildings of the first or dwelling-house class, and of the second or warehouse class, which shall be insulated, so far as relates to the distance thereof, from a public street or way,—

Every such building must be distant from any public street or alley one-third of the height thereof at the least; and if the building do not exceed twenty-four feet in height, then it must be so distant at the least eight feet.

And with regard to such building, so far as relates to the distance thereof from any other building, or from ground not in the same possession or occupation therewith, or connected therewith only by a fence or fence wall, it must be distant from such other building or such other ground at the least 30 feet.

And if such building be so distant from a public street or alley, and from any other building, or from ground not in the same possession or occupation therewith, then such building is not to be liable, in respect of the dimensions and materials thereof, to the rules and directions of this act.

Insulated Buildings afterwards divided.

Provided always, that if any such building be hereafter divided into two or more distinct buildings, and the several parts of such buildings so divided be not at the aforesaid distance from each other, and from other buildings and ground, then such several parts must be separated from each other by such party walls as are herein prescribed for the rates to which such several parts, if adjoining, would belong.

And if such requisites be not observed, then such several parts of such buildings in respect of which they are not so observed shall be deemed a public nuisance, and as such be taken down according to the provisions of this act in that behalf.

Toll Houses, &c.

And with regard to certain buildings which shall be built for the purposes of trade or the collection of toll,—

If such buildings be situate fifteen feet at the least from any other building, and do not cover an area of more than one square and one half, and the height thereof do not exceed twelve feet from the ground to the highest point of the roof, then every such building may be enclosed with any materials whatsoever, but the roof thereof must be covered as herein directed with regard to roofs, and the chimney and flue (if any) must be built as herein directed with regard to chimneys and flues.

SCHEDULE (D.)

PART I.—RULES concerning WALLS of whatever kind.

Foundations.

With regard to the foundations of walls:—

Every external wall, and every party wall, and every party fence wall, must be built upon a constructed footing, based upon solid ground, or upon other sufficient foundation.

Footings.

With regard to footings of walls, in reference to the materials thereof, to the width thereof, to the height thereof above the foundation, and to the depth below the surface:—

Materials.

1. In reference to the materials thereof:—

Every footing must be built either of sound bricks or of stone, or of such bricks and stone together, laid in and with mortar or cement in such manner as to produce solid work.

Width.

3. In reference to the width thereof:—

The bottom of the footing of every external wall and party wall of the first rate must be at the least 17½ inches wider than the wall standing thereon; and the bottom of every footing of every external wall and party wall of the second and third rates must be at the least 13 inches wider than the wall standing thereon; and the bottom of the footing of every external wall and party wall of the fourth rate, and of every party fence wall, must be at the least 8½ inches wider than the wall standing thereon.

The top of the footing of every party fence wall, and of every external wall and party wall, must be at the least four inches wider than the wall standing thereon.

Height.

4. In reference to the height above the foundation:—

The footing of every external wall and party wall of the first rate must be at the least eleven inches high above the foundation.

The footing of every external wall and party wall of the second and third rates must be at the least eight inches high above the foundation.

The footing of every party fence wall, and of every external wall and party wall of the fourth rate, must be at the least five inches high above the foundation.

Depth below Ground.

5. In reference to the depth thereof below the surface of the lowest ground or area adjoining:—

The top of the footing of every party fence wall, and of every external wall and party wall, must be at the least three inches below such surface.

Depth below lowest Floor.

6. In reference to the depth thereof below the surface of the lowest floor adjoining or intended to adjoin thereto:—

The top of the footing of every external wall and party wall must be at the least nine inches below such surface; and in any building of the first class the surface of the earth or of any paving on the outside (except the pavement of any public way) must not at any time be raised to within six inches of the surface of the lowest or first floor of such building.

Thicknesses of inclosing Walls to Stories of Buildings of whatever Rate.

With regard to the inclosing walls to stories of buildings of the first and second classes, each of the inclosing walls of any such story throughout the whole height thereof, from the top of the footing up to the top of such story, and with all the sets-off in addition required for such wall, to whatever rate or whichever class it may belong, and throughout at the least one-third of the whole length of such wall, in piers properly distributed, must be of the following dimensions (unless cross or return walls, coursed and bonded with the inclosing walls, shall in the opinion of the official referees, upon special application to them in each particular case, give sufficient strength with less thickness in such inclosing walls); that is to say,—

As to first class buildings:—If the story be in height more than 11 feet, then the thickness of its inclosing walls must be at the least 13 inches.

Or if the story be in height more than 15 feet, then the thickness of its inclosing walls must be at the least 17½ inches.

As to second class buildings:—If the story be in height more than 9 feet, then the thickness of its inclosing walls must be at the least 13 inches.

Or if the story be in height more than 12 feet, then the thickness of its inclosing walls must be at the least 17½ inches.

Or if the story be in height more than 15 feet, then the thickness of its inclosing walls must be at the least 21½ inches.

Or if the story be in height more than 18 feet, then the thickness of its inclosing walls must be at the least 26 inches.

Nevertheless as to any external wall of any building of the first class in which there are no apertures or recesses.— If there be another external wall and a cross wall of not less than 8½ inches thick coursing and bonding with such external wall, or if two such cross walls occur within a length of 24 feet of such wall, then such external wall may be built of the thickness of 13 inches, of any height not exceeding 18 feet, within any story, although the rate of the wall may require a greater thickness, but always upon condition that the substructure of such wall is 4 inches thicker at the least than such superstructure, and vertically under it.

And also if any such wall be abutted by cross or return walls within a length of 12 feet, and if not more than one aperture or recess occur within such length of 12 feet, and not more than one-half the quantity in length be taken out of such compartment of a wall by any such aperture or recess, then such external wall may be built of any thickness not less than 13 inches, notwithstanding the rate of such wall may require a greater thickness.

Part II.—External Walls.

Construction of Materials.

And with regard to the component materials of external walls to buildings of whatever class,—

Every such wall must be built of sound bricks or of stone, or of such bricks and stone together, laid in and with mortar or cement in such manner as to produce solid work; and every such wall must be carried up of its full thickness to the under side of the plate under the roof.

Nevertheless in such walls, besides all requisite openings for doors and windows, recesses may be formed, so that the back thereof be of the thickness of eight inches and a half at the least, and so that the stability and sufficiency of the wall be not injuriously affected by making such recesses.

And with regard to other substances than the component materials of external walls,—

There may be such wood and iron as shall be necessary.

And every plate, lintel, bond, corbel, being of wood, and ever wood-brick laid into any external wall, and all ends of joists, of girders, and of the heads and sills of partitions running into any external wall, must be fixed at a distance from the external face of the wall of four inches at the least.

And the frames of doors and windows must be fixed in reveals at a distance from the external face of the wall of four inches at the least.

And shop fronts must be fixed in such manner as is herein specially directed.

And the tiers of door cases to warehouses must be fixed in the openings left in such walls at a distance from the external face of the wall of two inches at the least.

But no timber must be laid into any external wall in such manner or of such length as to render the part of the wall above it wholly or in great part dependent upon the wood for support, or so that any such wood might not be withdrawn without endangering the safety of the superincumbent structure, except in the case of brestsummers.

Height and Thickness of Parapets.

And with regard to external walls, in references to the height and thickness of any parapet thereon,—

If an external wall adjoin a gutter, then such external wall must be carried up, and remain one foot at the least above the highest part of such gutter.

And the thickness of an external wall so carried up above the level of the under side of the gutter plate, and forming a parapet, must be at the least,—

In every such wall of the extra first rate of the first class, and in every such wall of the first rate of the second class, 13 inches thick; and—

In every other external wall, of whatever rate or whichever class, 8½ inches thick.

Brestsummers.

With regard to every brestsummer fixed to carry any front wall of a building,—

If such brestsummer have a bearing at one end upon a party wall, then it must be laid upon a template or corbel of stone or iron, which template or corbel must be tailed through such wall at least two-thirds of the thickness thereof; and the end of such brestsummer must not be fixed into, and must not have its bearing solely upon, such party wall, but must be supported by a sufficient pier built of brick or stone, or by an iron column, or iron or timber story post fixed on a solid foundation.

And if any such brestsummer have its bearing at each end upon a party wall, then it must be supported by at least two sufficient piers built of brick or stone, or by iron columns, or by iron or timber story posts fixed on solid foundations, and standing within and clear of the party walls.

Or any such brestsummer may bear upon constructed returns in the direction of the length of the brestsummer of four inches at the least, coursed and bonded with the substance of the party wall or party walls; and such constructed returns must be increased one inch at the least for every six feet in length that the brestsummer may be otherwise unsupported.

And if the height of the under side of any brestsummer laid from party wall to party wall to carry any external wall exceed 15 feet from the surface of the public foot pavement in front of the building, then there must be constructed returns in the direction of the length of the brestsummer from the inside of each party wall of 8½ inches at the least, and at the least of the full thickness of such brestsummer; and every such return must be increased one inch at the least for every foot or part of a foot the brestsummer may be in height from the surface of the public foot pavement more than 16 feet, whether the brestsummer be otherwise supported or not.

Materials to be used in Repairs.

And with regard to old external walls or other external inclosures of any building already built, in reference to materials to be used in the repair thereof,—

If any such wall or inclosure be not built of the materials required by this act for external walls or other external inclosures hereafter to be built, then every part of such wall or other external inclosure (except the inclosure of roofs, and the flats, gutters, dormors, turrets, lantern lights, and other erections thereon), may be at all times thereafter repaired with materials of the same sort as those of which such external wall or inclosure has been already built.

Materials to be used in rebuilding.

But if any such external wall or inclosure be at any time hereafter taken down or otherwise demolished for the height of one story, or for a space equal to one-fourth of the whole surface of such external wall, then every part thereof not built in the manner and of the several materials by this act directed for external walls must be taken down, and the same must be rebuilt in such manner, and of such materials, and in all respects as by this act directed for external walls hereafter to be built, according to the class and rate of the building to which such external wall or inclosure shall belong.

External Wall used as a Party Wall.

And with regard to external walls to be used as party walls to any building adjoining thereto (except an attached building or office as is herein-before described),—

If the external wall of any building have not such footings, or be not of such heights and thicknesses, or be not built in such manner and of such materials as are herein directed for party walls of buildings of the highest rate to which such wall shall adjoin, then such external wall must not be used as a party wall for any such building; but there must be a distinct external wall built as herein described for external walls of the rate to which it shall belong.

But if such external wall to any building already built be at the least 13 inches in thickness in every part, and be of sound and proper materials, and in good condition, then such wall may be used as a party wall; but if the house of which such wall forms a part be rebuilt within five years from the time at which the wall shall have been so first used as a party wall, then such wall must become subject to the provisions of this act in respect of party walls, according to the class and rate to which the said wall did first belong.

PART III.—PARTY WALLS.

Division of Buildings.

And with regard to walls used to divide single buildings into two or more,—

If it be intended to divide any building into two or more distinct parts, then every wall for that purpose must be built as a party wall in the manner and of the materials, and of the several heights and thicknesses for party walls of the highest rate of building to which

If such party wall shall belong or adjoin, as prescribed in reference to the thicknesses of party walls in schedule (C.)

And if any building already built or which shall be hereafter built be converted, used, or occupied as two or more separate buildings, each having a separate entrance and staircase, then every such building shall be deemed to be two or more separate houses, and such separate houses must be divided from each other by a party wall or party arch or arches built in the manner and of the materials required for party walls, or for party arches, for the class and rate to which the largest of the buildings so divided shall belong.

Site of Walls.

With regard to party walls, in reference to the site thereof,—

If the buildings be of equal rate then such party wall must be built on the line of junction of such buildings, one-half on the ground of the owner of one of such buildings, and one-half on the ground of the owner of the other of such buildings.

If such buildings be of different rates, then such wall must be built on the line of junction thereof, as follows; that is to say, one-half of the thickness of the wall required for the building of the lower rate on the ground of each of the adjoining owners; and the whole of the additional thickness of the wall required for the building of the higher rate on the ground of the owner of such building of the higher rate.

And if such building of the lower rate be thereafter enlarged or altered so as to become a building of a higher rate, then the owner of such first-mentioned building of the higher rate for the time being shall be entitled to receive from the owner of such building of the lower rate such sum of money as shall be a sufficient compensation for the ground occupied by that portion of the party wall, which according to the rate of the building enlarged ought to have been built by its owner on his own ground, as well as the value of so much of the wall itself as may be more than the owner of such building of the lower rate had already paid for.

Construction and Materials.

And with regard to party walls, in reference to the component materials thereof,—

Every part of such party wall must be built of sound bricks or of stone, or of such bricks and stone together, laid in and with mortar or cement in such manner as to produce solid work.

And as to the wood-work which it may be desired to connect with the party walls of any building, the bearing ends of wooden beams, brestsummers, girders, trimming joists, and the ends of partition heads and sills, and the bearing ends of the main timbers of a roof, and wood-bricks may be laid into the substance of a party wall; but no such beam, brestsummer, girder, joist, partition head, or sill, nor any part of a roof being wood, nor any wood-bricks, must be laid or placed within four inches of the centre of any party wall; and no other wood-work of any kind must be laid into, placed upon, or be run or driven into any part of the substance of any party wall.

But if the ends of timbers be carried on iron shoes or stone corbels, then such iron shoes or stone corbels must be built into the wall at the least one-half of the thickness of such wall.

And the top of every such party wall must be finished with one course of sound stock bricks, set on edge with good cement, or by a coping of any other properly secured and sufficient water-proof and fire-proof covering.

Height of Party Walls above Roof.

And with regard to party walls, in reference to the height thereof,—

If a party wall adjoin to any roof, then such party wall must be carried up and remain one foot six inches at the least above the part where the party wall and roof adjoin, measured at a right angle with the back of the rafters of such roof.

And if any party wall in any building of the first class adjoin a gutter, then such party wall must be carried up, and remain two feet at the least above the highest part of any such gutter.

And if any party wall in any building of the second class adjoin a gutter, then such party wall must be carried up, and remain three feet at the least above the highest part of any such gutter.

If there be fixed within five feet of a party wall, upon the flat or roof of the building, any turret, dormer, lantern-light, or other erection of combustible materials, then every such party wall must be carried up next to every such turret, dormer, lantern-light, or other erection, and must extend one foot six inches higher and one foot six inches wider than any such erection on each side thereof.

Openings in Party Walls.

And for the purpose of regulating the making of openings through any party wall between one dwelling-house and another, whereby two or more dwelling-houses shall be united,—

With regard to any dwelling-houses of any rate, such dwelling-houses may be united by means of openings in the party walls.

But with regard to any dwelling-houses which when so united will contain more than fourteen squares,—

If such dwelling-houses shall be and continue to be in the same occupation, then upon its being declared by the official referees that in their opinion the stability and security from fire of any or either of such dwelling-houses will not be endangered by making such openings, that they may be made accordingly.

Recesses and Chases.

And further, with regard to any party wall, as to recesses and as to chases in such wall,—

In every story recesses may be formed, but only with the consent and authority of the official referees first had and obtained, and so that such recesses be arched over, and so that the back of any such recess be not nearer than seven inches to the centre of the party wall in the first or lowest story, nor nearer than four inches to the centre of the party wall in any other story, and so that the stability and sufficiency of such party wall be not injuriously affected thereby.

If any chases be required for the insertion of ends of walls, of piers, of chimney jambs, of withes of flues, of metal pipes, or of iron story posts, then every chase for any such purpose must not be left or be cut nearer than four inches at the least to the centre of a party wall, nor within a distance of nine inches at the least from any front or back wall, and no two such chases must be made within a distance of seven feet six inches at the least from each other on the same side of a wall, and no such chase must be formed wider than nine inches.

Part IV.—Party Walls and Party Arches between intermixed Property.

And with regard to any building already built, having rooms or floors, the property of different owners, which lie intermixed, without being separated by any party wall or party arch or stone floor,—

If any such building be altogether rebuilt or to the extent of one-fourth of the cubical contents thereof, then such intermixed properties must be separated from each other, as follows:—

If they adjoin vertically, then so far as they adjoin vertically they must be separated by a party wall.

If they adjoin horizontally, then so far as they adjoin horizontally they must be separated either by a floor formed of brick, tile, stone, or other proper and sufficient incombustible materials, subject to the consent of the official referees, or by a floor formed of iron girders and brick arches, or stone landings, or tiles, or by a party arch or party arches of brick or stone of the thickness of nine inches at the least, if the span do not exceed nine feet, and thirteen inches at the least if the span exceed nine feet; and such floor or party arch or party arches must be built with sufficient abutments, and in a sufficient manner.

PART V.—BUILDINGS OVER PUBLIC WAYS.

And with regard to buildings extending over any public way, as to the part thereof which extends over such way, so far as relates to the separation of such part from such public way,—

If such part be rebuilt, then it must be separated from such public way, either by a floor or arch formed of brick or stone, or of other incombustible materials, subject to the consent of the official referees, or by a floor formed of iron girders and brick arches, or stone landings, or by an arch formed of brick or of stone; which arch, if the span thereof do not exceed nine feet, must be of the thickness of nine inches at the least, and which, if the span exceed nine feet, must be of the thickness of thirteen inches at the least.

And such floor or arch, with its abutments, must be built in such manner as shall be approved of by the surveyor; but there must not be formed over any public way a ceiling of lath and plaster, or of lath and cement.

SCHEDULE (E.)—(*See* § 5.)

RULES concerning external PROJECTIONS.

Porticoes projected over Public Ways.

And with regard to the portico or porticoes of any church, chapel, theatre, or other public building of the third class,—

If the building of the same shall have been previously sanctioned by the official referees, by writing under their hands; and if objection be not made by the party interested within one month thereafter, and if upon such objection or appeal, her Majesty's principal Secretary of State acting for the Home Department, do not decide in favour thereof, then such projections may be built over the foot payment of any street or alley which shall be fifty feet wide at the least (notwithstanding any act heretofore passed to the contrary).

Projections from Face Walls, &c.

And further, with regard to buildings hereafter to be built or rebuilt, in reference to projections therefrom,—

As to copings, parapets, cornices to overhanging roofs, blocking courses, cornices, piers, columns, pilasters, entablatures, facias, door and window dressings, or other architectural decorations, forming part of an external wall, all such may project beyond the general line of fronts in any street or alley, but they must be built of the same materials as are by this act directed to be used for building the external walls to which such projections belong, or of such other proper and sufficient materials as the official referees may approve and permit.

And as to all balconies, verandahs, porches, porticoes, shop fronts, open inclosures of open areas, and steps, and water pipes, and to all other projections from external walls not forming part thereof, every such projection (except such part of shop fronts, and the frames and sashes of the windows and doors, in reference to the necessary wood-work thereof,) may stand beyond the general line of fronts in any street or alley, but they must be built of brick, tile, stone, artificial stone, slate, cement, or metal, or other proper and sufficient fire-proof materials; and they must be so built as not to overhang the ground belonging to any other owner, and so as to obstruct the light and air or be otherwise injurious to the owners or occupiers of the buildings adjoining thereto on any side thereof.

Projections from Walls of Buildings over Public Ways.

And with regard to all buildings hereafter to be built or rebuilt, in reference to projections from the walls of such buildings, including steps, cellar doors, and area inclosures, the walls of all such buildings must be set back so that all projections therefrom, and also all steps, cellar doors, and area inclosures, shall only overhang or occupy the ground of the owner of such building, without overhanging or encroaching upon any public way.

Projected Buildings beyond the general Line of Buildings and from other External Walls.

And with regard to buildings already built or hereafter to be rebuilt, as to bow windows or other projections of any kind,—

Such projections must neither be built with nor be added to any building on any face of an external wall thereof, so as to extend beyond the general line of the fronts of the houses (which general line may be determined by the surveyor), except so far as is herein-before provided with regard to porticoes projected over public ways, and with regard to projections from face walls and shop fronts, nor so as to overhang the ground belonging to any other owner, nor so as to obstruct the light and air or be otherwise injurious to the owners or occupiers of the buildings adjoining thereto on any side thereof.

Projections from insulated Buildings.

Provided always, with regard to any insulated buildings, that if the projections be at the least eight feet from any public way, and if they be at least twenty feet from any other building not in the same occupation, then such projections are excepted from the rules and directions of this act.

Wooden Shop Fronts and Shutters.

And with regard to shop fronts and their entablatures, their shutters, and pilasters and stall boards made of wood,—

If the street or alley in which such front is situate be of less width than thirty feet, then no part of such shop front must be higher in any part thereof than fifteen feet; nor must any part, except the cornice, project from the face of a wall, whether there be an area or not, more than five inches; nor must the cornice project therefrom more than thirteen inches.

If the street or alley be of greater width than thirty feet, then no part of such shop front, except the cornice, must project from the face of a wall, whether there be an area or not, more than ten inches; nor must the cornice project therefrom more than eighteen inches.

And the width of such street or alley must be ascertained by measuring the same, as hereinafter directed with regard to the width of streets and alleys.

And the wood-work of any shop front must not be fixed nearer than four and a half inches to the centre line of a party wall.

And with regard to such wood-work, if it be put up at such distance of four and a half inches, then a pier or corbel built of stone or of brick or other incombustible material, and of the width of four and a half inches at the least, must be fixed in the line of the party wall, so as to be as high as such wood-work, and so as to project one inch at the least in front of the face thereof.

And the height of every shop front must be ascertained by

measuring from the level of the public foot payment in front of the building.

And every sign or notice board fixed against or upon any part of any house or other building standing close to any public way must be so fixed that the top shall be within eighteen feet at the most above the level of such public way.

SCHEDULE (F.)—(*See* § 5.)

RULES concerning CHIMNEYS hereafter built or rebuilt.

Construction.

With regard to chimneys and chimney stacks, except angle chimneys, in reference to the construction thereof,—

The foundations and footings of every such chimney and chimney stack must be built similar to those of the wall in or adjoining to which it shall be.

And every such chimney and chimney stack must be built from the foundation to the top thereof without any corbelling over, whereby any upper part of the brick-work of such chimney or chimney stack shall overhang any lower part of the brick-work on the front thereof.

Nevertheless, with regard to buildings of the first rate and extra first rate, the jambs, breast, and flue of any single chimney may be built upon brick, stone, or iron corbels above the ceiling of the third story of every such building.

And with regard to buildings of the second and third rates, the jambs, breast, and flue in any single chimney may be built upon brick, stone, or iron corbels above the ceiling of the second story of every such building.

But the projection both of such jambs and breasts must not in any case exceed nine inches before the face of the wall or stack to which the same shall adjoin.

And with regard to angle chimneys, such chimneys may be built in the internal angle of any building, so that the width of the breast thereof do not exceed five feet, and so that it be properly supported on iron girders with brick arches, or on strong stone landings not less than four inches thick, and tailed at least nine inches into each of the two walls forming such angle.

Dimensions and Materials.

And with regard to chimneys, in reference to the dimensions of the jambs thereof,—

The jambs of every chimney must not be less than eight and a half inches wide on each side of such opening.

And with regard to chimneys and flues, in reference to the thickness of the brick-work thereof,—

The breast of every chimney, and the front, back, withe, or partition of every flue, must be at the least four inches in thickness of sound bricks, properly bonded, and the joints of the work must be filled in with good mortar or cement, and all the inside thereof, and also the outside or face thereof next the interior of any building, must be rendered or pargetted.

And with regard to flues, in reference to the dimensions thereof, no flue may be used for a smoke flue which is of less internal diameter in any section than eight and a half inches.

Timber or Wood Work.

And with regard to chimneys, in reference to timber,—

No timber must be placed over any opening for supporting the breast of any chimney, but there must be an arch of brick or stone over the opening of every such chimney, to support the breast thereof, and an iron bar or bars must be built into the jambs, at the least nine inches on each side, to tie in the abutments whenever the breast projects more than four and a half inches from the face of the wall, and the jamb on either side is of less width than two-thirds of the opening.

And no timber or wood-work must be placed or laid in any wall under any chimney opening within eighteen inches at the least of the surface of the hearth to the fireplace of such chimney opening.

And as to any timber or wood-work, in reference to the fixing thereof in or against any wall containing flues or against any chimney breast or chimney jamb,—

If timber or wood-work be affixed to the front of any jamb or mantle, or to the front or back of any chimney or flue, then it must be fixed by iron nails or holdfasts, or other iron fastenings, which must not be or be driven nearer than four inches to the inside of any flue or to the opening of any chimney, and such timber or wood-work must not be nearer than nine inches to the opening of any chimney.

And no timber must be laid or placed within three inches of the face, or breast, back, side, or jamb of any flue, or of any chimney opening, where the substance of brick-work or stone-work shall be less than eight and a half inches thick, nor must any flooring board, batten, ground skirting, or other lining or fitting of wood, nor any wood staircase, nor any thing else of wood, be fixed or placed against or near to the face, or breast, back, side, or jamb of any flue, fireplace, or chimney opening, unless and until the brick or stone-work constituting the same shall have been thoroughly and efficiently rendered or pargetted with proper mortar or stucco, and such rendering must be in every case in addition to four inches at least of solid fireproof structure.

Slabs and Hearths.

And a slab or slabs of brick, tile, stone, slate, marble, or other proper and sufficient substance, at the least twelve inches longer than the opening of every chimney when finished, and at the least eighteen inches in front of the arch over the same, must be laid before the opening of every chimney.

And in every floor, except the lowest floor, such slab or slabs must be laid wholly upon stone or iron bearers, or upon brick trimmers; but in the lowest floor they may be laid on a brick fender, or bedded on the solid ground.

And the hearth of every chimney must be laid and bedded wholly on brick or stone, or other incombustible substance, which must be solid for a thickness of nine inches at the least, beneath the surface of any such hearth.

Backs.

And as to the back of every chimney opening of every building (except backs of chimneys in the lowest story of buildings of the fourth rate), every such back in the lowest story, must be at the least thirteen inches thick from the hearth to the height of twelve inches above the mantle, and in every other story at the least eight and a half inches thick up to the same relative height.

And as to the backs of chimney openings in the lowest story of buildings of the fourth rate, such backs must be at the least eight and a half inches thick to the height of twelve inches at the least above the level of the mantle:

Provided always, that if the chimney be built in any wall, not being a party wall, then the back of every such chimney opening may be four and a half inches less than the several thicknesses above described.

Chimney Openings, Back to Back.

And as to backs of all such chimney openings, if two chimneys be built back to back, then the thickness between the same must be at the least of the thickness herein-before described for the back of one chimney opening.

Angles of Flues.

And as to all flues, in reference to the angles thereof,—

If any flue be built with sufficient openings in it of not less size than nine inches square, and proper close iron doors and frames inserted in such openings, so that every part of such flue may be swept by machinery, then every angle in such flue may be of any degree.

But if it be not so built then every such angle must be one hundred and thirty-five degrees at the least.

And every salient or projecting angle within a flue must be rounded off four inches at the least, and protected by a rounded stone or iron bar.

Close Fires.

And as to every oven, furnance; cokel, or close fire used for the purpose of trade or manufacture, it must be six inches at the least distant from any party wall, and must not be upon nor within a distance of eighteen inches of any timber or wood-work.

And the floor on or above which such oven, furnace, cokel, or close fire shall be built or fixed must be formed and paved under, and for a distance of two feet all round the same, with stone, brick, tile, or slate, at the least two inches thick, or other proper incombustible and non-conducting materials.

Chimney Shafts.

And as to chimney shafts or flues,—

Every chimney shaft or flue hereafter built, raised, or repaired must be carried up in brick or stone work all round, at least four inches thick, to a height of not less than three feet above the highest part of such portion of the roof, flat, or gutter adjoining thereto, measured at the point of junction.

And as to any chimney shaft (except that of a steam engine, brewery, distillery, or manufactory), the brick or stone work of such shaft or flue must not be built higher than eight feet above the slope, flat, or gutter of the roof which it adjoins, measured from the highest point of junction, unless such chimney shaft be built of increased thickness, or be built with and bonded to another chimney shaft, or be otherwise rendered secure.

And as to the chimney shaft for the boiler furnaces of any steam engine, or for any brewery, distillery, or manufactory, such shaft may be erected of any height, so that it be built in such manner and of such strength and dimensions as shall be satisfactory to the official referees, upon special application in each case.

Chimney Pots, Tubes, &c.

And as to earthen or metal chimney pots, tubes, funnels, or cowls of any description whatsoever, if such pot, tube, funnel, or cowl be higher than four feet above the brick or stone work of the flue on which the same shall be placed, then it must be fixed two feet at the least into the brick or stone work of the flue on which it shall be placed.

Smoke Pipes.

And as to any metal or other pipe or funnel for conveying smoke, heated air, or steam, in reference to the position thereof, such pipe or funnel must not be fixed against or in front of any face of any building in any street or alley, nor on the inside of any building nearer than fourteen inches to any timber or other combustible material.

Cuttings into Chimneys.

And as to every chimney shaft, jamb, breast, or flue already built, or which shall be hereafter built, in reference to cutting the same, no such erection shall be cut into for any other purpose than the repair thereof, or for the formation of soot doors, or for letting in, removing, or altering stove pipes or smoke jacks, except as directed for building an external wall against an old sound party wall.

SCHEDULE (G.)—(*See* § 5.)

RULES concerning Roof Coverings.

Materials.

With regard to roof coverings, in reference to the materials thereof,—

If the external parts of any roof, flat, or gutter of any building, or of any projection therefrom, and of any turret, dormer, lantern-light, and other erection on the roof or flat of any building, be hereafter built or rebuilt, stripped,

ripped, or uncovered, then every such part (except the door frames and doors, window frames and sashes of such turrets, dormers, lantern-lights, or other erections,) must be covered with slates, tiles, metal, glass, artificial stone or cement, and such excepted parts may be made of such wood as shall be necessary.

Rain-water Pipes.

And with regard to the roof, flat, and gutter of any building, and of any projection therefrom, and also balconies, verandahs, and shop fronts, they must be so arranged and constructed, and so supplied with gutters and pipes, as to prevent the water therefrom dropping on to or running over any public way.

SCHEDULE (H.)—(*See* § 5 & 51.)

RULES concerning DRAINS to Buildings hereafter built.

Drains into Sewers.

With regard to the drains of buildings of any class, and of every addition thereto,—

Before the several walls of any such building shall have been built to the height of ten feet from their foundations the drains thereof must have been properly built and made good; (that is to say,) if there be within one hundred feet from any front of the building, or from the inclosure about the building, a common sewer into which it is lawful and practicable to drain, then into such common sewer; and if there be not in such situation and within such distance any such common sewer, then to the best outlet that can be obtained, so as to render in either case such drains available for the drainage of the lowest floor of such building, or addition thereto, and also of its areas, water-closets, privies, and offices (if any).

And the inside of the main drains under and from every building for carrying off soil must be in transverse section at the least equal to a circular area of at least nine inches in diameter.

And every such drain must be laid to a fall or current of at the least half an inch to ten feet, and so as that the whole of every such drain within the walls of such building shall be wholly covered over under the lowest floor, and independently thereof.

And every such drain within the walls of such building must

be built and covered over with brick, stone, or slate, and so as to render the drain air-tight.

And every part of such drain inside and outside the walls of every building must be built of brick, tile, stone, or slate, set in mortar or cement.

Cesspools and Privies.

And with regard to cesspools and privies,—

If there be a common sewer within fifty feet from any front of or from the inclosure about any house or other building, then a cesspool must not be made for the reception of drainage from such house or other building, unless there be or shall be built a good and sufficient drain from such cesspool to such common sewer.

And if any cesspool be built under a house or other building, then such cesspool must be built air-tight.

And every privy built in the yard or area of any building, or under any street or alley, must have a door, and be otherwise properly inclosed, screened, and fenced from public view.

SCHEDULE (I.)—(*See* § 5 & 52.)

RULES concerning STREETS and ALLEYS hereafter formed.

Width.

With regard to every such street or alley hereafter to be formed, in reference to the width thereof, every street or alley must be of at the least the following width from front to front in every part thereof respectively; that is to say,—

Every street (excepting any mews) must be of the width of forty feet at the least; but if the buildings fronting any street be more than forty feet high from the level of the street, then such street must be of a width equal at the least to the height of the buildings about such level.

Every alley and every mews must be of the width of twenty feet at the least; but if the buildings fronting any alley, or to any mews, be more than twenty feet high from the level of the alley or mews, then such alley or mews must be of a width equal at the least to the height of the buildings above such level.

Entrances to Alleys.

And with regard to every such alley, in reference to the entrance thereof, every alley must have two entrances thereto, each being at the least of the full width of the alley, and one of the two at the least open from the ground upwards.

Measurement of Width.

And with regard both to such streets and alleys, the aforesaid width is to be ascertained by measuring (at right angles to the course thereof) from front to front of the buildings on each side of such street or alley.

SCHEDULE (K.)—(*See* § 5 & 53.)

RULES concerning DWELLING HOUSES hereafter built or rebuilt, with regard to Back Yards and Areas, and Rooms under Ground and in the Roof.

Back Yards.

With regard to back yards or open spaces attached to dwelling houses,—

Every house hereafter built or rebuilt must have an inclosed back yard or open space of at the least one square, exclusive of any building thereon, unless all the rooms of such house can be lighted and ventilated from the street, or from an area of the extent of at the least three quarters of a square above the level of the second story, into which the owner of the house to be rebuilt is entitled to open windows for every room adjoining thereto.

And if any house already built be hereafter rebuilt, then, unless all the rooms of such house can be lighted and ventilated from the street, or from an area of the extent of at the least three quarters of a square, into which the owner of the house to be rebuilt is entitled to open windows for every room adjoining thereto, there must be above the level of the floor of the third story an open space of at least three quarters of a square.

And with regard to every building of the first class,—

Every such building must be built with some roadway, either to it or to the inclosure about it, of such width as will admit to one of its fronts of the access of a scavenger's cart of the ordinary size of such carts.

Lowermost Rooms.

And with regard to the lowermost rooms of houses, being rooms of which the surface of the floor is more than three feet below the surface of the footway of the nearest street or alley, and to cellars of buildings hereafter to be built or rebuilt,—

If any such room or cellar be used or intended to be used as a separate dwelling, then the floor thereof must not be below the surface or level of the ground immediately adjoining thereto, unless it have an area, fireplace, and window as required for rooms and cellars of existing buildings let separately, and used as a separate dwelling, and unless it be properly drained.

And with regard to every such lowermost room or cellar in any existing building, used or intended to be used as a separate dwelling,—

There must be an area not less than three feet wide in every part, from six inches below the floor of such room or cellar to the surface or level of the ground adjoining to the front, back, or external side thereof, and extending the full length of such side.

And such area, to the extent of at least five feet long and two feet six inches wide, must be in front of the window of such room or cellar, and must be open, or covered only with open iron gratings.

And there must be made for every such room or cellar an open fireplace, with proper flue therefrom.

And there must be a window opening of at least nine superficial feet in area, which window opening must be fitted with a frame filled in with glazed sashes, of which at the least four and a half superficial feet must be made to open for ventilation.

Attic Rooms.

And with regard to rooms in the roof of any building hereafter built or rebuilt, in reference to the number of floors of rooms in the roof, and to the height of such rooms, there must not be more than one floor of such rooms, and such rooms must not be of a less height than seven feet, except the sloping part, if any, of such roof, which sloping part must not begin at less than three feet six inches above the floor, nor extend more than three feet six inches on the ceiling of such room.

Rooms in other Parts.

And with regard to rooms in other parts of the building, in reference to the height thereof, every room used or intended to be used as a separate dwelling must be of at the least, the height of seven feet from the floor to the ceiling.

SCHEDULE (L.)

LIST of FEES payable to the SURVEYORS under this Act..

Fees for new Buildings.

For any Building erected on old or new foundations, as follows:	Dwelling House Class. £.	s.	d.	Warehouse Class. £.	s.	d.	Public Buildings Class. £.	s.	d.
If the Building be of the 1st rate - - - - -	3	10	0	3	10	0	3	10	0
Ditto - extra 1st ditto	5	5	0	-	-	-	5	5	0
Ditto - - 2nd ditto	3	3	0	3	3	0	3	3	0
Ditto - - 3rd ditto	2	10	0	2	10	0	2	10	0
If the Building be of the 4th rate, and contain more than two stories -	2	2	0	2	2	0	2	2	0
If the Building be of the 4th rate, and do not contain more than two stories -	1	10	0	2	2	0	1	10	0
And with regard to Buildings of the Warehouse Class, a further Fee to be paid in respect of any additional 200,000 cubic feet, or portion of 200,000 cubic feet, in any such Building, beyond the first 200,000 cubic feet -	-	-	-	Equal to One Half of the above Fees respectively.			–		
And for inspecting and reporting to the Official Referees (s. 24) on Party Walls and Intermixed Buildings,—									
If the Building be of the 1st rate -	3	10	0	3	10	0	3	10	0
Ditto extra 1st ditto	5	5	0	-	-	-	5	5	0
Ditto 2nd ditto	3	3	0	3	3	0	3	3	0
Ditto 3rd ditto	2	10	0	2	10	0	2	10	0
If the Building be of the 4th rate, and contain more than two stories -	2	2	0	2	2	0	2	2	0
If the Building be of the 4th rate, and do not contain more than two stories -	1	10	0	2	2	0	1	10	0
For every insulated Building -	1	1	0	1	1	0	1	1	0
For every detached Building built for the Purposes of Trade or Collection of Toll - - -	10s. 6d.								

For every attached or detached Building, distinctly rated (except any such attached or detached building built at the same time as the building to which it belongs, and carried up and covered in within 21 days after such building shall have been covered in within the meaning of this act), such fee as is hereby imposed in respect of additions to or alterations of buildings of the rate to which such attached or detached buildings shall belong.

Fee for Additions or Alterations.

For every addition or alteration made to any building (after the roof thereof shall have been covered in) which shall involve the execution of works subject to the regulations of this act, the following fees; that is to say,—

	£.	s.	d.
If the building be of the 1st rate -	1	15	0
Ditto - extra 1st ditto -	2	10	0
Ditto - 2d ditto -	1	10	0
Ditto - 3d ditto -	1	5	0
If the building be of the 4th rate, and contain more than two stories -	0	15	0
If the building be of the 4th rate, and do not contain more than two stories - - -	0	10	0

And with regard to buildings of the warehouse class, a further fee, equal to one-half of the above fees respectively, to be paid in respect of every additional 200,000 cubic feet, or any portion of 200,000 cubic feet, in any such building, beyond the first 200,000 cubic feet.

Fees for Special Duties.

For the following special duties performed by any surveyor, according to the enactments of this act, where such duties shall not be performed incidentally to the building or rebuilding of or adding to or altering any building in respect of which any other fees may be payable; that is to say,—

For attending to the cutting away of chimney breasts for external walls,—

	£	s.	d.
If the building be of the 1st rate -	3	3	0
Ditto extra 1st ditto -	3	3	0
Ditto - 2d ditto - / Ditto - 3d ditto -	2	2	0
If the building be of the 4th rate, and contain more than two stories - - -	1	1	0

	£	s.	d.
If the building be of the 4th rate, and do not contain more than two stories - - -	0	10	6
For condemning party fence walls -	0	10	6
For the inspection and removal of projections and ruinous buildings -	0	10	0
For surveying party walls not kept in repair, and consenting to notice of repair being served - -	0	10	0
For inspecting arches or stone floors over public ways - - -	0	10	0
For inspecting formation of openings in party walls - - -	0	10	0

Fees for Special Services not expressly provided for.

For any service performed by any surveyor which is required by this act, but not comprehended under any of the foregoing heads,—

Such fee, not exceeding 2*l.*, as the official referees shall by writing under their hands order and appoint, with the consent of the Commissioners of Works and Buildings.

SCHEDULE (M.)

METROPOLITAN BUILDINGS ACT.

SUMMARY of Proceedings to be taken or observed before and after Notices in relation to Buildings.

Section of the Act.	Stage of Proceeding.	Steps to be taken.	By whom taken.	With reference to whom taken.	Form of Notice to be given.	Place of Notice.	Subsequent Proceedings.
	WORKS GENERALLY.						
§13	Before commencing the operations specified in this section.	Two days' notice to be given.	By the builder. *See Definition,* § 13.	To the district surveyor.	*See* Form, No. 1.	At the district surveyor's office.	£20 penalty for neglect. Existing buildings altered, &c. without notice, to be abated as a nuisance.
§13	Before resuming operations, after being suspended for a period exceeding three months.	Two days' notice to be given.	By the builder. *See Definition,* § 13.	To the district surveyor.	*See* Form, No. 2.	At the district surveyor's office.	£20 penalty for neglect.
§13	On change of architect, master builder, or other superintendent.	Two days' notice to be given.	By the builder. *See Definition,* § 13.	To the district surveyor.	*See* Form, No. 3.	At the district surveyor's office.	£20 penalty for neglect.
§14	On the occurrence of any irregularity in building operations.	48 hours' notice to be given.	By the district surveyor.	To the builder.	*See* Form, No. 4.	At the builder's office, or place of building or of alteration.	Proceedings by surveyor or official referees.
§37	As to openings hereafter made in external walls abutting on adjoining ground or buildings.	Notice to stop up within one month.	By adjoining owner.	To owner of external wall.	*See* Form, No. 5.	According to sections as to notifications.	To be stopped up.
	SPECIAL SUPERVISION.						
§15	On completion of the carcass of a building subject to special supervision.	Notice for inspection thereof.	By architect or builder.	To the official referees.	*See* Form, No. 6.	At the official referees' office.	Survey and approval or disapproval by official referees. Prohibition of use of irregular buildings of this class, and penalty of £200 per day.
§15	On completion of amendments, or the entire com-	Notice relative thereto.	By architect or builder.	To the official referees.	*See* Form, No. 7.	At the official referees' office.	Survey and certificate.

§20, 21, 24, 25.	Before survey, repair, or pulling down of a party wall, party arch, or party fence wall.	Three months' notice before operations.	By the building owner. *See Definition*, § 13.	To the adjoining owner.	*See* Form, No. 8.	According to sections as to notifications.	§ 24.
§24	In the same case - -	Notice for survey.	By the building owner. *See Definition*, § 13.	To the district surveyor and official referees.	*See* Form, No. 9.	At the district surveyor's and the official referee's offices.	Inspection by surveyor, and report to official referees.
—	In the same case - -	Appointment of survey.	By the district surveyor.	To the owners and agents, &c.	*See* Form, No. 10.	To building and adjoining owners and agents.	Inspection by surveyor, and report to official referees.
§33, 34.	As to pulling down rooms in intermixed property, and repairing or rebuilding party fence walls.	Notice of intention to build a party wall, or as directed by official referees.	By the building owner.	To the adjoining owner and district surveyor. § 20.	*See* Form, No. 11.	According to sections as to notifications.	Erection of wall.
—	In the same case - -	Notice for inspection thereof.	By the building owner.	To the district surveyor and official referees.	*See* Form, No. 12.	At the district surveyor's and official referees' office.	Inspection of surveyor, and report to official referees.
—	In the same case - -	Appointment of survey.	By the district surveyor.	To the owners and agents, &c.	*See* Form, No. 13.	To building and adjoining owners and agents.	Inspection by surveyor, and report to official referees.
§26	As to pulling down a timber partition, and erecting or raising a party wall.	Three months' notice of intention to build or raise a party wall.	By the building owner.	To the adjoining owner.	*See* Form, No. 14.	According to sections as to notifications.	Erection of wall, or raising of wall.
§28	Excavation against existing party wall for a deeper story, and for the erection of an external wall.	One month's notice of intention to cut away footings or breast or shaft of a party wall.	By the building owner.	To the adjoining owner.	*See* Form, No. 15.	According to sections as to notifications.	Execution of operations.
§38	Building a party wall on line of junction of two pieces of vacant ground.	One month's notice for consent of adjoining owner.	By the building owner.	To the adjoining owner.	*See* Form, No. 16.	According to sections as to notification.	Execution of operations.
§38	In the same case - -	Notice of consent.	By the adjoining owner.	To the building owner.	*See* Form, No. 17.	According to sections as to notifications.	Erection of wall.
	MODIFICATIONS.						
§22, 23.	Modification or delay of intended works to suit adjoining owner.	Seven days' notice for consent.	By the adjoining owner.	To the building owner.	*See* Form, No. 18.	According to sections as to notifications.	If consent not given, commencement of works must be delayed for decision of official referees.
—	In the same case - -	Application for decision.	By the adjoining owner.	To the official referees.	*See* Form, No. 19.	At the official referees' office.	Delay in commencing of operations.
—	In the same case - -	Notice of application.	By the adjoining owner.	To the building owner.	*See* Form, No. 20.	According to sections as to notifications.	—

SCHEDULE (M.)—*continued.*

FORMS OF NOTICES AS TO WORKS.

METROPOLITAN BUILDINGS ACT, VICT. c. s. 13, 1844. (*a*)

1.—*Notice by the Builder to the District Surveyor Two Days before commencing Operations.*

I DO hereby give you notice, that I intend to (1) and that C. D. of is to be the (2) of the works to be executed; and that the said works will be begun on the day of

Dated this day of

(Signature and address.)

[*** Certain penalties are attached to neglect in giving this notice.]

METROPOLITAN BUILDINGS ACT, VICT. c. s. 13, 1844.

2.—*Notice by the Builder to the District Surveyor Two Days before resuming Operations.*

I DO hereby give you notice, that I intend to re-commence the (3) and that C. D. of is to be the (2) of the works to be resumed; and that the said works will be continued on the day of

Dated this day of

(Signature and address.)

[*** Certain penalties are attached to neglect in giving this notice.]

(*a*) Although the year and chapter are left in blank by the schedule, it may be proper to say: 8 Vict. c. 84, when any of these notices are served.

(1) *Describing the erection or intended operation in general terms, and whether it relate to any of the following matters :—*

"The erection of any building;"

or "The making of any addition to or alteration in any building;"

or "The building, pulling down, rebuilding, cutting into, or altering any party wall, external wall, chimney stack, or flue:"

or The making of "any opening in any party wall;"

or The doing of "any other matter or thing by this act placed under the supervision of the surveyor."

(2) *Insert* "architect," *or* "builder," *or other superintendent to have charge of the works.*

(3) *Describing in general terms the works referred to in notice No. 1, and which works may have been suspended three months.*

METROPOLITAN BUILDINGS ACT, VICT. c. s. 13, 1844.

3.—*Notice by the Builder to the District Surveyor as to Change of Builder.*

I DO hereby give you notice, that with reference to the works specified in my notice of last E. F. (1) is to be placed in charge of the said works, instead of C. D. the (1) mentioned in the said notice.

Dated this day of

(Signature and address.)

METROPOLITAN BUILDINGS ACT, VICT. c. s. 14, 1844.

4.—*Notice by the District Surveyor to the Builder as to any thing done in the Erection of any Building not conformably to the Act.*

I DO hereby give you notice, that the (2) now in progress (3) situate in (4) is not conformable to the statute in the portions thereof under mentioned; and I require you, within forty-eight hours from the date hereof, to amend the same.

Dated this day of at the hour of by the clock.

Note Irregularities referred to.

(Signature.)

METROPOLITAN BUILDINGS ACT, VICT. c. s. 37, 1844.

5.—*Notice by an Owner or Occupier to an adjoining Owner or Occupier to stop up an Opening in an external Wall abutting on his Premises.*

I DO hereby give you notice, that if within one month from the date hereof you do not stop up the opening made in the external wall of your premises situate in (5) and which abuts on my (6) I shall, at your expense,

(1) *Insert* "architect," *or* "builder," *or other superintendent of the work.*

(2) *Insert* "building," *or* "alterations," *or* "building operations," *as the case may be.*

(3) *Insert* "under your superintendence," *or* "in the building belonging to you," *as the case may be.*

(4) *Insert the situation as the case may be.*

(5) *Specify the situation.*

(6) *Insert* "ground," *or* "building adjoining."

cause the same to be stopped up, conformably to the statute.

Dated this day of

(Signature and address.)

FORMS OF NOTICES AS TO SPECIAL SUPERVISION.

METROPOLITAN BUILDINGS ACT, VICT. c. s. 15, 1844 (*a*).

6.—*Notice by an Architect or Builder to the Official Referees as to Completion of the Carcass of a Building subject to special Supervision.*

I DO hereby give you notice, that the building now erecting under my superintendence in ([1]) being a building of the ([2]) and having been completed to the full height of the walls thereof, and the timbers, floors, roofs, and partitions being fixed, I require you, in accordance with the statute, should you be of opinion that the building is subject to special supervision, to survey the same, and to certify accordingly.

Dated this day of

(Signature and address.)

[*** A penalty of two hundred pounds per day for using any such building without its being certified subsequent to notice as above and following.]

METROPOLITAN BUILDINGS ACT, VICT. c. s. 15, 1844.

7.—*Notice by an Architect or Builder to the Official Referees as to Completion of Amendments, and of Buildings subject to special Supervision.*

I DO hereby give you notice, that the buildings now erecting under my superintendence in ([1]) being a building of the ([2]) and having been completed in pursuance of your survey and notice subsequent, I require you, in

(*a*) See note (*a*) at p. 268.

(1) *Specify the situation.*

(2) *Insert* "first rate of second class," *or* "of the third class," *as the case may be.*

accordance with the statute, to survey the same, and to certify accordingly.

Dated this day of

(Signature and address.)

[*** This notice will be used both with reference to the completion of amendments and to the entire completion of a building.]

FORMS OF NOTICES AS TO PARTY WALLS, &c. (*a*)

METROPOLITAN BUILDINGS ACT, VICT. c. s. 20, 21, 24, 25, 1844.

8.—*Notice to be given (Three Months before commencing Operations) by an Owner or Occupier, to an adjoining Owner or Occupier, that the Party Wall or Party Arch or Party Fence Wall is out of repair.*

I DO hereby give notice, that I apprehend that the (1) or some part thereof, on the line of junction between my (2) situate, &c., and the (2) thereto adjoining, situate on the side thereof, is so far out of repair (3) as to render it necessary to (4) such wall or some part thereof; and that I intend to have such wall surveyed, pursuant to the statute; and also that I have given notice to the surveyor of the district and to the official referees to survey the premises for the purpose of certifying the condition of such wall, and whether the whole or any part thereof ought to be repaired or pulled down and rebuilt, and to certify accordingly.

Dated this day of

(Signature and address.)

(*a*) See note (*a*) at p. 268.

(1) *Insert* "party wall," *or* "party arch," *or* "party fence wall," *as the case may be.*

(2) *Insert* "house," *or* "building," *or* "ground," *as the case may be.*

(3) *Insert, when required,* "or has been rendered dangerous and ruinous by cutting away footings," *or* "breasts," *or* "chimney shafts."

(4) *Insert* "repair," *or* "pull down and rebuild," *as the case may be.*

METROPOLITAN BUILDINGS ACT, VICT. c. s. 20, 1844.

9.—*Notice, in the same Case, to the Surveyor and Official Referees.*

I do hereby give you notice, that I apprehend that the([1]) or some part thereof, on the line of junction between my ([2]) situate in and the ([2]) thereto adjoining, situate on the side thereof, is so far out of repair ([3]) as to render it necessary to repair or pull down and rebuild such wall or some part thereof; and that I require a survey thereof to be made, pursuant to the statute, and that in presence of such one or more surveyors or agents appointed by me, as under mentioned, or by *C. D.*, the owner of the adjoining property, for the purpose of certifying the condition of such wall, and whether the whole or any part thereof ought to be repaired or pulled down and rebuilt; and I do hereby also intimate that I have served a notice on *C. D.* to the like effect.

Dated this day of

(Signature and address.)

Names and Addresses of one or more Surveyors or Agents for Building Owner.

METROPOLITAN BUILDINGS ACT, VICT. c. s. 20 and 24, 1844.

10.—*Notice, in the same Case, by the District Surveyor to the Building Owner and adjoining Owner, and such One or more Surveyors and Agents by them appointed.*

I surveyor of the district, do hereby give you notice, that, in pursuance of an application made to the official referees and to me in that behalf, it is my intention to proceed to view the premises ([4]) situate in for the purpose of certifying the condition of the ([1]) and whether any part thereof is so far out of repair as to require to be either wholly or in part repaired or pulled down

(1) *Insert* "party wall," *or* "party arch," *or* "party fence wall," *as the case may be.*

(2) *Insert* "house," *or* "building," *or* "ground," *as the case may be.*

(3) *Insert, when required,* "or has been rendered dangerous and ruinous by cutting away footings," *or* "breasts," *or* "chimney shafts."

(4) *Designated by number or other name.*

and rebuilt; and such survey I do intend to make on the day of next, at by the clock in the noon, in the presence of any one or more surveyors or agents on behalf of the building owner and the adjoining owner.

Dated this day of

(Signature and address.)

METROPOLITAN BUILDINGS ACT, VICT. c. s. 33, 34, 1844.

11.—*Notice to be given, Three Months before commencing Operations, by an Owner to an adjoining Owner.*

I DO hereby give you notice, that I intend to (1) and that I intend to have such (2) surveyed conformably to the statute; and that I have given notice to the district surveyor and to the official referees to survey the premises, and to certify accordingly.

Dated this day of

(Signature and address.)

METROPOLITAN BUILDINGS ACT, VICT. c. s. 33, 34, 1834.

12.—*Notice, in the same Case, to the Surveyor and Official Referee.*

I DO hereby give you notice, that I intend to (1) and that I require a survey thereof to be made, pursuant to the statute, and that in presence of such one or more surveyors or agents appointed by me, as under mentioned, or by *C. D.* the owner of the adjoining property, for the purpose of certifying whether the whole or any part (3) ought to be pulled down and rebuilt; and I do hereby also intimate that I have served a notice on *C. D.* to the like effect.

Dated this day of

(Signature and address.)

Names and Addresses of one or more Surveyors or Agents for Building Owner.

(1) *Specify the kind of operation, as to whether it be intended*—
"To raise a party fence wall;"
or "To repair or rebuild a party fence wall;"
or "To pull down and rebuild rooms in intermixed property, &c.;"
and specifying the situation, &c.

(2) *Insert* "party fence wall," *or* "rooms in intermixed property."

(3) *Specify the kind of operation intended.*

METROPOLITAN BUILDINGS ACT, VICT. C. s. 33, 34, 1844.

13.—*Notice, in the same Case, by the District Surveyor to the Building Owner and adjoining Owner, and such One or more Surveyors and Agents by them appointed.*

I surveyor of the district, do hereby give you notice, that, in pursuance of an application made to the official referees and to me in that behalf, it is my intention to proceed to view the premises (1) situate in for the purpose of certifying whether any part of such (2) require to be (3) and such survey I do intend to make on the day of next, at by the clock in the noon, in the presence of any one or more surveyors or agents whom the parties concerned shall appoint for that purpose.

Dated this day of

(Signature.)

METROPOLITAN BUILDINGS ACT, VICT. C. s. 26, 1844.

14.—*Notice to be given, Three Months before commencing Operations, by an Owner to an adjoining Owner, where no Survey is required.*

I DO hereby give you notice, that I intend to (4) pursuant to the statute.

Dated this day of

(Signature and address.)

METROPOLITAN BUILDINGS ACT, VICT. C. s. 28, 1844.

15.—*Notice of Intention to build an external Wall against existing Party Wall, and for that Purpose to cut away Footings, Breast, and Shaft of an existing Party Wall.*

I DO hereby give you notice, that it is my intention, one month after the date hereof, to build an external wall against

(1) *Designated by number or other name.*

(2) *Specify the kind of operation intended.*

(3) *Insert* "raised," *or* "repaired," *or* "pulled down and rebuilt," *as the case may be.*

(4) *Specify the kind of operation, as to whether it be intended*—
"To pull down a timber partition, and instead thereof to build a party wall," *or* to rebuild a sound party wall.
or "To raise a party wall."

the existing party wall by which our premises are parted, situate , and to cut away such portion of the footings or chimney breast or shaft in such party wall as will be necessary for that purpose.

Dated this day of

(Signature and address.)

METROPOLITAN BUILDINGS ACT, VICT. C. s. 38, 39, 1844.

16.—*Notice of Desire to build a Party Wall on the Line of Junction of Two Pieces of vacant Ground.*

I DO hereby give you notice, that I desire to build partly on my land or ground adjoining your vacant ground, and partly on your vacant ground, on the line of junction of the said premises, (1) which will be of the under-noted thicknesses and dimensions; and should you consent thereto I require you to signify such consent in writing on or before the day of next.

Dated this day of

(Signature and address.)

Note of the Thickness and Dimensions.

METROPOLITAN BUILDINGS ACT, VICT. C. s. 38, 39, 1844.

17.—*Notice of Consent to the Building of a Party Wall on the Line of Junction of Two Pieces of vacant Ground.*

I DO hereby give you notice, that I consent to the building of a (1) partly on my land or ground adjoining your vacant ground on the line of junction of the said premises, which I require to be of the under-mentioned thicknesses and dimensions, and other particulars.

Dated this day of

(Signature and address.)

Note of the Thickness and Dimensions, and other Particulars.

(1) *Insert* "party wall," *or* "party fence wall," *or* "external wall," *as the case may be.*

FORMS OF NOTICES AS TO MODIFICATION OR DELAY OF INTENDED BUILDING OPERATIONS.

METROPOLITAN BUILDINGS ACT, VICT. C. s. 22, 23, 1844.

18.—*Requisition to a Building Owner by an adjoining Owner as to Modification or Delay of intended Work on his behalf.*

I DO hereby give you notice, that I require you to (1) the works specified in your notice of the day of in consequence of the inconvenience and loss that would arise to me if the same were executed at the time proposed by you; and if you do not consent hereto, or dissent therefrom, within days, then, in pursuance of the statute, you are hereby required to delay your intended operations until the official referees shall have determined thereon.

Dated this day of

(Signature and address.)

Note of Modifications.

METROPOLITAN BUILDINGS ACT, VICT. C. s. 22, 33, 1844.

19.—*Notice by an adjoining Owner to the Official Referees as to the Modification or Delay of intended Works of a Building Owner.*

I DO hereby give you notice, that *C. D.*, of having specified in his notice of the day of certain works to be executed subsequent to the day of next, and I having served upon him a requisition in reference to the (2) of the works so intended by him, in consequence of the inconvenience and loss that would arise to me if the same were executed at the time proposed by him, and he not having attended thereto, it is my desire

(1) *Insert* "modify, as under noted," *or* "delay until the day of ," *as the case may be.*

(2) *Insert* "modification as under noted," *or* "delay until the day of ," *as the case may be.*

that a survey be made, in pursuance of the statute, with reference to such works, and the notices referred to.

Dated this day of (1)

(Signature and address.)

Note of Modifications.

METROPOLITAN BUILDINGS ACT, VICT. C. s. 22, 23, 1844.

20.—*Notice by an adjoining Owner to a Building Owner as to Application to the Official Referees for Survey of intended Works with reference to the Modification or Delay thereof.*

I DO hereby give you notice, that, in consequence of your not consenting to the (2) of the works intended by you, as specified in my requisition of the day of last, I have applied to the official referees for a survey of the premises, pursuant to the statute.

Dated this day of (3)

(Signature and address.)

(1) *Within seven days after the previous requisition.*
(2) *Insert* "modification," *or* "delay," *as the case may be.*
(3) *Within seven days after the previous requisition.*

THE

LAW OF FENCES.

THE LAW OF FENCES.

CHAPTER I.

Of Fences, the Ownership of them, and other Incidents.

Of Fences.

FENCES, although they may have been occasionally used as boundaries for the division of property, are, nevertheless, treated by our law for the most part as guards against intrusion. A fence may consist of almost any kind of division or inclosure, but a hedge, ditch, or a wall will be most commonly found to answer that term. A bank without a hedge is likewise a defence (*a*), but this species of boundary or bulwark is more usually observed next the sea for the purpose of resisting the encroachments of the tide, and as it would then more properly belong to the law of sewers, we shall not interfere with such a matter in the present Treatise.

It is natural to make an inquiry here as to the mode by which fenciug between fields by the ordinary plan of hedging and ditching is accomplished. *Lawrence*, J., in an action connected with the question, gave the legal rule upon the point so clearly that it shall be transcribed at length.

"The rule about ditching is this. No man, making a ditch, can cut into his neighbour's soil, but usually he

(*a*) See 9 Bing. 3, Alston and others *v.* Scales, and *post*, chapter 2.

Of Fences.

cuts it to the very extremity of his own land: he is of course bound to throw the soil which he digs out, upon his own land; and often, if he likes it, he plants a hedge on the top of it: therefore, if he afterwards cuts beyond the edge of the ditch, which is the extremity of his land, he cuts into his neighbour's land, and is a trespasser; no rule about five feet and eight feet has any thing to do with it (*b*). He may cut the ditch as much wider as he will, if he enlarges it into his own land" (*c*).

This illustration of the learned Judge is, in fact, the most ordinary course of fencing in counties where stone walls are not in use, and we have, therefore, the ditch, the bank, and the hedge growing upon the base of the bank. No doubt, the more useful method was for the maker of the hedge to have four feet for the area of his ditch and then four feet farther for the surface of his bank, and in order to meet this convenient enclosure, the neighbour might, probably, have agreed that his own soil might be disturbed for the purpose of carrying out that breadth of line. The obligation of repair on the part of the maker might have been a sufficient ground for a surrender of the adjacent ground for so valuable an end. But it did not follow as a legal consequence that the eight feet were to be extorted without an agreement, and, therefore, the defendant in an action upon the case for an injury to the plaintiff's reversion in vain attempted to set up a common law right of this nature. He succeeded, however, in the action, the jury having found for him, because the declaration did not apply to the close where the injury was done, but to one quite different (*d*). From hence it follows, that where two

(*b*) See *post*, as to this.
(*c*) 3 Taunt. 138.
(*d*) 3 Taunt. 137, Vowles *v.* Miller.

Of Fences.

adjacent fields are separated by a hedge and ditch, the hedge belongs *primâ facie* to the owner of the field in which the ditch is not (*e*). For when the fence was made the party would necessarily have thrown the soil upon his own land, and as two ditches would not have been needed, the bank where the hedge was planted would be upon a level with the field on the other side of the hedge. This consideration in general decides the ownership of a hedge. And the property of a wall would ensue in like manner where, as is often the case, a ditch appears on one side of it. But there may be two ditches, and but one bank and hedge. Each owner might have thought fit to throw up a bank as far as the verge of his own boundary, so that, in effect, the banks would become united, and thus as soon as the hedge grew there would appear but one bank. A question might then arise at a subsequent period and in the absence of a deed, as to the ownership of the hedge. The hedge might be claimed for its trees, or might come into issue as involving the important consideration of repair. The law, in this case, will not presume, from the mere circumstances, a tenancy in common of the hedge, and yet as both neighbours would have thrown their soil towards each other's land instead of the contrary way as in the instance of a solitary hedge, it might appear to have been a joint concern. Acts of ownership, therefore, are required as evidence of the right where a dispute arises (*f*). Should those acts prove to be joint, a tenancy in common will present itself, and on the contrary, proof, entirely or for the most part, on one side only, will satisfy the jury that there is an undivided property in the fence. If it

(*e*) 2 Selwyn, N. P., 1329, 8th edition, *per* Bayley, J., in Guy *v.* West.

(*f*) *Per* Bayley, J., in Guy *v.* West, *ut supra*.

Of Fences.

could be shewn that the hedge stood half on one land and half on the other, and mutual acts of ownership were to be disclosed, the severalty of the hedge would be manifest.

The principles which govern a tenancy in common apply to interference with fences. So that if a tenant in common were to alter the joint wall, or do any other act calculated to injure his co-tenant, an action on the case and not of trespass or abatement must be the remedy. So a person clipping a hedge cannot be sued in trespass by his fellow (*g*). But if the wall be wholly destroyed, or the hedge grubbed up by a tenant in common, the act of destruction makes it impossible for the other tenant to exercise his right, and therefore trespass will lie in such cases (*h*). It may be remarked, that much care is indispensable if the remedy by abatement be pursued. It is not always easy to calculate the consequences of an injudicious act of this kind, as in the case of the party who broke down a wall erected as a guard against the sea.

In this case the plaintiff proceeded to repair his wall, but before he had finished, a storm arose and destroyed the new works upon which it was made a question whether the defendant ought not to answer for this new damage, it being no other than the sequel of his own illegal conduct (*i*).

(*g*) See Gow Rep. 201.

(*h*) Gow, 201, Voyce *v.* Voyce, and Others. The plaintiff and defendant were tenants in common of a hedge, and the defendant grubbed it up. See also 5 Taunt. 20, Matts *v.* Hawkins. 8 B. & C. 259, Cubitt *v.* Porter.

(*i*) 12 Mod. 543.

CHAPTER II.

Of the Obligation to make or repair Fences.

Of the Obligation to make or repair Fences.

In discussing the subject proposed for consideration in this chapter, it will be found that the results of neglect to make or repair a fence wall, for the most part, involve the legal obligation concerning that matter. For a party, unless bound by a particular act of Parliament, is not, from the mere circumstance of having a neighbour, compelled to raise a ditch, or bank, or other defence against the contiguous property (*a*). He may continue to preserve the "ideal invisible boundary," which the law recognises as separating the close of one man from that of another, without using any visible or tangible fence (*b*).

The inconvenient consequences, however, of this exposure give at once the reason why such works are of value, and the right to create and keep them in repair comes in question so soon as the mischief, whether it be by the intrusion of cattle or otherwise, has occurred. Because the law (notwithstanding the rule that one man shall not, in general, be held to an enclosure for the benefit of another,) interferes immediately upon the accession of injury, and accords a remedy according to the event (*c*).

(*a*) The general rule of law is, that a man is only bound to take care that his cattle do not wander from his own land and trespass upon the lands of others. 6 B. & C. 337, by Bayley, J.

(*b*) See 2 Selw. N. P., 8th ed., 1327. 3 Com. 210, ed. 1809.

(*c*) See Bro. Trespass, pl. 345.

Of the Obligation to make or repair Fences.

Thus it became the interest of men, in the first instance, to guard against mutual encroachment and incursion, and this was effected through the medium of a fenced boundary. Therefore, when it is said that a person ought, of common right, to keep up his own hedges (*d*), the legal meaning seems to be that when a damage accrues, he will become fixed with the consequences. As where the lord of a manor sold fifty acres of his land: it was held, that although the vendee ought certainly to have made a hedge in this case, yet that the lord also was bound to raise an enclosure on such parts of his property as might adjoin the land of a neighbour (*e*). So where a commoner suffered his cattle to escape from the common into the land of J. S., he was held liable in trespass (*f*). And so strict is the rule, that it would be no defence to allege that the beasts of a third person had invaded the land of the plaintiff, and so not the defendant's beasts. As where A. and B. were neighbours, but B. was bound to repair. A.'s cattle travelled over B.'s field, and thence into one belonging to C. C. recovered in trespass against A., upon which A. sued B. in an action upon the case, and it mattered not that the trespassing beasts were not those of the defendant B., as he was the defaulter (*g*). Nor is it a defence that the cattle were driven forcibly upon the land, as by wild dogs, &c. (*h*).

The principle above laid down is not shaken by an

(*d*) 2 Ro. Rep. 289.

(*e*) Dy. 372 (*b*). See also Vin. Ab. Fences, (C.) 1, 2. 1 Taunt. 529, Churchill *v.* Evans.

(*f*) Bro. Tres. pl. 345. S. P., Vin. Ab. Fences, (B.) 3. See *post*, Chapter III., under the head of "Defect of Fences."

(*g*) Cro. Jac. 665, Holbach *v.* Warner; S. C., but the same facts do not appear. 2 Ro. Rep. 288.

(*h*) 20 E. 4, 16. F. N. B. 128.

Of the Obligation to make or repair Fences.

observation of the Court upon one occasion, that the charge laid upon the defendant of repair was *against common right*, for that the law bounded every man's property, and was his fence, whereas here was an obligation upon one man to make a fence for another (*i*). In the case cited the action was upon the case, and rested the defendant's liability upon a prescriptive duty that the tenants and occupiers of a certain close had always made and repaired the fence between the close of the plaintiff and that of the defendant. This was, evidently, (to use the language of the Court,) against common right, and is quite distinguishable from the ordinary actions of trespass or case where there is not any such immemorial burthen.

In former days likewise, a writ was granted for one vill against another to compel the repair of fences, but the Court said it should be in the nature of a *scire facias* returnable before them (*k*).

It may just be remarked that an ecclesiastical person is liable to this repair of enclosures as soon as the consideration attaches upon him. And the law and custom of England makes the amendment of the fences a subject of dilapidation if it be neglected (*l*).

Looking at the principle mentioned above, it might be supposed that as the advantages of a fence are so mutual, there would be found a double bank and hedge at the verge of each inclosure. This, however, so far from being the case universally, is even very rare, the boundaries of property being usually confined within one defence. And it may be added as a general rule, that

(*i*) 1 Salk. 335, Starr *v.* Rookesby.

(*k*) Sty. 26, Anon.

(*l*) See 2 Lind., edit. Ox., p. 253, 254. Gibs. Codex, p. 752. 2 Burn. Eccl. Law, ed. 1824, p. 152. 2 Adol. & El. 773.

Of the Obligation to make or repair Fences.

the repair of the defence ensues upon the ownership thereof. This condition of things must be attributed to agreement between the respective proprietors. This agreement is either developed by a deed, or presumed where no deed exists. In the one case, the instrument itself sufficiently manifests the intention of the parties, in the other, (and the majority of instances is of this nature) the obligation to fence arises by prescription. Whether the compact was originally made by reason of tenancy, or in what manner the consideration arose in cases of prescription, it is not our business to inquire in this place. The bargain might have been made by an agreement that A. should make the fence if B. would submit to repair it: the consideration might have sprung from a money payment by one owner to his neighbour: it might have been owing in some cases to the necessity of a retribution for damage occasioned by a trespass: the relation of landlord and tenant (*l*), again, might have occasioned it; or both the raising and amendment of the fence might have been the voluntary acts of one individual in order to suit his own convenience by lessening the hazards of trespass. Setting aside these speculations, it is plainly our object here to deal with the obligation to repair a fence already made, since the creation of new boundaries, except by acts of Parliament, has been disposed of by the observations which have been above suggested. The right to repair fences has sometimes been the subject of litigation where there has existed an express covenant, but it has been more especially so when the liability has rested upon prescription.

It seems clear that a man is not bound to fence against his own land. As if A. should have a close named

(*l*) See 2 Ro. Rep. 288.

Of the Obligation to make or repair Fences.

Whiteacre and one contiguous called Blackacre. Although A. might be under an obligation to fence against the land contiguous to Blackacre, he is, nevertheless, under no such liability to defend Whiteacre against Blackacre. Thus where one who was bound to enclose against his neighbour, purchased one acre contiguous to the enclosure of twenty acres against which he was compelled to enclose, it was held, that he should not be answerable with reference to the one acre (*m*). For if it were so, he would be obliged to fence against his own land, a duty which the law does not recognise. A. has land adjoining to his park—it belongs to him to fence his park; yet he is not, therefore, to fence against that portion where his own land lies (*n*). The same case is put differently thus: A. was seised of the park of C., in C.; B. was seised of thirty acres adjoining. A. was under a prescriptive obligation to make a fence between this park and certain land which lay between the park and the thirty acres; B. sent his beasts into the thirty acres, and for want of a fence they entered the park. Trespass being brought, B. pleaded that A. was bound to fence, upon which A. replied that one C. was seised of ten acres lying between the said thirty acres and the park, and because B. had confessed the trespass, A. had judgment; for A. was bound to fence except against him who had the land next his park, unless in a special case, by which we may understand a particular agreement or covenant (*o*).

It will readily occur to the reader that the property of adjoining closes may become severed, and, again, that

(*m*) 21 H. 6, 5.

(*n*) 22 H. 6, 7, Sagevill *v.* Midward.

(*o*) 21 H. 6, 33; S. C., 22 H. 6, 7. And see F. N. B. 299. 13 Vin. Ab. 163, Fences, (A.) 1, (D.) 3 and 4.

Of the Obligation to make or repair Fences.

after the disunion they may be once more centered in the same owner. In the first case, where no enclosure exists, it has been debated whether the seller or the buyer should maintain the fence in the absence, of course, of an express stipulation upon the subject. If there be an incloeure already, unless there be an agreement to the contrary, the person on whose side the hedge is, and the ditch is not, is under the obligation to repair. In the second case, where the closes have returned to the same owner, *and they are once more divided*, it has been considered that the usual principle of extinguishment upon unity of possession governs the transaction, and, moreover, that the consideration does not revive after the severance. With respect to the first point, in seems clear, that where there is not any enclosure, the principle concerning mutual trespass must prevail notwithstanding some ancient controversies to the contrary. As where A. had, time out of mind, two closes adjoining, and the question was who should make the hedge, and the Court were divided as to the liability of the vendor or purchaser (*p*). So where it was said that if A. sell to B. a piece of pasture lying open to another piece of pasture belonging to A., the vendee must keep his cattle from running into A.'s piece (*q*). This case and opinion, although plainly calculated to raise questions between the seller and buyer are nevertheless of inferior authority to the case in Dyer, where the true principle appears. A. was seised of 200 acres of common moor, and he enfeoffed B. of 50. It was held, that the purchaser should enclose and keep the beasts within the fifty acres, and

Query
t

(*p*) Mo. 775, Doyly *v.* Drake. Yelverton and Williams, Js., that the vendor should make it; Popham, C. J., and Fenner, J., *é contrà*.

(*q*) 6 Mod. 314.

Of the Obligation to make or repair Fences.

that A. ought to do the like in respect of the residue (*r*). From thence the inference, as we have mentioned in a former page, is, not that either party is under a legal obligation to make the enclosure, but that each will be respectively answerable in case of damage, a circumstance which highly favours the creation of a fence (*s*).

As to the second point, it is the rule that a duty of fencing becomes extinguished by unity of possession, and that it is incapable of a revivor though the closes came afterwards into severalty (*t*). The plaintiff sued, in a modern case, as the owner and occupier of certain land called the Deans. The defendant was the owner and occupier of the next adjoining field called Dead Moor. These lands were separated by a fence and gate on the defendant's close. Both belonged to one C. thirty years before the action, and about that period C. sold the Deans to the plaintiff's father, and two years afterwards the Dead Moor to the defendant. The closes thus lost the unity. The repair of the gate lay upon the tenant of Dead Moor whilst C. was the sole proprietor of the property in both fields. An injury having occurred in consequence of the defendant's act in removing the gate mentioned above, the plaintiff brought an action upon the case, and proved that the tenant of Dead Moor had repaired the gate once under a threat of impounding between the time when the plaintiff's father had bought Deans and the defendant Dead Moor. He then shewed, that after the defendant's purchase of Dead Moor, the defendant himself repaired the gate at the instance of the plaintiff. These two examples of repair were relied on by the plaintiff's counsel as evidence of an agreement on

(*r*) Dy. 372 (*b*).

(*s*) See likewise Law Mag. vol. i. 590, "Law of Fences."

(*t*) 1 Ventr. 97, Polus *v*. Henstock.

Of the Obligation to make or repair Fences.

the part of the occupier of Dead Moor to do the repair in question, and the learned Judge left it to the jury to say whether they would presume such an agreement, for, if so, the verdict would be for the plaintiff. The jury found that the defendant was bound by agreement to repair this gate. But the defendant's counsel, upon a motion for entering a nonsuit, urged strongly that a deed, which must have existed within thirty years in this case, could hardly have been laid aside or lost, and he added, that the Judge should have presented that suggestion more fully than he did to the minds of the jury. And of this opinion was the Court, who considered that the verdict ought to have been for the defendant upon this evidence. Upon no occasion had the defendant or his predecessor been acquainted that in case of trespass, the owner of Deans would look for compensation from the occupier of Dead Moor. The fact of repair, although done twice, did not distinctly shew that the occupier of Dead Moor had done so by virtue of any legal obligation. With respect to the extinguishment, Mr. Justice Bayley, who delivered judgment, observed, that a pre-existing obligation to repair is destroyed by unity of ownership, and, further, that it would not revive unless words should be introduced for that purpose into the deed of conveyance (*u*). Still, as there was evidence for the jury, slight indeed, but yet sufficient for their consideration, the rule was made absolute for a new trial, instead of a nonsuit, but without costs (*x*).

Making and repair of Fences by virtue of Acts of Parliament.]—Fences are frequently repairable by virtue of particular acts of Parliament. The general Enclosure

(*u*) 6 B. & C. 337.
(*x*) 6 B. & C. 329, Boyle *v.* Tamlyn.

Of the Obligation to make or repair Fences.

Act, for instance, affords an example of this nature. By 41 Geo. 3, c. 109, sect. 9, carriage roads set out, shall be well and sufficiently fenced on both sides by the owners of allotments, and within such time as commissioners shall direct in writing, but no person may set up or erect any gate across any such carriage road. By sect. 24, if any allottee, or any guardian, &c. shall neglect to fence the land allotted within the time directed by the commissioners in writing, the commissioners may cause the allotments to be fenced, and the expenses of such fencing must be reimbursed before the allottee can have possession of his land. By sect. 25, the proprietors of allotments may set up and erect posts and rails, or other dead fences, on the outside of the ditches bounding their respective allotments, not exceeding three feet from such ditches, for the preservation of their quickset hedges, at any seasonable time within seven years after the fencing of their allotments, and may likewise take and carry away the materials of such outside fence, at any seasonable time before the expiration of the said term. By sect. 26, no fences or hedges standing upon the lands to be enclosed at the time of passing any enclosure act shall be cut down or destroyed by the owners until the execution of the award, unless the consent of the commissioners in writing shall first be had. If any such fences or hedges shall be assigned or approved of by commissioners as boundary fences, or subdivision fences to any allotments, all such fences and hedges shall be left uncut for the benefit of the proprietor of the allotments, and such proprietor shall make compensation in money to the former owners thereof, as the commissioners shall in writing appoint (*y*). By sect. 27, however, where the

(*y*) See section 29, as to the mode of recovering it.

Of the Obligation to make or repair Fences.

boundary of any common fields or enclosed grounds shall happen to be a mound, fence, brook, or rivulet, the proprietors shall not be compelled to fence, but such mound, &c. shall be maintained and cleansed by the respective proprietors of the same in the same manner as before the passing of the act, or in such other manner as the commissioners may direct. Provided, nevertheless, that in case it shall appear to the commissioners that any proprietor may have a greater proportion of fences to make and maintain upon any allotment than, in the judgment of such commissioners, he ought to have, it shall be lawful to award a sum of money to be paid to that proprietor in respect of such repair, out of the money to be raised for defraying the expenses of the act, so that the boundary fences may be brought as near as may be to a just and equal proportion. By sect. 28, any person wilfully and unlawfully breaking down, destroying, carrying away, or damaging any fence, stile, post, rail, gate, bridge, or tunnel, which may be placed or put up under the authority of the act, shall forfeit, upon conviction before a justice for the county where the land is situate, the sum of *5l.*, and any proprietor of lands within or inhabitant of the parish may give evidence notwithstanding he may be the owner of such fence, &c. (z).

By 7 & 8 Geo. 4, c. 29, s. 40, if any person shall steal, or shall cut, break, or throw down with intent to steal, any part of any live or dead fence, or any stile or gate, he shall, upon conviction before a justice for the first offence, pay a sum, over and above the value of the article stolen or the damage done, not exceeding *5l.*, and for any subsequent offence, he shall be committed to the house of correction for a term not exceeding twelve

(z) See section 39, for the recovery of the forfeiture.

Of the Obligation to make or repair Fences.

calendar months, there to be kept to hard labour, and may, moreover, if a male, be once or twice publicly or privately whipped after the expiration of four days from the conviction. By 7 & 8 Geo. 4, c. 30, s. 23, similar punishments are ordained against such as shall unlawfully and maliciously cut, break, throw down, or in anywise destroy any fence of any description whatsoever, or any wall, stile, or gate, or any part thereof respectively (*a*).

The reader will not have failed to notice the words "mound, brook, or rivulet," in the 27th section of 41 G. 3, c. 109, above set out. Upon the construction of a similar clause, it was made a question whether a ditch could be said to come within the description of a "sufficient fence;" the term employed, amongst others, in the particular enclosure act to which we refer. The clause alluded to was that the allotments of certain impropriators of tithes should be enclosed by fences of good and thriving quickset except where it should be directed that any other proprietor should fence, or where such allotments should adjoin to any enclosed lands, or be *bounded by any river or other sufficient fence*. The whole costs and expenses of making and keeping such fences, stiles, and

(*a*) An ancient remedy for prostrating fences was by suing out a writ of noctanter. This was given by the statute of Westm. the Second, 13 Edw. 1, c. 46, which ordained that if the destroyer of a dyke or hedge could not be known by the verdict of an assise or a jury, and if men of the towns would not indict such as were guilty of the fact, then the towns near adjoining should be distrained to levy the hedge or dyke at their own cost, and to yield damages. This writ, however, is entirely out of use. See, however, upon the subject, 2 Inst. 476. Cro. Car. 280, 439, 580. 1 Sid. 107, 212. 2 Show. 255. 1 Lev. 108. 1 Lutw. 170. 3 Salk. 167. 10 Mod. 157. An information has, however, been preferred for a riot and prostrating fences, and so it would be now, for the riot would be the principal misdemeanor, and the destruction of the fences the aggravation, or accessory. See 1 Show. 106, Rex *v.* Berchet and Others.

Of the Obligation to make or repair Fences.

gates in good repair for seven years, to be deemed and considered as part of the expenses of carrying the act into execution, and to be borne by the persons whose lands and grounds were to be discharged from tithes by virtue of the act in such proportions as the commissioners should direct. The clause went on further to enact that such fences should, after the expiration of the said term of seven years, be maintained and kept in repair by the persons whom the commissioners should, by their award, direct to perform the same. An old deep ditch or drain was the fence in question upon this occasion. It had been immemorially the boundary between the common and the two adjoining townships. No hedge or rail protected this ditch, but the surveyor to the commissioners swore, that the fence was, in the judgment of the commissioners, a sufficient fence, in its then state.

Abbott, C. J., referred to the general Enclosure Act, 41 Geo. 3, c. 109, s. 25, 26, and 27, and construing the act before him with the general act, held, that a mere ditch could not be a fence within the meaning of those provisions. A verdict was therefore found for the plaintiff upon the issue, but his Lordship gave leave to enter a verdict for the defendant. A rule was moved for, accordingly, and it was said that "fence" meant nothing more than a sufficient guard to fend, or keep off, or shut out, and the Court considering that a ditch might in legal construction be a fence, directed that the rule should be absolute for entering the verdict as prayed for (*b*).

By 4 Geo. 4, c. 95, s. 66, where, in private grounds, or across any public or private footway, an old road is altered, or a new one made, or where any fence is taken

(*b*) 1 B. & C., 70, Ellis *v.* Arnison; S. C., 2 D. & Ry. 161.

Of the Obligation to make or repair Fences.

away for the purpose of widening or improving a road, the trustees shall have proper quickset hedges planted, or have proper fences or walls made on both sides of the newly made road, or on the side from whence the fence has been removed, with sufficient ditches and sufficient posts and rails, or other fence on both sides of such quickset hedge to protect its growth, so as effectually to guard and fence off the adjoining lands from trespass or injury by horses, asses, cattle, sheep, or swine. They are also to make proper gates, stiles, posts, bridges, and arches where necessary, out of such road into the lands adjoining, and must keep the fences so to be made in good order and repair for five years, unless the owners should agree to repair from an earlier period. We, therefore, see that, under these acts of Parliament, the burthen of repair is often cast upon the trustees or makers of the road for a certain number of years, and then upon the proprietors of the lands. Where, however, no liability is imposed upon those who meddle with the road, or who are charged with carrying out the enclosure, the owners become clothed, in the first instance, with the duty of repair as in an ordinary case at common law. Even although trustees may have repaired fences for twenty years, they cannot be compelled to continue such repair in the absence of a special provision to that effect. A mandamus was applied for, commanding certain trustees to repair a wall on each side of a road leading through the churchyard of Llandilofour, in Carmarthenshire. The clause in their act ordered that the tolls should be applied towards repairing and widening the roads within their respective districts, but was entirely silent on the head of fences. The Court, therefore, were quite clear that the application must fail. And *Grose*, J., added, " Suppose that trustees under an act of Parliament make

Of the Obligation to make or repair Fences.

a road through private property, for which the party is entitled to satisfaction, the jury in assessing the damages must be taken to give him as much as will, besides the value of the land, indemnify the party for the expense of keeping up the fences between the road and the enclosure" (c). So where a person gave permission to trustees to make a way through his land, but omitted to obtain from them a promise to put up a fence upon the completion of their undertaking, he was held personally responsible to his neighbour for damage done in consequence of the want of a fence, for it was his fault, and not that of the plaintiff, that the proper stipulation had not been originally asked at the hands of those who made the alteration in the premises (d). Nevertheless, a mandamus will probably lie where trustees are directed to make good and permanent enclosures, but where instead thereof they only erect insufficient fences (e).

By 6 & 7 Wm. 4, c. 115, the act for facilitating the enclosure of open and arable lands in England and Wales, sect. 27, ring or outer fences which may be necessary, and which shall be ordered by commissioners for dividing the various parcels of land, are to be made. But if the proprietors of enclosures shall desire and shall give notice in writing to that effect, that their allotments should remain unfenced, except the ring or outer fence above-mentioned, the commissioners need do no more than set out the respective parcels by metes and bounds, without requiring any subdivision fences to be erected. By sect. 30, after premising that rectors or vicars may require interior or subdivision fences for their allotments,

(c) 2 T. R. 232, R. v. Commissioners of Llandilo District of Roads.

(d) 3 Y. & Jer. 308, Winter v. Charter.

(e) See 2 Adol. & El. 781.

Of the Obligation to make or repair Fences.

and that such fences will be attended with considerable expenses, it is enacted, that such fences may be made by the rectors or vicars under the direction of the commissioners, and, moreover, that for the payment of the expenses, the allotments may be charged with two years' annual value to be set apart for the purpose of defraying the same. By sect. 32, if any proprietor shall not have an equal or proportionable quantity of boundary mounds or fences allotted to him, the commissioners may make an equitable apportionment, so that contribution shall be afforded by the other proprietors to the person whose boundary is unequal, and the money awarded in respect thereof shall be levied and recovered in the same manner as other expenses incurred under the act.

By sect. 49, the expenses of the act, and, amongst others, of the fences, are to be borne by all the proprietors of the land authorized to be divided, allotted, and enclosed in such proportions as the commissioners shall determine, and such expenses shall be paid according to the commissioners' order, notice thereof being previously given thirty days before the payment shall be required.

Provisions under the Highways Act, 5 & 6 Wm. 4, c. 50, with respect to Fences.]—By the 65th section of this act it is provided that if the surveyor shall think that any carriageway or cartway is prejudiced by the shade of any hedges, or by any trees (except those trees planted for ornament or for shelter to any hop-ground, house, building, or court-yard of the owner thereof), growing in or near such hedges or other fences, and that the sun and wind are excluded from such highway, to the damage thereof, or if any obstruction is caused in any carriageway or cartway by any hedge or tree, it shall be lawful for any one justice of the peace, on the application of the

Of the Obligation to make or repair Fences.

said surveyor, to summon the owner of the land on which such hedges or trees are growing next adjoining to such carriageway or cartway to appear before the justices at a special sessions for the highways to shew cause why the said hedges are not cut, pruned, or plashed, or such trees are not pruned or lopped, in such manner that the carriageway or cartway shall not be prejudiced by the shade thereof, and that the sun and wind may not be excluded from such carriageway or cartway to the damage thereof, or why the obstruction caused in such carriageway or cartway should not be removed: and the question as to the cutting, pruning, or plashing such hedges, or the pruning and lopping such trees, or the removal of such obstruction as aforesaid, shall, upon proof of the service of such summons, and whether the said owner attend or not, be determined at the discretion of such last-mentioned justices; and if such justices shall order and direct that such hedges shall be cut, pruned, or plashed, or such trees pruned, or lopped, in manner aforesaid, or such obstruction removed, the said owner shall comply therewith within ten days after a copy of such order shall have been left at the usual place of abode of the said owner or of his steward or agent, and in default thereof shall forfeit on conviction a sum not exceeding forty shillings; and the said surveyor, if the order of the said justices is not complied with, shall, and he is hereby authorized and required to cut, prune, or plash such hedges, and to prune and lop such trees, for the benefit and improvement of the highway, and to remove such obstruction as aforesaid, to the best of his skill and judgment, and according to the true intent and meaning of this act, and the said surveyor shall be reimbursed by the owner as aforesaid what charges and expenses he shall be at in cutting, pruning, and plashing

Of the Obligation to make or repair Fences.

such hedges, and pruning and lopping such trees, and the removal of such obstruction, over and above the said forfeiture; and it shall and may be lawful for the justices, at a special sessions for the highways, upon proof to them made upon oath, to levy as well the expenses of cutting, pruning, and plashing such hedges, or pruning and lopping such trees, or removal of such obstruction as aforesaid, as the several and respective penalties thereby imposed, by distress and sale of the offender's goods and chattels in such manner as distresses and sales for forfeitures are authorized and directed to be levied by virtue of this act. Provided always, by section 66, that no person shall be compelled, nor any surveyor permitted, to cut or prune any hedge at any other time than between the last day of September and the last day of March; and that no person shall be obliged to fell any timber trees, growing in hedges at any time whatsoever, except where the highways shall be ordered to be widened or enlarged, or then to cut down or grub up any oak trees growing in such highway or in such hedge, except in the months of April, May, or June, or any ash, elm, or other trees in any other months than December, January, February, or March.

By section 69, if any person shall encroach by making or causing to be made, (amongst other things) any hedge, ditch, or other fence, or any carriage or cartway, within the distance of fifteen feet from the centre thereof, he shall forfeit a sum not exceeding forty shillings. The surveyor shall cause such obstruction to be removed at the expense of the person to whom the same shall belong. And the justices at special sessions, upon proof made to them upon oath, may levy the expenses of such removal and the penalty by distress and sale of the

Of the Obligation to make or repair Fences.

offender's goods and chattels in the manner prescribed by the act for that purpose (*f*).

It is no ground for breaking in upon the exception in the early part of the 65th section, that the ornamental trees are doing damage to the highway (*g*).

With regard to the order for cutting the hedges, some nicety is required. The manner of cutting the trees must appear upon the face of that document, and if an obstruction be alleged, the nature of that obstruction must be set forth. The plaintiff brought trespass for cutting down his hedges, and destroying his trees, bushes, shrubs, and thorns. The defendants were surveyors, and at a special session for the highways they had obtained an order upon the plaintiff to cut his hedges and pay certain costs to the surveyor. The order was served, and the plaintiff cut a part of the hedge. However, an information was subsequently laid, and the plaintiff was fined five shillings with costs, for not obeying the order. The surveyors then cut the hedges, and the plaintiff brought his action. The defendants relied upon the order, but it was objected, that a mere order to cut, prune, or plash was insufficient for want of specifying in what manner the plaintiff should cut the hedge. The order, moreover, stated that obstructions were caused in the carriage or cartway, but omitted to explain what the nature of these obstructions might be. There was a verdict for the defendants, upon which it was moved to have a new trial, on the ground of misdirection. And the Court made the rule absolute. The objections to the order were not merely of a formal character. The defect was one of substance, for the owner should have

(*f*) See sections 101, 103. 1 Adol. & El., N. S., 726, Sellwood *v.* Mount; S. C., 1 Gale & D. 358.

(*g*) 2 Jurist, 986, Hampton *v.* Tiffin.

Of the Obligation to make or repair Fences.

been ordered to do the acts in manner and so as to produce the particular effect specified in the statute (*h*).

The latter part of the clause relates to the levying of expenses. Here it is observable, that a demand must first be made upon the person sought to be charged. So that in moving for a mandamus to compel justices to make a levy, it must appear that this demand was made, and, further, it must be brought home to the justices, that it was made (*i*).

Under the 69th section, it is worthy of remark that the obstruction complained of must be *on* the highway (*k*).

By section 80 of this same statute, cartways leading to any market town must be twenty feet wide at the least, and horseways eight feet wide, and footways by the side of carriage and cartways three feet wide, if the ground between the fences, including the same, will admit thereof. This enactment, however, will not enable the surveyor to pare away a bank in order to make the way twenty feet. Where the plaintiff's property was separated from the carriageway by a ragged bank with elder bushes growing on the top, it was held, that a removal of soil from the bank, although slight, formed a ground for an action by the reversioner of the premises. It tended to alter the evidence of title, and besides, the projecting sides of the bank formed a portion of the plaintiff's fence, as well as the bushes on the top (*l*).

Provisions under the Turnpike Acts, with respect to Fences.]—By 3 Geo. 4, c. 126, s. 116, it is enacted, that

(*h*) 2 Adol. & El., N. S., 265, Brook *v.* Jenney and Another.

(*i*) 8 Dowl. P. C., 431, Whitemarsh, *ex parte*.

(*k*) 4 B. & C. 3, Lowen *v.* Kaye.

(*l*) 9 Bing. 3, Alston and Others *v.* Scales. With reference to the erection of gates across turnpike roads, highways, or statute labour

Of the Obligation to make or repair Fences.

the owners or occupiers of the land next adjoining to every turnpike road, shall cut, prune, and trim their hedges to the height of six feet from the surface of the ground, and also cut down, prune, or lop the branches of trees, bushes, and shrubs, growing in or near such hedges, or other fences adjacent thereto (such fences, trees, bushes, or shrubs, not being in any garden, orchard, plantation, walk, or avenue to a house, nor any tree, bush, or shrub, being an ornament or shelter to a house, unless the same shall hang over the road, or any part thereof, in such a manner as to impede or annoy any carriage or person travelling thereon) in such manner, that the turnpike road shall not be prejudiced by the shade thereof, and that the sun and wind may not be excluded from such turnpike road to the damage thereof; and that if such owner or occupier shall not, within ten days after notice given by the surveyor for that purpose, cut, prune, and trim such hedges, or cut down, prune, or trim such branches of trees, bushes, and shrubs in manner aforesaid, it shall and may be lawful for the said surveyor, and he is hereby required to make complaint thereof to some justice, of the limit where such turnpike road shall lie, who shall summon the occupier of such lands before him to answer the said complaint; and if it shall appear to such justice that such occupier has not complied with the requisites of this act in that behalf, it

roads, by the proprietors of railways, see 5 & 6 Wm. 4, c. 50, s. 71. 2 & 3 Vict. c. 45. As to the width of gates across public cartways and horseways, see 5 & 6 Wm. 4, c. 50, s. 81. That gates on turnpike roads are to open inwards, and such as open outwards are to be removed upon pain of a forfeiture of such sum as the alteration by the surveyor shall amount to, and likewise of a further sum by way of penalty, not exceeding forty shillings, unless the owner of the gate shall remove it upon fourteen days' notice being given to him by the surveyor, see 3 Geo. 4, c. 126, s. 125.

Of the Obligation to make or repair Fences.

shall and may be lawful for such justice, upon hearing the surveyor and occupier of such land or his agent (or in default of his or her appearance, upon having due proof of the service of such summons) and considering the circumstances of the case, to order such hedges to be cut, trimmed, and pruned, and such branches of trees, bushes, and shrubs to be cut down or pruned, or trimmed in such manner as may best answer the purposes aforesaid; and if the occupier of such lands shall not obey such order within ten days after it shall have been made, and he or she shall have had due notice thereof, he or she shall forfeit the sum of two shillings for every twenty-four feet in length of such hedge which shall be so neglected to be cut, trimmed, and pruned, and the sum of two-pence for every tree, bush, or shrub which shall be so directed to be cut down, pruned, or trimmed; and the surveyor, in case of such default made by the occupier shall, and he is hereby required to cut, prune, and trim such hedges, and to cut down, prune, or trim such branches of trees, bushes, and shrubs, in the manner directed by such order, and such occupier shall be charged with and pay, over and above the said penalties, the charges and expenses of doing the same, or in default thereof, such charges and expenses shall be levied, together with the said forfeitures, upon his or her goods and chattels, by warrant from a justice of the peace, in such manner as is authorized for forfeitures incurred by virtue of this act (*m*).

Provided by section 117, that no person or persons shall be compelled, nor any surveyor permitted, by virtue of this act, to cut or prune any hedge at any other time than between the last day of September and the last day of March.

(*m*) Section 141.

Of the Obligation to make or repair Fences.

By section 118, if any person shall make, or cause to be made (amongst other things) any hedge or other fence on or at the sides of any turnpike road, in such manner as to reduce the breadth or confine the limits thereof, or any hedge or other fence on any common or waste land on the side or sides of any turnpike road, within the distance of thirty feet, if within three miles of any market town, or if beyond that distance, within twenty-five feet from the middle or centre thereof: every such person shall forfeit forty shillings to the informer, and the trustees or commissioners may cause the obstruction to be removed at the expense of the person to whom the same shall belong. Any justice of the county where the offence is committed, may, upon proof made to him upon oath, levy, as well asthe expenses of removing the obstruction as the penalties imposed by distress and sale of the offender's goods and chattels, rendering the overplus (if any) to the owner on demand.

And by section 121, if any person shall (amongst other acts) cause any injury or damage to be done to the hedges, posts, rails, or fences of a turnpike road, or suffer any pigs or swine to root up such fences, hedges, or banks, he shall pay for every such offence a sum not exceeding forty shillings over and above the damages occasioned thereby (n). Moreover, by section 60, the property of fences is vested (amongst other things) in the trustees.

By 6 & 7 Vict. c. 30 (An Act to amend the Law relating to Pound breach and Rescue), sect. 2, justices are restrained from entering into certain questions, such as title, &c., and, amongst others, as to "the obligation of maintaining, repairing, or keeping in repair any wall, hedge, paling, ditch, sunk fence, or fence whatsoever."

(n) See section 141. And see, likewise, to the same effect, 4 Geo. 4, c. 95, s. 72.

CHAPTER III.

Of the Proceedings after damage done in consequence of Non-repair. Of the remedies in respect thereof: and by or against whom Actions may be brought, together with the defences set up in bar to such Actions.

Proceedings and Remedies.

The most natural and ordinary proceeding in cases of intrusion by cattle or otherwise is for the owner to drive the beasts, or remove the offending matter from his field; or give the trespasser notice to come and do the like; or to distrain damage feasant. If the trespasser should himself take away the cause of the mischief, without notice, he would, in strictness, be liable in trespass for that act, although it is unlikely that the owner of the close would shape his remedy in that way. But if the owner elect to send notice to the trespasser for the purpose of expelling the intruder, he gives, of course a license to enter his land, and he cannot sue the party who obeys his mandate, otherwise than for the damage committed. Indeed, as soon as notice is sent to the owner of the cattle, so far from his being a trespasser by coming to retake the beasts, he is guilty of a tort if he do not forthwith comply (*a*), and therefore, he has a right to recover them under such circumstances. And it makes no difference that the owner of the land is under an obligation to repair the fence, if notice be given to remove the cattle, for the defaultof the tenant shall not excuse the disregard

(*a*) See 2 Wm. Saund. 285; note (4). Com. Dig. Plead. 3 M. 29.

Proceedings and Remedies.

of the notice (*b*). And not only is the owner of the cattle in danger from the tenant if he do not hasten to retrieve his beasts; he runs a chance likewise of their being distrained for rent by the landlord of the tenant's close. And so it was held where A.'s beasts escaped into B.'s land, which B. was bound to fence. For it was the fault of A. in this case that he did not make fresh pursuit instead of allowing the beasts to be levant and couchant on his neighbour's ground, and rent being due of common right, and the land the debtor, the landlord of B. was not bound to inquire whose cattle they were when he took his distress (*c*).

There are distinctions between different landlords upon these occasions, and between cases where cattle are suffered to be levant and couchant, or the contrary. The landlord who distrains for services may take cattle after they have become levant and couchant, for this lord has nothing to do with the land or the fences, and whether there be a defect in the fence or not, or notice given or otherwise, is to him an immaterial matter (*d*). As where the chief lord or the grantee of a rent-charge distrains the beasts of a stranger which have escaped through a defect of fences which either the lessor or lessee should have repaired. Here the absence of notice makes no difference, and as soon as the cattle are levant and couchant the lord, unless the owner immediately make suit (*e*), may take the distress damage feasant (*f*). But the landlord who distrains for rent reserved under a lease is in a dif-

(*b*) 2 Leon. 93, citing 22 Edw. 4, 49; S. C., Poph. 46.

(*c*) 2 Ro. Rep. 124, Gill *v.* Gawin.

(*d*) See Dy. 317, 318.

(*e*) See 1 Brownl. 170. For if freshly pursued, they cannot be taken unless they have broken down the fence, or made an entry without any excuse.

(*f*) 2 Lutwy. 1573, 1580, Kimp *v.* Crewes and others.

Proceedings and Remedies.

ferent position. Where there is a defect of fences, and an obligation on the part of the tenant to repair, the landlord of the lease cannot take the trespassing cattle for his rent, either before or after their levancy and couchancy, unless there be notice to the owner, and a contempt of that notice. For, as he himself, with reference to third persons, ought to repair, or to provide for repair on the part of his tenant, it would be to allow him the advantage of his own wrong if a distress were thus sanctioned (*g*). It is true, that upon one occasion the distrainor had judgment in replevin, although he was under an obligation to repair. He took certain cattle levant and couchant for his rent without giving any notice, and upon his avowing accordingly, the plaintiff pleaded in bar this duty on the defendant's part; the defendant then demurred, and after argument in the Common Pleas and again in the King's Bench upon error brought, the judgment was affirmed (*h*). Nevertheless, *Saunders* was dissatisfied with the decision, and he observed in his report, that the case was hard to be maintained, and he pointed out the diversity, above illustrated, between the lord of a seignory and the landlord of a lease (*i*). Indeed, it had been received for law in very early times, that upon the escape of beasts, the distress would be good as soon as the cattle became levant and couchant, but the contrary if the owner made suit and carried away the animals before they lay down. And it was said, that if the cattle were on trespass for forty days, yet that the lord could not distrain if the owner got possession of his beasts first, whereas if they were on the land but for an hour, that is to say, being levant and

(*g*) By Holt, C. J., 6 Mod. 198. 3 Salk. 136.

(*h*) 2 Saund. 282, 289. Poole *v.* Longuevill and others; S. C. 2 Keb. 660, 680, and see id. 729.

(*i*) 2 Saund. 290.

Proceedings and Remedies.

couchant, they might be taken as a good distress by the seignior (*k*). Soon afterwards, this opinion of *Saunders* was confirmed and the distinction fully recognised, and the case of *Poole and Longuevill* was set aside as contrary to law (*l*). And such is the received doctrine at the present day (*m*).

We will now suppose that there is not any defect of fence, or that the tenant of the land has no duty fixed upon him to repair. This circumstance varies the transaction and enables the landlord of the lease, and *à fortiori*, the lord of the chief rent, to distrain. And it signifies not whether the cattle be levant and couchant, and so, of course, no notice is necessary, for there is no colour of excuse for the entry of the cattle, and thus are the cases to be understood where a distress has been approved of before levancy and couchancy occurred. (*n*) If the distress, nevertheless, be a long arrearage of rent, the owner may be relieved in equity (*o*). It may be added, that if the owner of a close be under an obligation to repair, it is not a trespass on the part of the owner of the cattle to enter his neighbour's land without notice, in order to redeem his beasts (*p*), for he has committed no

(*k*) 10 H. 7, 21 B.

(*l*) 2 Lutwy. 1480. And again by Holt, C. J., 6 Mod. 198, Elmore *v.* Tucker.

(*m*) 2 Wm. Saund. 290, note (7).

(*n*) See 2 Wm. Saund. 290, note (7). Hob. 265, Reynolds *v.* Okeley. Palm. 43, Lacie's case. 5 B. & C. 647, Jones *v.* Powell. 3 Com. Dig. Distress (B 1.)

(*o*) 2 Vern. 131.

(*p*) Keilw. 30, 13 Hen. 7. 2 Ro. Ab. 565, pl. 4. And so it has been said in the case of a forester who enters a close, which the owner ought to keep fenced, in order to rechase wild animals into the forest. Keilw. *ut suprà*, Brian, C. J., *contrà*, because there could be no property in the "savages," and so no remedy but the writ *de parco fracto*. But it seems that the distinction would be

Proceedings and Remedies.

wrong, and no distress can be made as for damage feasant until after notice given to take away the animals.

There is one other course, which, if pursued by the owner of the close trespassed upon, deserves our attention. He may think fit to drive away the cattle instead of impounding them. And doubtless he is at liberty to eject intruders in any manner and without risk of consequences, where there has been a trespass, but it is incumbent upon him to consider before he so acts whether he may not himself be under an obligation to fence against invasion. For if he be so liable, the least he can do is to put back the cattle into the place from whence they have strayed, if he be in a condition to ascertain it (*q*), or to acquaint their owner, and use precautions to prevent injury from happening to them till their removal. The defendant was charged with chasing and driving the plaintiff's sheep, whereby they were damaged. He pleaded that they were wrongfully in his close, upon which he turned them into the highway. The plaintiff replied that the sheep got into the defendant's close through a defect in the fence, and set out a prescription to repair on the part of all those who had occupied the close of the defendant. To this the defendant rejoined, denying the escape and the defect in the fence. Upon this issue was joined, and the plaintiff had a verdict. But it was sought to arrest the judgment, or have a repleader, because the defendant, although bound to repair, might yet drive out the sheep; he could not, indeed, complain of their being on his close, nor distrain damage feasant

where the land lay within the purlieus, or where quite out of the forest; in the former case, the forester might enter, but not otherwise, even although there should be a default of impaling or repair. See Id. Vin. Ab. Tresp. (I. a. 5).

(*q*) See 8 Adol. & El. 117.

Proceedings and Remedies.

without notice; still as the highway might have been the nearest road to the plaintiff's close, he was justified in placing them there. But the Court held that the escape of the cattle had been caused by the defendant's default, and that he was not justified in driving them into the highway and leaving them without further security, and the rule was refused (*r*).

We proceed to mention the legal remedies which are commonly adopted when a recompense for injury done in consequence of non-repair or of the want of a fence is required. These are principally actions of trespass, upon the case, and distress of the cattle damage feasant. The actions in question are of common right where there is no obligation to repair on the side either of the plaintiff or the defendant, but if the defendant be charged with the duty to fence, they are against common right, and the plaintiff must shew a title by prescription or otherwise (*s*). Trespass may be maintained where there is an absence of any consideration to repair, but if, for instance, the occupiers of a particular close have been accustomed, time out of mind, to repair it, and a default happens; either trespass or case may be had, the former because it is the plaintiff's ground which is invaded; and case, because the first wrong was a nonfeasance and neglect to repair, and that omission would be the gist of the action, the trespass being only consequential damage (*t*). A parallel case, although not connected with the question of repair was where the cattle of A. broke the fence of C. B. was injured by this intrusion, but he could not sue in trespass because the assault was made upon another man's fence,

(*r*) 8 Ad. & El. 113, Carruthers *v*. Hollis and another.

(*s*) 1 Salk. 335, Starr *v*. Rookesby.

(*t*) *Ibid.*

Proceedings and Remedies.

and, therefore, an action on the case lay for him against A. (*u*).

The third course is to distrain the matters which are found upon the land of the party who has been trespassed upon.

Mandamus.]—But it should be added here, that, in the case of public bodies or companies, or persons authorized to do certain acts under the provisions of a statute, (as the commissioners of an Inclosure Act,) a mandamus will probably lie to compel the making or repair of fences. As if the commissioners were to make insufficient fences under an act which contemplated the erection of good and permanent enclosures (*x*).

By whom Actions may be brought.]—The next point for our consideration has reference to the parties by whom actions may be brought, and likewise against whom they will lie for damages incurred by reason of the non-repair of fences. A very plain principle is, that neighbours may sue each other where there is no especial consideration on either side to keep up a division between their lands. And it has been shown (*y*), that even a third person, whose field lies beyond the mere vicinity of the next field, may, nevertheless, bring his action where he himself is not in fault. The true ground with regard to neighbourhood, is that a man, who is plaintiff, must be himself free from blame, as far as the defendant is concerned. For if a man be bound to repair a fence between my land and his adjoining, I may justify in trespass brought by him for damage done by my cattle in consequence of his neglect to fence (*z*). A. had land on the side of a large field, and B. had land on

(*u*) Sty. 131.

(*x*) 2 Ad. & El. 782.

(*y*) *Ante*, in this Chapter.

(*z*) 2 Ro. Ab. 565, pl. 3.

Proceedings and Remedies.

the other side. Both A. and B. were mutually bound to fence. A.'s beasts escaped through the default of repair across the large field, and entered B.'s land. Here B. was held entitled to have trespass against A., since as between A. and B., A. was wrong in not keeping up his fence, and was, therefore, bound to meet the consequences (*a*). So if there had been an obligation for A. to enclose against B., and the beasts of C. crossed over into A.'s land, A. might have trespass, since C. was a trespasser upon B. and thence upon A. (*b*), otherwise if C. had had common or a way in the land of B. (*c*)

But supposing one C. to have been the owner of the large field, with A. on one side and B. on the other, and that A. was liable to fence against C. and C. against B. Here if the beasts of B. were to cross C.'s field, and come upon A.'s pasture, A. may not have trespass, because there would be no fault in B., the defendant (*d*). On the contrary, both A. and B. are found neglectful of their obligation to repair (*e*). But if B.'s beasts were to invade the land of a stranger, the stranger might sue B. and leave B. to his remedy against A. (*f*) So if A.'s beasts or those of a stranger were to come upon C.'s land under such circumstances, C. might sue A. in trespass as a defaulter, and if C. were to sue the stranger likewise, the stranger in his turn, might bring case against A. for the consequences of non-repair, of course, assuming that he himself lay under no obligation, and that his beasts were lawfully in the place from whence they escaped into the land of C. And, indeed if the stranger's beasts should do

(*a*) Vin. Ab. Fences, (B. 2,) citing Bro. Cur. Claud. pl. 2.
(*b*) F. N. B. 298. (Hale), note (3).
(*c*) *Ibid, per* Newton, C. J.
(*d*) See F. N. B. 298. (Hale), note (*a*).
(*e*) *Id. ibid*, (B. 3.)
(*f*) *Ibid.*

Proceedings and Remedies.

damage in the land of C. through A.'s default, C. might also bring an action on the case against A. So if beasts come upon A.'s land from the highway and thence advance upon B.'s land which B. ought to fence, as against A., B. may sue the owner of the beasts, because as between him and the defendant he is not answerable for the conduct of the defendant in allowing his cattle to leave the highway (*g*). But it is added, that A. shall not have trespass, although the cattle trample on all his closes contiguous to the highway (*h*), and the reason is, because A. is bound to guard his land from the highway (*i*), and it is not possible for a driver to prevent an occasional trespass if the land lies open at the side of the road. The cattle are, therefore, lawfully in the highway, and A. is, with reference to repair, a defaulter. So again, if A. be bound to fence on the side of his park, and he buy land adjoining, on the other side of which is B.'s land, but A. is under no obligation to fence against B.; here if B.'s cattle escape into the park of A., A. shall have trespass because as between him and B. there was no default, it being B.'s duty to hinder the cattle from straying upon the land immediately contiguous to his. For a man, (A. for instance) is not bound, without a special agreement to fence against his own land, although in this case A. was obliged to guard his own park before the purchase, by virtue of a particular covenant (*j*).

Bailee.]—A gratuitous bailee is competent to sue in

(*g*) Noy. Rep. 107. Harvey *v.* Gulson.

(*h*) *Ibid.*

(*i*) 2 Ro. Ab. 565, pl. 7. F. N. B. Hale, 298, note (*a*). But trespass would lie for A. if he were to give notice to the driver or owner of the cattle, and such notice were not attended to.—*Ibid.*

(*j*) Vin. Ab. Fences, (D. 4.)

Proceedings and Remedies.

case of damage for neglect to repair a fence. This point was adverted to and recognised in a case where the plaintiff's brother sent him a horse to take care of. The plaintiff turned the horse out, after dark, into his close, but, on the following morning the animal was found dead in the close of the next neighbour, the defendant, having fallen from the one into the other. An action on the case being brought, the defendant admitted that he had neglected to repair his fence, but the defence was, that the plaintiff had not such a property in the horse as would entitle him to maintain the action. The Court, was, however, against him, for a gratuitous bailee is under an obligation to run no unnecessary hazard. In this case, the plaintiff owed it to the owner of the horse not to put it into a dangerous pasture, and, in the absence of a proper degree of care he was liable for any damage which might result. Then the defendant having by his negligence rendered the field unsafe, became answerable to the plaintiff for the death of the horse (*k*).

Owner of Inheritance not in general liable.]—The owner of the inheritance is not liable for the defect of fences. This was considered quite a clear point where it appeared that another person was tenant in possession under the defendant in an action on the case for non-repair (*l*). "It is so notoriously the duty of the actual "occupier to repair the fences, and so little the duty of "landlord, that, without any agreement to that effect, "the landlord may maintain an action against his tenant "for not so doing, upon the ground of the injury done "to the inheritance. And deplorable indeed would be "the situation of landlords, if they were liable to be

(*k*) 1 B. & Ald. 59. Rooth *v.* Wilson.
(*l*) 4 T. R. 318. Cheetham *v.* Hampson.

Proceedings and Remedies.

"harassed with actions for the culpable neglect of their "tenants." (*l*) But if there were an agreement on the part of the landlord to repair, the case would be altered, and, to avoid circuity of action, the landlord would be held answerable. As where the plaintiff met with an accident in consequence of a hole in the foot pavement, upon which he sued the owner, and not the occupier of the house. The defence was the action should have been brought against the actual occupier, and that the occupier ought, as between himself and the public, to see that the repairs were duly made, although the landlord might be under the obligation to repair, and *Cheetham* v. *Hampson* was cited as authority. To this authority the Court fully agreed, but here was the fact that the landlord, not the occupier, was bound to this repair, and therefore as the tenant would have a remedy against the landlord, there would be an encouragement of double actions if the plaintiff were to have judgment of nonsuit (*m*).

Executor of Vicar.]—The representative of a beneficed clergyman is liable for dilapidations of fences (*n*), although the burden be imposed by a modern Act of Parliament, and although other persons ought, perhaps, to have made better fences in the first instance. As where land was allotted to a vicar under an Enclosure Act in lieu of tithes and was to be well and sufficiently fenced as the commissioners should direct, but subsequently are to be repaired by the vicar and his successors. An action on the case

(*l*) *Id.* 319, by Lord Kenyon, C. J.

(*m*) 2 H. Bl. 349. Payne *v.* Rogers.

(*n*) 4 M. & S. 183. Young *v.* Munby, where the question was whether the executor could be sued in separate actions for dilapidations of the house, gates, and hedges, and likewise for dilapidations of the chancel, and of a pew.

Proceedings and Remedies.

having been brought against the executrix, it was alleged in defence that this charge of repair thrown on the vicar by a modern act could not survive as against the representative, and further, that the fences had not been well made according to the provisions of the act, being calculated to last for three or four years only. But the Court decided against the defendant, the executrix. For, first, the action was not brought upon the provision of the act which directed the vicar to repair the fences, but upon the liability arising upon the law and custom of England, and that law and custom must certainly attach upon this allotment of land. This custom is not a custom from time immemorial, but merely the common law. This determination would not compel a vicar to fence where land came to him unfenced, but here the ground became the vicar's in an enclosed and fenced state, and, if so, even without the direction in the act, the common law would attach upon it, and oblige the vicar to keep up the enclosure for the benefit of his successors. Then, secondly, if the fence were improperly made, a mandamus might, possibly, have been enforced against the commissioners; but no interference took place, and as a period of four months was awarded by the act within which parties aggrieved by the proceedings under it might appeal, the executrix was too late to relieve herself in any way from the consequences of the supposed neglect (*o*).

Defences.]—The next subject for discussion is the nature of the defences which are tendered in opposition to actions for non-repair. Of these the principal and most common is where in answer to the plaintiff's action the defendant places an allegation upon the record that

(*o*) 2 Ad. & El. 773. Bird *v.* Relph.

Proceedings and Remedies.

the tenants and occupiers of the close where the trespass was committed have been always accustomed to repair the fences immediately contiguous to that close, and that the fence in question was out of repair for want of proper amendment, whereby the defendant's cattle escaped into the close of the plaintiff. This is the plea of defect of fences (*p*), a plea available by one who has an interest in the land adjoining as a common path, highway, license, lease, &c. (*q*). It is not, however, necessary to enlarge upon this mode of defence in this place, because the subject has been already in a great measure exhausted in the chapter of repair, and also above, where the parties who may bring actions have been particularly mentioned. It will be remembered, that the material principle was that the plaintiff should not himself be a defaulter as to the obligation of repair, but that where he lay under no such charge, he might proceed against the owner of beasts trespassing on his ground, and might resist any action against him for damage happening to the cattle by reason of the trespass. The plea of defect of fences would apply to the first class of these cases where the plaintiff himself appears to be in fault, but would be unsuccessful where it cannot be proved that there is any claim upon him, either by agreement or prescription, to make the fence, or do the amendments pointed out.

It should, notwithstanding, be noticed here, that although there may be, as between the plaintiff and the defendant, such a default as might prevent him from suing the defendant upon ordinary occasions, yet if the plaintiff can make out that the defendant's beasts were unlawfully in the close from whence they strayed into the land of the plaintiff, it seems that the plea of defect

(*p*) See Vin. Ab. Trespass (I. a 3).
(*q*) F. N. B. 298. Hale (n. 3).

Proceedings and Remedies.

of fences will not avail the defendant (*r*). For the defendant shall not take advantage of his own wrong to justify an injury which might not have happened if his cattle had been in their right pasture.

Another defence has been that, upon an exchange of lands between the plaintiff and the defendant, the plaintiff had actually agreed to make and keep up the fence, but that he had failed to do so, whereupon the defendant's beasts strayed, and so the defendant justified the trespass. But the Court held, that this agreement was not a bar to the action of trespass. Had it even been by deed, it would not have been a bar, and it was added that the defendant should be put to his action of assumpsit for the breach of this agreement (*s*). However, *Popham*, C. J., did not assent to this opinion of his brethren, holding, that the plaintiff was under an absolute obligation to make the fence after his pledge, as much as though he had been under a prescription, and, therefore, that the action for non-performance was not the sole remedy on the part of the defendant, since he might likewise well justify in trespass (*t*).

Another line of defence has been, that the damage done was too remote to effect the defendant. The fences of the defendant were out of repair, and the horses of the plaintiff broke into the defendant's close by reason of the defect. A haystack fell down whilst the animals were there, and killed them. After a verdict for the plaintiff in an action upon the case, it was moved to arrest the judgment by reason of the remoteness of the injury, and it was alleged that the mischief ought not to depend upon a substantive event which took place subsequently to

(*r*) By Wilmot, C. J. 3 Wils. 126.
(*s*) Cro. El. 709. Sir A. Nowel *v.* Smith.
(*t*) S. C.

Proceedings and Remedies.

the trespass caused by the default, and over which the defendant could not have any control. But the Court of Exchequer held, that the injury here must be considered to be the immediate consequence resulting from the act, and the rule was discharged (*u*).

It has been attempted to interpose the liability of third persons as a defence, although the defendant would otherwise have admitted the right of action. The law, however, has not lent a favourable hand to this mode of meeting an action, as we have already seen in the case of the executrix of a clergyman, who objected, but in vain, that certain commissioners had not made her hedges in a sound and permanent condition. She was, therefore, held liable for dilapidations (*x*). So, again, where a road had been diverted, it became desirable to make a passage from the new road to the close of A. This was done before the stopping up of the old road, but it was necessary, in order to effect it, that B.'s fence should be broken down. B., who was the defendant, gave leave for this purpose, in writing, unstamped and unsealed, and the alteration was made accordingly; the trustees of the road, nevertheless, did not put up either a gate or a fence upon B.'s land. A.'s cattle, consequently, strayed over B.'s land, and from thence into a highway, and other cattle strayed from the highway over B.'s land into A.'s land, whereupon A. sued B. upon the case for this inconvenience and damage. It was admitted that B. had always repaired the fence, but his counsel urged that the nonfeasance of these trustees could not make him responsible, as he had relinquished all his right to them, and had not appealed against their act. But the Court was against him, for as the trustees had no autho-

(*u*) 2 Y. & Jer. 391. Powell *v.* Salisbury. And see 1 Vent. 264.
(*x*) 2 Ad. & El. 773. Bird *v.* Relph, *ante*, p. 317.

Proceedings and Remedies.

rity to make the passage over his land without his consent, they must be taken to be agents. He ought to have so stipulated as that the obligation cast upon him by law might be complied with. The postea was delivered to the plaintiff (y). In this case the trustees were wrong doers on two grounds. First, they ought to have secured to the plaintiff a permanent right of way, which was not done, since the license, being by parol, was revocable at will (z). Secondly, they were bound to fence and put out the adjoining lands from trespasses, and this they likewise neglected (a). Not having acted, therefore, in pursuance of the act, the defendant was without redress, for he could not sue them for doing that which he himself had authorized, although the plaintiff might, perhaps, have treated them as trespassers.

(y) 3 Y. & Jer. 308. Winter *v.* Charter.

(z) *Id.* 312, 315.

(a) *Id.* 312, 317.

CHAPTER IV.

Of the Pleadings, Evidence, &c., in Actions relating to Fences.

WE have seen (*a*) that actions of trespass and upon the case are the most common remedies for damage caused by a nonfeasance in fencing. The issues, however, which are sometimes necessary to raise questions of law between parties upon disputes of this nature can also be raised in replevin when cattle are taken damage feasant. In an action upon the case the plaintiff declares upon his possession of land and states a possession likewise of the land in the defendant (*b*), by reason of which the defendant ought to have repaired the hedge or fence in dispute. The neglect of the defendant is then averred, and lastly, the damage, whether it be injury to the cattle of the plaintiff from their straying into the defendant's land, or mischief to his own close from the wandering of the defendant's beasts, or of those of other persons, owing to the want of repair, or, perhaps, both of these ill con- Pleadings, Evidence, &c.

(*a*) *Ante*, Chapter III.

(*b*) See 1 Vent. 264, Anon. In this case, likewise, it was determined that the manner of stating the time was good. As that the fence was down from the 23rd of April to the 25th of May, and afterwards, saying also, that the plaintiff's mare was drowned through the defect of the fence. For, 1st, The Court would intend as much after verdict; and 2ndly, They would, at all events, intend it, as the accident was laid to have happened through the defect of the fence, and the objection, therefore, that the fence might have been good on the 28th of May, when the cause of action arose, was held of no avail.—See also, 1 Salk. 22.

Pleadings, Evidence, &c.

sequences. It seems, that although there might be an agreement to repair, the plaintiff might still declare upon the possession of the defendant (c), and would not be constrained to say that the defendant was bound to repair by virtue of the agreement (d). This statement of possession shews the necessity of disclosing the plaintiff's right to bring this action. As where a mare belonging to the plaintiff met with an accident in consequence of a supposed default on the defendant's part through neglect in mending his fences. The declaration alleged the liability, and stated the damage, but failed to shew that the plaintiff had any right to have his beast in the place whence she escaped, so that here was *damnum absque injuriâ*, and judgment was given for the defendant (e).

In an action upon the case for damage done through the falling of a haystack, by which the plaintiff's horses were killed, the plaintiff employed three counts. 1. Stating the respective possessions of the plaintiff and defendant, and the obligation of the defendant to repair certain fences in order to prevent the escape of cattle, and then alleging that the defendant suffered the fences to be in bad condition whereby the injury occurred. 2. Stating that the haystack mentioned in describing the injury in the first count was in an improper and dangerous state through the default of the defendant, whereby, &c. 3. Stating a depasturing of the plaintiff's grass and herbage by the cattle of the defendant (f).

The declaration in trespass merely states the damage

(c) 6 B. & C. 338, *per* Bayley, J.

(d) See an observation of Littledale, J., *id.* 333, and the dictum of Bayley, J., *id.* 338.

(e) Cro. Jac. 158, Blyth *v.* Topham.

(f) 2 Y. & Jer. 391, Powell *v.* Salisbury.

Pleadings, Evidence, &c.

without alleging any lawful possession or consideration to repair, and this is the most ordinary form of action where the mischief complained of consists simply of an invasion by the defendant's beasts. For the action upon the case, although in this instance it may be used as well as trespass, is mostly applied to matters of consequential injury, which cannot be the subject of trespass; as the falling down of the haystack (*g*), the damage to the sheep which the defendant occasioned by driving them illegally into the highway (*h*), and so on.

An avowry for taking cattle damage feasant is in the nature of a declaration, but the defendant merely states that the place in question was his freehold, or copyhold, &c. (as the case may be,) and that the cattle of the plaintiff in replevin were wrongfully depasturing and doing damage there, whereupon he well avows the taking of the same.

The actions of covenant and assumpsit not unfrequently arise in matters connected with fences upon an alleged breach of covenant or agreement by a tenant. The landlord rightly deems this neglect to be a mischief done to his inheritance, and is entitled to recover accordingly.

Pleas.]—To an action upon the case not guilty may sometimes be pleaded alone.

Defect of Fences.]—The defence of a broken and unrepaired hedge is placed upon the record as an answer to an action of trespass to a plea of distress damage feasant, and also in bar of an avowry. After adverting to the trespasses, the defendant in trespass says, that he was lawfully possessed of a close next adjoining to that of the

(*g*) 2 Y. & Jer. 391. (*h*) *Ante*, 8 Ad. & El. 113.

Pleadings, Evidence, &c.

plaintiff, and he then prescribes (*i*) against the plaintiff that the plaintiff and all the tenants and occupiers (*j*) of the plaintiff's close have been accustomed, &c. to repair the hedge and fence between the two closes (*k*). The defendant then avers the breach of the fence, by means of which the cattle escaped, and, of necessity, did a small portion of damage. Sometimes it is added, that the defendant drove his cattle from the plaintiff's close as soon as he was made acquainted with or had notice of their intrusion, and, thereby, unavoidably and without unnecessary damage, trampled upon the plaintiff's grass, &c. (*l*)

This form varies but little where it is employed as a bar to the avowry. Instead of the defendant's possession, that of the plaintiff is stated in the first instance, and the plaintiff then lays down his prescription against the defendant, concluding sometimes that the defendant took away the cattle before the plaintiff could have had any notice of their having strayed. A slip in pleading was once made where a plea of this nature alleged an immemorial obligation upon the defendant to amend and repair the fence between the close in which the cattle were taken and a certain highway lying contiguous. The plea went on thus: "when and so often as need or occasion hath been or required, or shall or may be required to prevent cattle *being* in the said highway from erring and

(*i*) Cause must be shewn for the repair, as by prescription, covenant, or otherwise. Yelv. 74, 75, Faldo *v.* Ridge.

(*j*) See 1 Salk. 336, Starr *v.* Rookesby. 2 Ld. Raym. 804, *per* Holt, C. J.

(*k*) Or it might be a common or highway. Com. Dig. pl. 3, M. 29. 2 Lutwy. 1357.

(*l*) See, as to the old mode of pleading, Dy. 365. It is not now necessary to set out the title, Yelv. 74. 3 Salk. 278. Com. Dig. pl. 3, M. 29.

Pleadings, Evidence, &c.

escaping," &c. Now as the cattle could not be in the highway lawfully except as *passing* there, it was by no means a correct allegation of the prescription to speak of them as *being* there. They might have been passing and repassing, but they might have been trespassing on the road, and, consequently, upon a special demurrer, judgment was given for the defendant (*m*).

This plea of a defect of fences is an answer likewise to a justification in trespass for driving cattle that the defendant drove the cattle into a highway. For the defendant had no right to drive beasts from his close and leave them in the road when he had himself been guilty of a breach of duty through non-repair. Thus, the plaintiff brought trespass for chasing his sheep into a highway. The defendant said that the sheep were depasturing unlawfully in his close, wherefore he ordered his servant to drive them into the highway and leave them there. Upon a replication of defect of fences, and a denial of the escape by way of rejoinder, a verdict passed for the plaintiff, and it was urged that the defendant's plea had not been answered, since the defendant had a full right to turn out the strange sheep, although he could neither bring an action, nor distrain damage feasant. But the Court refused a rule for a repleader or to arrest the judgment, being of opinion that the replication was an answer to the defendant's allegations (*n*).

Care must be taken that a declaration in assumpsit or covenant by a landlord against his tenant for non-repair should receive a right answer if a defence be attempted. The plaintiff charged his tenant with using the premises let to him otherwise than in a husband-like

(*m*) 2 H. Bl. 527, Dovaston *v.* Payne.

(*n*) 8 Adol. & El. 113, Carruthers *v.* Hollis and Another.

Pleadings, Evidence, &c.

manner, by neglecting to repair fences upon an implied promise to do so. The defendant pleaded that the fences became out of order through natural decay, that there was not proper wood assigned by the plaintiff for repairs, and that the plaintiff ought to have set out the wood necessary for the purpose. The plea did not specify the wood required: no request to set out this timber was averred, nor was any custom of the country cited so as to warrant a presumption that no such request was necessary. The plea was held bad (*o*).

Again, where the landlord sued the defendant in assumpsit for not repairing hedges, the pleas were,—1st, That no timber had been assigned by the landlord for repair; 2nd, That there was not any proper timber for the defendant which he had a right to take. Both these pleas were held bad, both in form and substance, for, in the first place, the tenant had failed to make a request to his landlord according to the record, which contained no mention of such a request, and the tenant might, on refusal, take the timber (*p*). Secondly, by saying that there was no timber to which he had a right, the jury were left to determine a matter of law which could not be correct. The plaintiff, therefore, had judgment (*q*).

It was once held to be no answer to an action of trespass (*r*), that there had been an exchange of lands between the plaintiff and defendant upon condition that the plaintiff should make the fences (*s*); but the authority of this case may well be doubted, for the exist-

(*o*) 2 Chit. Rep. 685, Whitfield *v.* Weedon.
(*p*) 2 Lutwy. 1480.
(*q*) Lofft. Rep. 43, Anon.
(*r*) By three Justices, against the opinion of Popham, C. J.
(*s*) Cro. Eliz. 709, Nowel *v.* Smith.

Pleadings, Evidence, &c.

ence of an agreement may be presumed in an action upon the case, under the plea of not guilty (*t*), and there seems to be no good reason why an agreement or deed, if pleaded, should be a bar to an action of trespass. Circuity of action is, at all events, avoided.

Replications, &c.]—If the defendant should plead a distress damage feasant to trespass, the plaintiff may reply that there was a defect of fences. If this plea should itself be used, the plaintiff may answer that the fences were good, but that the cattle of the defendant were unruly and accustomed to break down fences, and so destroyed the plaintiff's hedge, doing the damage complained of, and the plaintiff may then deny the defect, which ought to be done simply without a formal traverse, and with a conclusion to the country (*u*). The first of these replications arises where the plaintiff seeks to charge the defendant with the repair, and the other where the defendant alleges a breach of the same duty against the plaintiff, but the plaintiff parries the accusation by a denial of the defect. Again, the plaintiff may reply that the defendant wilfully turned the cattle upon his close, for it is not an excuse on the behalf of a defendant in trespass that the fence was out of repair if he, the defendant, drove the beasts onwards to do the trespass (*v*). Or he may say that the defendant threw down the fences. And, in another plea, if the fact be so, the plaintiff may, of course, deny his obligation to repair, and put that matter at once in issue. And so may the defendant in his replication to a plea in bar to an avowry charging the like defect. By comparing the action of replevin with other proceedings, it is easy to accommo-

(*t*) 6 B. & C. 332, 340.

(*u*) 1 Saund. 103 (*c*).

(*v*) See Com. Dig. pl. 3, M. 29.

Pleadings, Evidence, &c.

date the replications to the altered position of plaintiffs and defendants. So may the plaintiff reply that he gave the defendant in trespass notice to remove the cattle, and this will operate as a *new assignment to a plea of escape* in an action to recover damages accrued after notice. And the same replication will avail in replevin (*x*).

The rejoinder of the defendant to the replication of the plaintiff mentioned above, stating that the cattle of the defendant were unruly, and that the breach of the fence was thus occasioned, would be that the cattle escaped through the defect, and not the breach of the fence, a denial which necessarily involves a conclusion to the country, and presents the issue. The ordinary replication, however, in trespass is *de injuriâ* (*y*). But sometimes the plaintiff traverses the prescription, or the want of repair, *i. e.* the defect of fences, or the escape *modo et formâ* (*z*).

Evidence.]—We will be sparing in our remarks concerning the evidence, because the proofs upon this subject will be found in the books of writers upon that head, and likewise because such proofs either depend upon individual circumstances, or, on the other hand, are, upon many occasions, the same. As, in trespass, where the plaintiff has to show the invasion of his territory. In case, where he must disclose by his witnesses the particular injury which he has sustained through the act of the defendant. In replevin, where the taking is most commonly acknowledged by the defendant. In assumpsit, where the terms of the letting or agreement are brought forward, or the deed in actions of covenant. The plea of defect of fences is also made out by proving

(*x*) 2 Wm. Saund. 285, n. 4.
(*y*) See 1 Chit. on Pleading, 639.
(*z*) Com. Dig., tit. Pl., 3, M. 29. 1 Chit. on Pleading, 628.

the broken condition of the enclosure, and the immemorial obligation to repair on the part of the occupier, or, if there be a deed, or agreement, the liability to repair by virtue of a covenant or clause in those instruments respectively.

Pleadings, Evidence, &c.

With reference to matters which are contested by opposite testimonies, the jury will be of course the judges, unless a point of mere law should intervene. Thus we have seen that where there are two ditches, one on each side of a hedge, the ownership of the hedge, if that be the question in dispute, must be decided by proof of acts of ownership on one, or on both sides (*a*). The jury will determine by their opinion the right so contended for. If it be wished to shew the extent of an occupier's land, it is open to both parties to prove the ancient width of his ditch. And as the occupier may not cut beyond the outer edge of the ditch (*b*), it is for his interest to claim for himself as enlarged a ditch as possible.

The occasional repair of a fence is not, of itself, evidence that the person who has done it must, therefore, be fixed with a permanent obligation. The question is one which may, most properly, be submitted to a jury. Upon the trial of an issue between the owner of certain land called Deans and the owner of Dead Moor Close, two instances were brought forward in support of the duty to repair on the part of the latter, one where a tenant of Dead Moor repaired a gate upon being required to do so by the owner of Deans; the other where the defendant, the present owner and occupier, did so upon a similar order given by the same person. This evidence was left to the jury by *Littledale*, J., who said

(*a*) 2 Selwy. N. P. 1329.
(*b*) 3 Taunt. 137, Vowles *v.* Miller.

Pleadings, Evidence, &c.

that an agreement between the plaintiff and defendant might be presumed, but the learned Judge did not sufficiently point out to the attention of the jury the improbability of the existence of such a deed, and the Court came to the conclusion that the weight of evidence was greatly in favour of the defendant, and granted a new trial (*c*), so that, under these circumstances, two examples of repair were deemed quite insufficient. And, indeed, *Littledale*, J., had, at the trial pointed out a distinction which existed between rights of way or common, and the present. In every user of a way or common, an act is done by one man upon the land of another, and unless done with the acquiescence of the owner, express or implied, it must be a wrongful act. The long user of the way or common raises an inference that it is rightful, and affords evidence for a jury to presume in fact that there has been a grant or conveyance of the easement by the owner of the land to the person who has so used his land. But, in this case, the owner of Dead Moor, had, in no instance, allowed the plaintiff to do any act upon his, the defendant's, land. The defendant might fairly say that he repaired the fence for his own benefit, and to prevent his cattle from trespassing upon his neighbour's land (*d*). And then the learned Judge tendered the presumption to the jury which they accepted, and found against the defendant, but which presumption was, nevertheless, too weak for the Court to admit of without a new trial and a more express opinion on the part of the Judge that there was no good ground to entertain such a supposition.

(*c*) 6 B. & C. 329, Boyle *v*. Tamlyn. (*d*) *Id.* 332.

AN INDEX

TO THE

PRINCIPAL MATTERS.

*** *The Reader will please to refer to the Table at the commencement of the Work, entitled*

"Duties and Liabilities of Officers,"

To prevent unnecessary repetition, the Duties and Liabilities of such Persons have not been repeated in this General Index.

A.

D.

E.

I.

J.

L.

M.

R.

S.

T.

LONDON:
PRINTED BY RAYNER AND HODGES,
109, Fetter Lane, Fleet Street.

Nabu Public Domain Reprints:

You are holding a reproduction of an original work published before 1923 that is in the public domain in the United States of America, and possibly other countries. You may freely copy and distribute this work as no entity (individual or corporate) has a copyright on the body of the work. This book may contain prior copyright references, and library stamps (as most of these works were scanned from library copies). These have been scanned and retained as part of the historical artifact.

This book may have occasional imperfections such as missing or blurred pages, poor pictures, errant marks, etc. that were either part of the original artifact, or were introduced by the scanning process. We believe this work is culturally important, and despite the imperfections, have elected to bring it back into print as part of our continuing commitment to the preservation of printed works worldwide. We appreciate your understanding of the imperfections in the preservation process, and hope you enjoy this valuable book.

The Law Of Party Walls And Fences: Including The New Metropolitan Buildings Act, With Notes

Humphry William Woolrych

Reading Borough Council

3412601047509 6